The Fear of Chinese Power

NEW APPROACHES TO INTERNATIONAL HISTORY

New Approaches to International History covers international history during the modern period and across the globe. The series incorporates new developments in the field, such as the cultural turn and transnationalism, as well as the classical high politics of state-centric policymaking and diplomatic relations. Written with upper level undergraduate and postgraduate students in mind, texts in the series provide an accessible overview of international diplomatic and transnational issues, events, and actors.

Published:

Decolonization and the Cold War, edited by Leslie James and Elisabeth Leake (2015)
Cold War Summits, Chris Tudda (2015)
The United Nations in International History, Amy Sayward (2017)
Latin American Nationalism, James F. Siekmeier (2017)
The History of United States Cultural Diplomacy, Michael L. Krenn (2017)
International Cooperation in the Early 20th Century, Daniel Gorman (2017)
Women and Gender in International History, Karen Garner (2018)
International Development, Corinna Unger (2018)
The Environment and International History, Scott Kaufman (2018)
Scandinavia and the Great Powers in the First World War, Michael Jonas (2019)
Canada and the World since 1867, Asa McKercher (2019)

The First Age of Industrial Globalization, Maartje Abbenhuis and Gordon Morrell (2019)
Europe's Cold War Relations, Federico Romero, Kiran Klaus Patel, Ulrich Krotz (2019)
United States Relations with China and Iran, Osamah F. Khalil (2019)
Public Opinion and Twentieth-Century Diplomacy, Daniel Hucker (2020)
Globalizing the US Presidency, Cyrus Schayegh (2020)
The International LGBT Rights Movement, Laura Belmonte (2021)
Global War, Global Catastrophe, Maartje Abbenhuis and Ismee Tames (2021)
America's Road to Empire: Foreign Policy from Independence to World War One, Piero Gleijeses (2021)
Militarization and the American Century, David Fitzgerald *(2022)*
American Sport in International History, Daniel M. DuBois (2023)
Rebuilding the Postwar Order, Francine McKenzie (2023)
Soldiers in Peacemaking, Beatrice de Graaf, Frédéric Dessberg, Thomas Vaisset (2023)
From World War to Postwar, Andrew N. Buchanan (2023)

Forthcoming:

China and the United States since 1949, Elizabeth Ingleson

The Fear of Chinese Power

An International History

JEFFREY CREAN

BLOOMSBURY ACADEMIC
LONDON • NEW YORK • OXFORD • NEW DELHI • SYDNEY

BLOOMSBURY ACADEMIC
Bloomsbury Publishing Plc
50 Bedford Square, London, WC1B 3DP, UK
1385 Broadway, New York, NY 10018, USA
29 Earlsfort Terrace, Dublin 2, Ireland

BLOOMSBURY, BLOOMSBURY ACADEMIC and the Diana logo are trademarks of Bloomsbury Publishing Plc

First published in Great Britain 2024
Reprinted in 2024

Series design by Catherine Wood
Cover image © Military vehicles parade past the Tiananmen Rostrum in Beijing, China, 3 September 2015.
Imaginechina Limited/Alamy Stock Photo

A catalogue record for this book is available from the British Library.

A catalog record for this book is available from the Library of Congress.

ISBN: HB: 978-1-3502-3395-9
PB: 978-1-3502-3394-2
ePDF: 978-1-3502-3397-3
eBook: 978-1-3502-3396-6

Series: New Approaches to International History

Typeset by Deanta Global Publishing Services, Chennai, India
Printed and bound in Great Britain

To find out more about our authors and books visit www.bloomsbury.com and sign up for our newsletters.

To Heather, with all my heart

Contents

Figures

Acknowledgments

First and foremost, I wish to thank my parents for all they have done to bring me to this stage in my life. I can never thank them enough for all the sacrifices they have made. Second, I wish to thank my graduate school adviser Jason Parker and all the faculty at the Texas A&M History Department for helping make me the historian I am today.

I offer my gratitude to Thomas Zeiler for offering me the opportunity to contribute this volume to Bloomsbury's "New Approaches in International History" series of books. Thank you to the editors at Bloomsbury and my anonymous reviewer for helping me to improve on my initial draft. I also wish to commend Lilly Smith at the Tyler Junior College Library for tracking down the hundreds of books I have requested through interlibrary loan so I could research this book. In addition, thank you to my good friend Chris Gilson for the cover design.

Finally, I must note that this labor of love could have never been produced without the love and support of my wife, Heather. She has been with me throughout my research and writing, offering encouragement, guidance, and most importantly inspiration. I could never have written this book without you, my darling.

Introduction

Let Him Sleep

"Not only we but all the people of the world will have to make our best effort if we are going to match the enormous ability, drive, and discipline of the Chinese people." President Joseph Biden could have spoken these words in 2021 when he signed the United States Innovation and Competition Act into law. It was the first piece of legislation to pass Congress with bipartisan support during his administration. By allocating a quarter of a trillion dollars for investment in semiconductor production and other related technologies, the legislation was designed to help the United States compete with the Chinese. Very few things can bring today's Democrats and Republicans together. The threat of a powerful China is one of them. Yet this quotation is a half-century old. It was written in the diary of President Richard Nixon late at night in Beijing, during the first-ever visit by a sitting US president to China. Nixon then added, ominously, "otherwise, we will one day be confronted with the most formidable enemy that had ever existed in the history of the world."[1]

Around the world, many believe humanity has arrived at this moment. It is a moment that has been anticipated for a very long time. In 1879, former president Ulysses S. Grant became the first American leader to visit China. At that time, the Qing Dynasty was still recovering from a series of massive internal rebellions and licking its wounds from repeated foreign military incursions. China was vast, but it was also backward and therefore vulnerable. Still, based on his observations, Grant predicted: "the day is not very far distant when they will make the most rapid strides toward modern civilization, and become dangerous rivals to all powers interested in the trade of the East."[2] Like Nixon nearly a century later, he could not help but see the potential in this land and its people to achieve great things and inspire even greater worries.

This book is the story of those worries, what their sources were, and how they developed in the United States, among China's neighbors, and across continents. It begins a year after Grant's visit and extends down to our own time. I show how consistent these fears have been over the decades and generations, across very different Chinese regimes, and through multiple eras in the international system. I argue that these fears have been based on persistent racialized stereotypes of the Chinese. These negative and positive stereotypes have interacted to create anxieties about Chinese power that are unique to China. Its people are seen as both quantitatively and qualitatively unique. Not only are there multitudes of them, but as individuals they possess unique capacities not only for hard work, endurance, and intelligence but also for cruelty and indifference. As represented by the Fu Manchu archetype in popular culture, they are seen as imbued with "both superhuman and inhuman qualities."[3] These fears have always been about more than mere demographic arithmetic, as reflected by the absence of a concept of an "Indian Peril."[4]

The fears embodied in the phrase "Yellow Peril" take four primary forms. The first is cultural, bound up in a conception of Chinese culture as alien and threatening, particularly to civilizations based upon European culture. The second is demographic and is usually expressed through fears of Chinese migration abroad. The third is economic, based upon the notion of Chinese people as dangerously productive and excessively frugal. This form can be applied to Chinese both in China and abroad, and in the latter manifestation has fueled opposition to Chinese immigration. The fourth is strategic and focuses on the military power of the Chinese state. This often interacts with cultural fears, whereby a powerful China can be seen as a danger to non-Chinese cultures. At different times, and in different places, some forms are more prominent than others. All of them react not only to China's actual present power but its potential future power, what Michael Barr, a China scholar at the University of Newcastle, has labeled China's "imagined power."[5] Were this book to focus on the history of China's actual power, it would be much shorter, and cover a smaller time frame. But fears of China's imagined power dating back to the late nineteenth century have conditioned how people view China's actual power in the early twenty-first century.

For China's neighbors, such fears have been predominantly pragmatic. China is and has usually been the colossus of East Asia, possessing by far the region's largest population and military. With the exception of the white settler colonies of Australia and New Zealand, their fears usually lack an obvious racial component. This is not to say China's non-white neighbors abjure anti-Chinese prejudice, just that these nationalist and ethnic prejudices are extended to other less powerful neighbors as well. In Europe, where the term *gelbe gefahr* or "Yellow Peril" originated, the fears began as a manifestation of imperial anxieties of reverse colonization. Appearing as the continent's economic power and military might were peaking, Europe's political and intellectual leaders imagined what could happen were China to become as politically organized and economically developed as their own lands. This was a marked shift from earlier in the century, when European elites viewed Chinese civilization as inherently inferior, and Chinese elites mocked for their undeservingly arrogant attitude toward foreigners. As European power declined, so did worries about China. They have only reemerged quite recently, and in a very different and less fanciful form, based now on China's penetration of European economies.

It is in the United States that the disparate strands of Sinophobia have most thoroughly intertwined. As an Atlantic nation derived from a European heritage, a Pacific nation which has long seen Asia as its future, and a nation of immigrants, the United States is a veritable *gelbe gefahr* melting pot. In the nation's earliest years, the fears centered around the immigration of individual Chinese who were viewed as uniquely unassimilable. Americans shared this anti-Chinese backlash with all nations bordering the Pacific Ocean. Along with Europe, American elites in the early twentieth century shared eugenics-based fears of racial conflict where the Chinese might emerge victorious. But such fears intermingled with a uniquely American attachment to the people of China, most notably felt among the thousands of Protestant missionaries who flocked to China from the mid-nineteenth century onward. As the noted historian of East Asia Bruce Cumings puts it, "China has not been a nation for Americans, but a metaphor."[6] The notion of a special relationship between Americans and Chinese peaked in the 1930s and 1940s during the reign of Chiang Kai-shek, only to be shattered by Chiang's defeat and expulsion to Taiwan at the hands of Mao Zedong's Communist armies. That epochal event popularized American Sinophobia as never before by merging the Yellow Peril with the Red Menace.

This book's eleven chapters are arranged in chronological order, revealing themes and beliefs that were unique to each period and connecting those that have reappeared across the decades. Part One, entitled "The Dragon Stirs," lays the groundwork, explaining over Chapters 1–4 the historical origins of the various strains of Sinophobia which developed between 1880 and 1920, as well as reactions to the establishment of the Guomindang regime under Chiang Kai-shek. Part Two, entitled "The Dragon Roars," consists of Chapters 5–8, which follow the rise of the Chinese Communist Party to power and the nearly three decades of Mao's rule. During this period, China alternately fulfilled long-standing Yellow Peril prophecies, failed to attain its potential, inspired admiration from outsiders, and upended international geopolitics as never before. Part Three, entitled "The Dragon Soars," features Chapters 9–11 and takes on the most recent four decades, which have been defined by the meteoric economic rise of China. The first half of this period witnessed a return of idealistic hopes that as the Chinese grew wealthier they would also become freer, and therefore less of a strategic threat to the United States and its allies. The second half saw such hopes dashed, with naivete replaced by alarmism.

The evidence I use to tell this story reflects the sentiments of statesmen, journalists, and academics, as well as novelists, filmmakers, and other producers of popular culture who have had at least as much impact on the general public's views of China over the past fourteen decades. I also detail what the Chinese thought of what the rest of the world thought of them in these various periods, and how the nation's leading citizens sought to mold this image to benefit China. In addition, for readers unfamiliar with the contours of modern Chinese history, I provide a running narrative of the important political events involving modern China to contextualize my arguments and evidence. If the material presented here appears excessively focused on the United States, that is due to the unique breadth and depth of American concern with this topic. When it comes to fearing China, the United States has long conceded second place to no one.

This is far from the only recent book on the topic of fears of a rising China. But it is the only one to provide a detailed history of these fears over the entire period of their existence. Most works on China's rise deal only with recent decades and do so from the viewpoint of an international relations scholar rather than a historian. My hope is that this work will enable curious readers to better understand and evaluate both this voluminous body of literature as well as ongoing daily news reports on events related to this topic. Many of these recent works include some version of Napoleon's alleged quote "China—there lies a sleeping giant. Let him sleep, for when he wakes he shall shake the world."[7] Variations of this quote have Napoleon identify China as a sleeping giant, a sleeping lion, or a sleeping dragon. But the meaning is always the same, and the sentiment always attributed to the Corsican general-turned-emperor-turned-prisoner.

These variations in the quote are perhaps an indication of its apocryphal nature. It is confirmed that on his way back from a diplomatic mission to China, British official Lord Amherst met Napoleon during his captivity on the South Atlantic island of Saint Helena. It is also known that while on that island, Napoleon had access to accounts of British ambassador George McCartney's 1793 visit to China more than two decades earlier, which was one of the rare cases before 1840 of a European receiving an audience with the Chinese emperor.[8] Napoleon no doubt was curious about Asia's largest nation. As to his supposedly high rating of its strategic potential, that would be less in character for Napoleon and his European contemporaries. Like them, Napoleon believed in the racial and cultural superiority of Europeans over people from other continents. Predictions of rising powers in this period tended to focus on the United States or Russia, such as those made by Alexis de Tocqueville in his 1830's work *Democracy in America*. A prophecy in the early nineteenth century of a non-Western great power would have been most anomalous indeed.

In addition to the lack of a definitive citation of the origin of this supposed quote, there are two other crucial pieces of evidence indicating its inauthenticity. First, the quote only became widely cited in the 20th century.

Second, and far more noteworthy, is the fact that the Chinese used variations of this metaphor to describe themselves nearly a half-century before outsiders began regularly claiming its Napoleonic origin. A 1904 book by Great Britain's acting minister in Peking claimed that "Chinese statesmen have been fond of saying that 'China is a sleeping dragon.'"[9] In the period after the abdication of the final Qing Emperor Pu Yi in 1912, Sun Yat-sen often referred to China as a "Sleeping Lion."[10] It is quite possible that Westerners borrowed this metaphor from the Chinese themselves, and later attributed its provenance to a famous European already well-known for numerous sayings and maxims. The Chinese themselves have proudly appropriated the supposed prophecy. For instance, a state-run Chinese newspaper in 1996 wrote "the French hero Napoleon long ago said 'Asia's China is a sleeping lion. Once it awakes, it will shake the entire world.' The sleeping lion of the East has already awoken to an obsessively ambitious America, and has roared."[11] The leaders of plenty of large nations predict an eventual rise to greatness. There is no national pride in citing such home-grown statements. But when it comes out of the mouth of a legendary figure from thousands of miles away, who never even set foot in your land, it carries serious weight. Ultimately, it's a quote that's too good not to be true.

PART ONE

The Dragon Stirs: 1880–1937

1

The Birth of the Yellow Peril

1880–1900

It began as a nightmare. The manifestation of the addled fears of Kaiser Wilhelm II's mercurial mind. On that night, the subconscious of the leader of Europe's largest economy and most powerful military did not fear Great Britain, which possessed the world's largest empire. He did not fear the United States, which boasted the world's largest economy. Nor did he fear the Russian Empire, his vastly more populous neighbor to the east, which the previous year had made an alliance with France, Germany's resentful and revanchist neighbor to the west. Instead, he feared peoples half a world away, who had yet to fight a single war against Germany and were in that era the recurrent victims of European aggression.

As reported by the Kaiser, his dream took the form of a prophetic vision of a Buddha riding a dragon which was flying across Eurasia to attack and destroy Europe. He interpreted the Buddha as representing Japan, and the dragon as China.[1] The apparent stimulus for this vision was Japan's recent victory over China in the Sino-Japanese War, which had recently concluded with the Treaty of Shimonoseki, in which Japan acquired Taiwan and China acquiesced to the end of its traditional dominant influence in Korea. But beneath this near-term cause were underlying, longer-term, and heavily racialized fears Wilhelm had harbored for many years. His vision was years in coming—a merging of current geopolitical events with the burgeoning fantasy literature of invasion novels, of which the Kaiser had admittedly read deeply.

The German monarch was never one to let any idea of his go unheard—or, in this case, unseen. Thus, he commissioned a professional illustration of his vision, with the caption "Nations of Europe! Join in the Defense of Your Faith and Your Homes." He then had the illustration disseminated to newspapers and magazines across Europe and North America. In the foreground of the black-and-white sketch are a mixture of Wagnerian Germanic heroes and Christian warrior angels. Obscured in the background is a massive if poorly detailed Buddha atop a dragon. The religious aspect of the symbolism was made blatant in Wilhelm's original version of his caption: "Nations of Europe, defend your holiest possessions!"[2]

With its fantastical mixture of pagan, Christian, and racial imagery, the drawing encapsulated *fin de siècle* anxieties as vividly as Bram Stoker's *Dracula* or H. G. Wells's *The Time Machine*. Or, at least, it could have. Wilhelm was let down either by an unimaginative artist or by the paucity of his own vision. The drawing fails to live up to its description. The Buddha as a religious icon is associated with peace and meditation, and the mere thought of him raising a sword in anger is the stuff of parody. The notion of him riding a dragon into battle is one-part Revelations, one-part Ring Cycle, and one-part psychedelic acid trip, worthy of the pen of the scandalously notorious contemporary illustrator Aubrey Beardsley. It should be given prominence, instead of the scene's banal and derivative cookie-cutter heroes.

Yet Wilhelm felt overweening pride in his creation, even printing up large numbers of postcards containing the illustration, which he would use for years in his personal correspondence.[3] He proudly became the avatar of the *gelbe*

FIGURE 1 *"Peoples of Europe Guard Your Dearest Gods," 1895. Kaiser Wilhelm II coined the term "Yellow Peril" after he had a nightmare of Europe being attacked by a Buddha riding a dragon. Illustration by Hermann Knackfuss, Courtesy of Harvard University, Harvard-Yenching Library, ss_26084140.*

gefahr, most directly translated as "Yellow Danger" but which can also be rendered "Yellow Risk," "Yellow Threat," "Yellow Hazard," or "Yellow Peril." His persistence paid off, as the idea gradually entered the zeitgeist in the opening years of the ensuing decade. It was popularized in Britain by Matthew Shiel's 1898 novel *The Yellow Danger*, whose Chinese villain was the primary inspiration for Sax Rohmer's later creation Fu Manchu.[4] Attacks on Europeans living in China during the Boxer Rebellion of 1900 helped solidify an image of the Chinese as potential bloodthirsty hordes, even though the rebellion itself led to foreign occupation of the Qing Dynasty capital of Peking and the imposition of a crippling indemnity. Resistance to European aggression somehow implied aggressive intent toward Europe (Figure 1).

By using the mass media to popularize the notion of China and the Chinese as both a security and a civilizational threat, the Kaiser inspired the sorts of novelists and intellectuals who had inspired him. This chapter illustrates how the Yellow Peril was conceived and promulgated in the petri dish of a burgeoning mass media by writers and statesmen who interpreted the events of the day through the prevailing paradigm of Social Darwinism, from which they drew the counterintuitive conclusion that they had the most to fear from the least successful of the world's major polities. They feared an imagined China which had successfully adopted the technologies and institutions of Europe, and which the Chinese would inevitably use to torment their current tormentors. Expanding European power overseas bred confidence and insecurity in equal measures, and the more powerful the European predator, the greater the fear of becoming prey. Chinese intellectuals were also drawn to these ideas. Yan Fu's 1894 book *Heavenly Evolution* was a translation of Thomas Huxley's *Evolution and Ethics* and introduced Chinese readers to Social Darwinism. Yan and his Chinese readers cared not for the biological implications of Darwinism but instead focused on national struggles for survival.[5]

At this stage, China could not live up to these fears by itself. In Wilhelm's illustration, the Chinese dragon was merely a beast of burden—albeit a most frightening one—in need of someone to ride it. The British academic Halford Mackinder is widely labeled the "Father of Geopolitics," an innovator in the study of geography who very much reflected the profound insecurity of the powerful that so defined the period leading up to the First World War. A proud citizen of the world's leading naval power, he posited that land power was now the key to global dominance. Britannia might rule the waves, but whichever rival power controlled the Eurasian landmass had the potential to turn the British into slaves. His "Heartland Theory" argued that whichever power gained control of the "pivot region" of the vast Eurasian steppe—as Genghis Khan and Tamerlane once had—could use this central position to dominate both Western Europe and East Asia. Since the Russian Empire controlled most of this territory at that time, Mackinder was participating in the long-standing British habit of vastly inflating the chances of a Russian invasion of British India, providing an intellectual justification for the "Great Game" of seeking a controlling influence in Central Asia in general and Afghanistan in particular. In 1904, Mackinder published his seminal work "The Geographical Pivot of History," laying out the ideas for which he is best remembered.

That same year, in an essay entitled "The Pressure of Asia," he used the start of the Russo-Japanese War to inflate a new threat. Following in the Kaiser's footsteps, Mackinder warned "were the Chinese, for instance, organized by the Japanese, to overthrow the Russian Empire and conquer its territory, they might constitute the Yellow Peril to the world's freedom just because they would add an Oceanic frontage to the resources of the great continent, an advantage yet denied to the Russian tenant of the pivot region."[6]

First Sea Lord Jackie Fisher, himself something of a strategist, was not a supporter of Mackinder's ideas. He was also a noted dissenter to the extremely popular views of US naval strategist Alfred Thayer Mahan, against whom Mackinder very much directed his Heartland Theory. Mahan's 1890 book *The Influence of Sea Power Upon History* is a celebration of the rise of British naval dominance from the wars against the Dutch in the mid-seventeenth century through those against the French in the late eighteenth century. In the telling of this unabashed Anglophile, Britain's nineteenth-century success proved that control of the oceans was the key to global economic and military success. Fisher countered that "man does not live on water. He lives on land" to emphasize the need to integrate naval and army actions. In a way, he split the difference between Mackinder and Mahan. Yet he saw completely eye-to-eye with Mackinder on the threat of a rising China. According to Fisher, "when by-and-by the Chinese know their power, they have only to walk slowly westwards, and, like the locusts of Egypt, no pharaohs in Europe with all their mighty boats will stop them. They won't wait to fire guns or bombs. They'll just all walk along and smother Europe."[7]

The term "Yellow Peril" appeared shortly after Europeans began defining the peoples of East Asia as having skin the color yellow. Before the nineteenth century, European travelers to China and its neighbors tended to describe the inhabitants as having white skin. The belief that this geographical branch of humanity had yellow skin became commonplace only in the second half of the nineteenth century.[8] Moreover, while Chinese writers had long made racial distinctions based on the darkness or lightness of the skins of various groups of foreigners, they themselves only self-identified as yellow after contact with white missionaries, who had classified them as such.[9] This adoption was eased by the fact that in traditional Chinese culture yellow was regarded as the most favorable of the five "pure" colors.[10] In a rainbow, Yellow was the central color, mirroring China's conception of itself as the Middle Kingdom. It was the official color of Chinese emperors and of the

Yellow River upon the banks of which Chinese civilization first developed. The color white, meanwhile, symbolized death to the Chinese.[11] The label stuck throughout the region, with white journalists calling the Sino-Japanese War "The Yellow War" while it was ongoing, reflecting the period's racialization of foreign relations.[12]

Developing in tandem with increased fear of China after 1880 was increased, and often disproportionate, coverage of events in that nation by European and American journalists.[13] Merchants dreamed of 400 million new customers, while missionaries prayed for an equal number of converts. Both would be disappointed by their eventual meager returns. Familiarity created as much fear as admiration. Often the two could be intertwined. Admiration for the frugality and work ethic of Chinese peasants, supposedly inured to suffering and privation, could create fears of what would happen if they were turned into factory workers or soldiers. To quote Lord Wolseley in the British magazine *Cosmopolitan* in 1895, "this hardy, clever race, whose numbers are to be counted in hundreds of millions, needs only the quickening, guiding, controlling hand and mind of a Napoleon to be converted into the greatest and most powerful nation that has ever dictated terms to the world!"[14] Conversely, cross-cultural encounters often led to contempt. To many from the industrialized world, China and its people seemed filthy, and—what was worse—entirely unconcerned with cleanliness. The British in particular were profoundly scandalized by the state of Chinese hygiene and sanitation in the later nineteenth century.[15]

One European observer during this period was Joseph-Arthur de Gobineau. He is known to history as one of the founders of what came to be called "Scientific Racism," and the author of the four-volume work *Essai sur l'inégalité des races humanes*, first published between 1853 and 1855. But before becoming a writer, Gobineau was a French diplomat who visited China and served in multiple posts nearby.[16] A minor intellectual figure during his lifetime, his magnum opus only became widely known with the printing of its second edition in 1884, two years after his death. In the final years of his life, Gobineau became fixated on the possibility that the Chinese, in league with either the Russians or the Germans, would overrun and colonize Europe, destroying its superior civilization. He articulated these fears in the 500-page, 12,000-verse epic poem *Amadis*. Published posthumously in 1887, the epic concludes with its heroes, not dissimilar to the figures in Wilhelm's illustration, literally drowning in the blood of the hordes of Chinese they had slain.[17] Wilhelm later reported that as a young man he was an avid reader of Gobineau's work and that these were significant influences on his worldview. Furthermore, Gobineau had been a close friend of Prince Philipp of Eulenburg, who was one of the Kaiser's intimates, providing a personal connection between them.[18]

After an 1881 British novel on the Chinese conquest of those islands and an 1881 article in Germany about a Chinese invasion of that country, Gobineau's work was the first of the major Chinese invasion stories in Europe and helped set the template for many later efforts.[19] Most of these works would come, not from Britain or Germany, but from the United States and Australia. By the 1890s, these two nations had decades of experience with Chinese immigration, and both had reacted with intense hostility. In both Australia and the West Coast of the United States, sparse white populations worried about being overrun by Chinese migrants in search of work. These invasion stories invariably featured local Chinese acting as Fifth Columns in support of Chinese invasion, along with other non-white inhabitants. As a rule, the Chinese could not win so long as the opposing country was sufficiently united.

William Ward Crane's short story "The Year 1899," published in a California magazine in 1893, fits this pattern well and added class and religion to race as additional fault lines. In the near future of 1895, a war between Britain and Germany on one side and the rest of non-Teutonic Europe on the other leads to an Anglo-German defeat, only to be followed swiftly by mutinies within the "Latin and Slavic armies" and socialist revolutions in their home countries. With Britain severed from its overseas empire, the Chinese emperor encourages the populations of India and North Africa to revolt, and then adds them to his massive army of invasion "in a holy war against the white race everywhere."[20] These armies quickly overrun and depopulate a European continent scarred by war and revolution, "working with the never-flagging steadiness of ants and bees."[21] Meanwhile, in the United States, Chinese migrate to the Deep South, where they organize Black sharecroppers, with Native Americans fomenting their own uprising on the Great Plains. The Qing emperor prepares a million-man invasion force to cross the Pacific in 1899. Before the Chinese-led forces can land, the US Navy, in cooperation with the Japanese Navy, defeat the Chinese fleet, and then successfully attack China itself. Meanwhile, Britain is spared due to a civil war breaking out between the Hindu and Muslim forces preparing to cross the channel and exterminate their former overlords. Crane concludes with a plea for racial solidarity, noting how, in this story, "Asiatic strength was less important than European weakness" and that "the white race, united, need fear nothing the world contains."[22]

In 1898, Matthew Shiel incorporated non-state actors in his invasion novel *The Yellow Danger.* This work established character archetypes which would directly inspire Saxe Rohmer's iconic Fu Manchu character. Like Fu, Shiel's villain, Dr. Yen How, possesses superhuman intelligence and moves easily in both European and Asian high society. Born of a Chinese mother and a Japanese father, receiving his medical degree from the University of Heidelberg, and working as a doctor in San Francisco, Yen was "an epitome of the West, as he was an embodiment of the East."[23] What distinguished

Yen from Fu Manchu—but gave him much in common with the villain in *The Red Napoleon*, published three decades later—was his emotional and sexual passion. His emotions are hyperbolic, especially the negative ones, and "he cherished a secret and bitter aversion to the white race," while his lifelong goal was "to possess one white woman, ultimately, and after all."[24] Yen took Social Darwinism to genocidal extremes, professing a firm conviction that "the yellow man is doomed—if the white man is not." Believing that ongoing technological advances in Europe would eventually render Asia's population advantage irrelevant in a military conflict, he chose the option of preventive war.

Yen's plan was to use Europe's military superiority against itself while exploiting China's weakness. Becoming the chief adviser to the Qing emperor, Yen accepted European demands for territorial concessions in China at a rate faster than the Europeans expected. As the British, French, Germans, and Russians further encroached upon Chinese territory, they came to blows with one another—first in Asia and then back home in Europe, triggering a continent-wide conflagration. While Europe tore itself asunder, Yen forged a union of China and Japan, and raised an immense army of Chinese conscripts and Japanese officers.[25] After Europe had exhausted itself, Yen's massive host crossed Eurasia and attacked, destroying all in its path. In keeping with Yen's own emotionalism, Shiel depicts Chinese soldiers as monstrously ferocious, writing "the intensity of the Chinese instinct of Vengeance is a mystery—it is not human—it is not bestial—it may be demonic." Shiel combined this image of the subhuman-cum-superhuman Chinese with a hive metaphor, writing that when on the march "every Chinaman was feeling the thrill of that electrical cobweb spreading over the land, of which the brain of Yen How was the centre."[26]

Like Fu Manchu, Yen How is opposed by a heroic and debonair British secret agent, a man named John Hardy.[27] Hardy proposes a union of Britain with the United States, but the leaders of the latter country refuse to participate out of fears of massive inflows of penniless refugees from the devastated European continent. Britain now stands alone, defended only by its navy, which Yen soon sinks with his torpedoes. But then, in a twist uncannily similar to H. G. Wells's later bestseller *War of the Worlds*, before it can cross the English Channel, the Chinese host becomes infected with bubonic plague and cholera—both diseases Europeans at the time associated with the Chinese, and believed had originated in China.[28] Whereas Wells's aliens were felled because of their unfamiliarity with the Earth's pathogens, the Chinese perished due to their purportedly innate disease-carrying nature. The British proceeded to repopulate Europe and became the rulers of the entire globe. *The Yellow Danger* proved a bestseller, going through three printings in 1898 alone. Its cover, which featured a thin, bald Chinese man with long fingernails and a thin handlebar mustache clutching the globe, became an iconic piece of Yellow Peril imagery.[29]

In 1893, five years before Shiel's novel, and two years before Wilhelm's vision, the Oxford Fellow and Minister of Education in the Australian Territory of Victoria Charles Pearson published an academic study entitled *National Life and Character*. It was a pathbreaking link between the late nineteenth-century fears of Gobineau and the post-First World War pessimism of Lothrop Stoddard, and became a highly influential bestseller on multiple continents. Kaiser Wilhelm was in the process of reading Pearson's book when he had his "Yellow Peril" dream, and Australian parliamentarians cited and read from Pearson's book during their 1901 debates on immigration restriction.[30] Upon reading it in 1894, Theodore Roosevelt developed an avid interest in natalist eugenics, since it was Pearson who informed him that there were 400 million Chinese. As a result, during his presidency, Roosevelt tried to encourage all white American women to have at least five children. In 1908, Roosevelt recalled that *National Life and Character* "shook the self-confidence of the white races and deprived them of the absolute sense of assured superiority which had hitherto helped them to dominate."[31] Roosevelt's close friend, naval theorist Alfred Thayer Mahan, was inspired by Pearson's book to declare that the ultimate question of the age was whether "Eastern or Western civilization is to dominate through the earth and control its future."[32]

During his lifetime, Pearson would be credited with inventing the notion (though not the actual term) of the Yellow Peril.[33] As a European intellectual of the 1890s, Pearson predictably and fervently embraced a race-based Social Darwinist approach to international relations. However, he turned the conventional assumptions of this school of thought on their heads. A large measure of this was due to Pearson having spent the previous two decades of his life in Australia, where, looking northward, white dominance appeared far less secure than it might from London or Berlin. The 1890s were the height of modern imperialist expansion, as the European powers carved up Africa, the United States annexed Hawaii and the Philippines, and the Japanese took Taiwan and set their sights on Korea. It was also the peak of white racial arrogance. Pearson saw this moment—somewhat correctly—as the pinnacle before an inevitable decline and retreat. He achieved this by taking (pseudo)-Scientific Racism back to its eighteenth-century Enlightenment roots when writers hypothesized climatic explanations for racial traits.[34]

At issue was the common late Romantic conception of Pearson's time that "the character of a race determines its vitality more than climate."[35] Pearson argued centuries of European colonization proved that white people were only fit to live in the temperate zones of the northern and southern hemispheres: the United States and Argentina, but not Guatemala; South Australia, but not northern Australia. In between these temperate zones was "The Black and

Yellow Belt" of tropical and subtropical climates which girdled the equator, where few whites chose to settle and those who did struggled with diseases and heat.[36] Most of this "Black and Yellow Belt" was currently under European control, but due to the lack of colonial settlers, could not remain so indefinitely. Furthermore, Europe was at a demographic disadvantage, since in terms of population growth "the lower race increases faster than the higher."[37]

Into this inevitable void would step the Chinese. The Chinese were the world's most populous ethnicity and were climatically adaptable in ways that the white peoples were not. Why this was so, Pearson does not explain. China, like Europe, is largely in the temperate zone, though it also contains subarctic and subtropical regions, and the Chinese thrived in all. The author focuses on the adaptability of the southern Chinese to subtropical and tropical climates, particularly the large and thriving Chinese populations in Singapore, Malaya, the Philippines, South America, the Caribbean, and the northern coast of Australia. While intellectually less creative than "Aryan" Europeans, the Chinese—in addition to their proven climatic adaptability—worked harder than Europeans, successfully competing against white labor in the western United States and Australia. Pearson predicted that, absent government intervention, the future of his adopted homeland would be identical to that of Southern Africa, part of which was also in the temperate zone. Just as in those colonies the British and Dutch settlers came to rely on African labor, white Australians would—if the free market prevailed—utilize Chinese manual labor in preference to white workers. Soon, northern Australia would become "a Natal," with the Chinese constituting over 90 percent of the population, while more temperate southern Australia would be "a Cape Colony," and only one-quarter white.[38]

In Chapter 1, Pearson stoked one aspect of the Yellow Peril—the fear of Chinese immigrants. In Chapter 2, he dealt with two others—fear of the potential economic and military power of China proper. Its rise to becoming the planet's leading power was as inevitable as gravitational attraction: "with civilization equally diffused, the most populous country must ultimately be the most powerful; and the preponderance of China over any rival—even over the United States of America—is likely to be overwhelming."[39] Chinese preponderance would inevitably influence European civilization, and "it is not assumed that this effect would necessarily be all evil," since the Chinese people were harder working, more frugal, and less hedonistic than Europeans.[40] Pearson considers the possibility of a China led by "a man with the organizing and aggressive genius of Peter the Great or Frederick the Second" and the threat this would pose to Russian Asia and British India.[41] He makes no overt claim that Chinese sovereignty would follow Chinese migration to lands from Indochina to New Guinea. Pearson also posits no timeline for these predicted developments. Nor does he present any possible remedies, excepting immigration restrictions, declaring in the book's introduction that "we may circumscribe the growth of China, though we cannot altogether arrest it."[42]

Perhaps the most intriguing work in the invasion subgenre of proto-science fiction was Jack London's controversial short story "The Unparalleled Invasion," written in 1907 and published in *Collier's* magazine in 1909. London traveled through Korea and into Manchuria with the Japanese army during its war with Russia in 1904, publishing in the *San Francisco Examiner* on September 25 of that year a soon-to-be famous essay on the epochal significance of that war entitled "The Yellow Peril." Written in Manchuria that June, the essay argued Japan's military successes would soon "awaken" the Chinese people who—rather than the Japanese—constituted the true Yellow Peril and threat to white dominance.[43] This essay provided the basis for "The Unparalleled Invasion," and portions of it appeared verbatim in that story's text. London identified China's threat as primarily economic rather than military. "The Chinese was the perfect type of industry," he wrote in both the story and the essay, adding in the essay that "he is not so ill-disposed toward new ideas and new methods as his history would seem to indicate."[44]

In the story, Japan's economic and military penetration of China "awakens" that nation to modernity. The people rise up and expel the Japanese in 1922, driving them not only out of China proper but also Korea and Taiwan. However, "contrary to expectation, China did not prove warlike," and "after a time of disquiet, the idea was accepted that China was to be feared, not in war, but in commerce."[45] Industrial development and trade enable China to break its Malthusian shackles and increase its already gigantic population by hundreds of millions. In the 1970s, tens of millions of Chinese migrated to French Indochina and British Malaya, Burma, and Nepal. When the French colonial army resisted, it was annihilated by China's massive and "splendidly efficient militia," which it chose to develop in lieu of a professional standing army. A large-scale invasion and naval blockade by an outraged France proved fruitless, the army was annihilated on its march to Peking, and the blockade was ineffective against an economically self-sufficient nation.[46]

"The world trembled," not because of China's territorial expansion (Britain, interestingly, did not protest or resist Chinese penetration of its colonies as the French had) but because "there were two Chinese for every white person in the world." All conventional uses of force proving useless, the Western powers—upon the suggestion of an American scientist—resort to large-scale biological warfare, dropping vials containing "a score of plagues" onto Chinese territory on May 1, 1976, from thousands of "tiny airships" launched from warships loitering off China's coast. Massive European armies prevented the stricken Chinese people from fleeing and soon they all succumb to disease. According to "the democratic American program," the "howling wilderness" China had become was resettled by whites in "a tremendous and successful experiment in cross-fertilization," essentially creating a second United States of America in the year of its bicentennial. Shortly afterward, on the eve of a war between France and Germany over Alsace-Lorraine, the white nations sign a treaty, pledging to never use such weapons of "ultra-modern war" upon each other.[47]

Many scholars have taken London's story at face value. Cultural historian Bruce Franklin called it an "exultation of the superweapon and Asian genocide."[48] Yet recent literary scholars of London's work have argued London "satirized the West's paranoia about Asians" with that story.[49] Rather than an example of racism, the story was "a very stern warning of what can happen if racial hated is allowed to flourish" as well as "an ironic indictment of the behavior of imperialistic governments per se."[50] London's essay "The Yellow Peril" appears to support this revisionist contention. In that dispatch, London heaps contempt upon Koreans, whom he views as backward and cowardly, finds the Japanese gifted only in military matters, but has nothing but praise for every characteristic of the Chinese individuals he meets after crossing the Yalu River into Manchuria. He terms them a people "deft, intelligent, and unafraid to die," who are brave in battle, industrious in labor, insistent but honest in business matters, and "not dead to new ideas."[51] London contradicted nearly a century of American conventional wisdom concerning the Chinese people. His affection for them was unmistakable. One is left with the distinct impression that it is highly doubtful he would wish to see them wiped off the face of the earth. The inescapable conclusion would be that Jack London intended "The Unparalleled Invasion" to be at least in part a dark satire, though readers of *Collier's* most likely failed to appreciate this.[52]

At the start of the twentieth century, even China's weaknesses could pose a threat. Images of contemporary China more often than not emphasized not China's future power but instead its present state of degeneracy, decay, and disease. Calling China the "Sick Man of Asia" had a double meaning not applied to the Ottoman Turkish "Sick Man of Europe." To Europeans, China was the purported origin site of bubonic plague, the source of the nineteenth-century urban scourge of cholera—sometimes called "the pestilence of the East"—and the alleged "cradle of smallpox."[53] Long absent from Europe, plague struck Hong Kong in 1894. It was during this outbreak that British doctors in the colony discovered that plague was transmitted to humans by fleas traveling on rodents, solving a mystery extending back to the fourteenth century.[54] Such was China's reputation as an incubator for diseases that during the worldwide influenza pandemic of 1918, a US Army doctor named James Joseph claimed the disease was actually pneumonic plague transmitted from Northeast China to Europe by "Chinese Coolies" used as laborers on the Western Front.[55]

Geopolitically, the notion of an ailing China carried strong metaphorical weight in an era of Social Darwinism. British Prime Minister Salisbury reflected both this reality and its dangers in a May 1898 address widely known as his "Dying Nations" speech. Most famously, and prophetically, Salisbury predicted that "the living nations will gradually encroach on the territory of the dying and the seeds of conflict among civilized nations will gradually appear." His worries about imperial competition spawning great power war centered upon ongoing events in China. The previous year, Germany seized the village of Qingdao, establishing a colony in Shantung province. In response, Britain gained rights to the nearby northern Chinese port of Weihaiwei to complement their southern Chinese base in Hong Kong, while Russia obtained Port Arthur, denied three years earlier to Japan. After decades of expectation, a genuine "Scramble for China" appeared to finally be underway. Meanwhile, only weeks before, the United States Navy under Commodore Dewey destroyed a Spanish fleet in Manilla Bay, opening the door to US occupation of the entire Philippine archipelago, much to Germany's chagrin. While loudly and self-righteously proclaiming its lack of interest in acquiring any Chinese territory, a key motivation for the establishment of a base at Manilla was to strengthen American diplomatic and economic leverage in China.

A key player in laying the groundwork for the United States in East Asian diplomacy was John Watson Foster. One of America's first career diplomats, Foster briefly served as Secretary of State in Benjamin Harrison's administration in the early 1890s. Today, he is best known as father-in-law to Edward Lansing, Secretary of State under Woodrow Wilson, and as the grandfather of Eisenhower's Secretary of State John Foster Dulles, who proudly kept bound volumes of Foster's papers and correspondence in his Foggy Bottom office, making a point of pulling out a volume when meeting with other officials, as if seeking guidance. Like his grandson, Foster was a religiously devout lawyer-turned-diplomat, and he viewed the Christianization of China by American missionaries as inevitable in the twentieth century. Unlike his grandson, he was uncomfortable with saber-rattling and ardently supported peaceful arbitration of international disputes. He advocated a US policy in Asia based upon "a spirit of justice, forbearance, and magnanimity," and believed in the US mission of "giving the world a freer market, and the inhabitants of the Orient the blessings of Christian Civilization."[56] He opposed the exclusion of Chinese immigrants from the United States, arguing the best approach was to treat their people and leaders with respect. Most importantly, he realized that military belligerence toward the Qing Empire and economic exploitation of the Chinese people were the surest paths to creating a China that could threaten the Western world. Foster worried that "four hundred millions, sturdy and passionately devoted to their ancient customs, might in time, under the influence of an all-prevailing race hatred, be changed from a peace-loving community into a warlike people, bent upon avenging their wrongs."[57] In Foster's estimation, if Europeans, Americans, and Australians feared future Chinese power, they had only themselves to blame.

Shortly after China's humiliating military defeat at the hands of the neighboring Japanese, the editors of *Harper's Weekly*, in an essay which assessed the potential Japanese threat and found it wanting, referenced widespread speculation about China's potential. They noted how "a great many thoughtful people have believed that if we should succeed in teaching our methods to the Chinese we might pay dearly for it." They warned, with measured understatement, that "if we could teach China to use her resources in war as Germany has used hers, the result might be unpleasant." Swiftly shifting tone, the authors speculated that "a Mongolian domination of the human race would be a calamity worse than the Deluge." Still, the magazine concluded, "this danger, if it ever existed, was always remote."[58] After all, at that time, the Western powers were waxing, and the backward, corrupt, seemingly incurious Qing Dynasty was rapidly disintegrating. Yet China's defeat also led to fears, like those of Kaiser Wilhelm's, that Japan could harness and exploit China's human and material potential. The Boston-based magazine *Living Age*, in an essay analyzing Wilhelm's term and Pearson's "thoughtful book," worried that "the yellow giants may turn to the yellow dwarfs, and this if they do the struggle may be at least more protracted than any one in Berlin, or indeed in Europe, now expects."[59]

Defeat at the hands of its neighbors stung the Chinese far more than the Opium Wars or other European incursions had. It was one thing to be bested by distant white barbarians. But to lose to neighboring Japan, whose culture the Chinese had long regarded as an inferior facsimile of their own, and whom they had long called "dwarf pirates," was particularly stinging. It awakened the nationalistic fervor of both Chiang Kai-shek and Mao Zedong and is remembered by the Chinese as nearly as psychologically damaging as the far more grievous acts of Japanese aggression during the Second World War.[60] But that which the Chinese viewed as a profound setback was seen by Western observers as a spur to China's modernization and awakening. In fact, during the final decade of the Qing Dynasty, foreigners proved far more sanguine than the Chinese themselves about their progress and prospects. In 1898, the missionary-affiliated journal *The Congregationalist* claimed that "the slow Chinaman is awakening from his sleep of centuries. The war with Japan brought a revelation to him." As missionaries, they saw this as a "beneficent revolution," especially if it was inspired by their own teachings in China.[61]

Other observers were decidedly less sympathetic to the prospect of an awakening China. An 1899 article in the *Washington Post* entitled "Peril of Yellow Menace" warned of "a dreadful Eastern specter formed by a fusion of China, Japan, and other the other yellow races in Asia." The newspaper foresaw an incipient Sino-Japanese alliance which would make Kaiser Wilhelm's nightmare "an accomplished fact and a proven reality." Parroting Wilhelm's imagery, the paper warned of the prospect of "the most populous, industrious and prosperous empire in the world, possessed of undeveloped wealth to an incalculable extent," lashed to an aggressive and expansionist Japan.[62] The use of the awakening metaphor brings to mind the quote about China attributed to Napoleon, though at this time no source cited it, providing evidence to doubt its veracity. The British periodical *Review of Reviews* in fact cited the mid-nineteenth-century Russian anarchist revolutionary Nikolai Bakunin as "the first to prophecy eruption of the Yellow Race into Europe."[63]

The subsequent Russo-Japanese War in 1904–5 over control of and influence in Korea and Manchuria, another event seemingly confirming China's continuing decline, was presented at the time as a boon to the Qing Empire. American observers predicted a Japanese victory, and since they assumed Russia was a greater threat to China's territorial integrity, believed this would redound to the Qing Empire's benefit. *Living Age* claimed Japan's victory "has freed China" from Russia's grip, enabling the Qing to continue reforms after the crushing of the Boxer Uprising provided "the death-throw of that conservative and bigoted reverence for the past."[64] During the conflict, Frederick Seward, son of Lincoln's Secretary of State William Seward and an influential figure in Republican Party foreign policy circles, claimed Japan was fighting on behalf of China and of all Asia. At this time, and in fact for several decades afterward, Westerners could not conceive of Japan as a threat to China, in spite of accumulating evidence to the contrary. Seward also warned Yellow Peril fears incited aggression against China which would inevitably foment "the most disastrous war" among Western powers for control of China, echoing Salisbury's "Dying Nations" speech from the previous decade.[65]

In 1901, a British diplomat in China named Claude MacDonald praised the Chinese and predicted great things for their future, saying "they are so sober and industrious and will work so cheap and so hard that they will develop very rapidly if they get a chance." He concluded that "there may be a yellow peril or there may not, but there will certainly be a yellow wonder."[66] But while China as a nation remained weak and poorly governed, the millions of Chinese who ventured overseas in the nineteenth century provided a current, clear, and present danger. As the Australian Prime Minister T. Price said on a visit to Liverpool in 1908, "the Australians see the yellow peril ahead," and were preparing to face it. Sensing British complacency, Price warned that "with the awakening of the East, if you are going to retain Australia," then "someone has to stand up and fight to keep it."[67] At the dawn of a new century, the dual fears of potential Chinese national power and the actual presence of Chinese individuals abroad combined to produce a global backlash.

2

Worldwide Opposition to Chinese Immigration

The readers misunderstood the poem's meaning, and this misunderstanding made the poet a star. Without intending to, a young San Francisco writer named Bret Harte captured the national zeitgeist. As with Jack London, what had been meant as satire was taken in all seriousness. A send-up of bigotry became an anthem for hatred. Over the next two decades, it was the inspiration for numerous hit songs, enhancing the repertoire of the popular minstrel character "John Chinaman," who had been created in California in the 1850s.[1] Appealing not just to lowbrow tastes but to highbrow culture as well, its success prompted the University of California at Berkeley to offer Harte the position of "Professor of Recent Literature and Curator of the Library and Museum," which he turned down for a far more lucrative offer to write for the *Atlantic Monthly*. In the poem "Plain Language from Truthful James," the Chinese immigrant Ah Sin, who has a "childlike" smile, defeats the Irish immigrant William Nye in a high-stakes game of euchre, out-cheating a cheater who suspected nothing until it was too late. Upon realizing that the tables had been turned, Nye exclaims "Can this be? We are ruined by Chinese cheap labor." The final stanza of the poem was its most memorable: "Which is why I remark/ And my language is plain/ That for ways that are dark/ And for tricks that are vain/ The heathen Chinee is peculiar/ Which the same I am free to maintain."

First appearing in the local literary journal *Overland Monthly*, which Harte at the time edited, "Plain Language from Truthful James" was over the next year reprinted in numerous newspapers and magazines, often with a new title—"The Heathen Chinee"—which became how most people referred to it. It also appeared in stand-alone book or pamphlet form, with numerous illustrations of the scenes described. The poem ends with allusions to hazily defined violence. Upon realizing he is the one who has been conned, William

Nye attacks Ah Sin, with others possibly joining in. It was a fictionalized representation of countless attacks on Chinese immigrants during this period. But whereas Harte sympathized with Ah Sin, his readers identified with, and cheered on, William Nye. At a time of great tension between Irish and Chinese workers in northern California, Harte's intention was to humorously critique prevailing white stereotypes about the Chinese. In his newspaper articles, Harte had put himself on record condemning white violence against the local Chinese community, as well as toward nearby Native Americans. His 1874 short story "Wan Lee, the Pagan" similarly sought both to undermine negative stereotypes of the Chinese and to portray white Americans as the true barbarians. Originally written as an afterthought, with no intention to publish, Harte would later refer to the poem as "the worst poem I ever wrote, possibly the worst poem anyone ever wrote."

As the first voluntary non-white immigrants to arrive in the United States in noticeable numbers, the Chinese tested how welcoming America could be to cultural outsiders, and how accommodating of racial diversity.[2] Previous acts of Congress presented mixed signals. The Naturalization Act of 1790 provided an easy path to citizenship for all immigrants who could be classified as white, buttressing the notion of antebellum America as a *Herrenvolk* Democracy welcoming only to European outsiders. However, the Fourteenth Amendment, ratified in 1868, extended the rights of citizenship to all born on US soil—excepting members of Indian nations—regardless of race. Congressional debate indicated that the intent was not merely to grant citizenship rights to the formerly enslaved. While that was the primary goal, those who supported the amendment made clear that it would also apply to other non-whites—including the Chinese. There was thus an inherent tension between racialist immigration regulations and a now-potentially racially inclusive Constitution. To paraphrase Roger Taney's majority opinion in the 1857 case *Dred Scott v. Sanford*, it remained to be determined if the Chinese had any rights that white Americans were bound to respect.

In the end, the US political system arrived at the same conclusion reached in every other place experiencing the arrival of Chinese, regardless of regime type, constitutional rights, or political traditions. Throughout the periphery of the Pacific Ocean and beyond, wherever people had the power to prevent or restrict the arrivals of new Chinese, and to circumscribe the rights of those already present, they did so. With the enactment of the Chinese Restriction Act in 1882, the US government set a precedent on immigration—not only for itself but for all the lands to which the Chinese migrated. In each instance, the justification was a combination of fears of economic competition, demographic change, and cultural degeneracy. This chapter begins with the reaction to Chinese arrivals in the United States, before discussing similar patterns in Canada, Latin America, Australia, Russia, South Africa, and Britain.

In all cases, the Chinese were classified as uniquely different from other newcomers, and as uniquely threatening. They were seen not as immigrants, but rather as invaders.

Pulled by economic opportunity abroad, and pushed by civil war and overpopulation at home, beginning in the 1850s, a steady stream of Chinese migrated out of the Pearl River Delta region (near the modern metropolis of Guangzhou, then the growing port city of Canton). An estimated quarter million migrated to the Caribbean, where British and Spanish landowners and colonial administrators intended to use them to replace formerly enslaved Black labor forces. Approximately 300 thousand would seek their fortunes in the gold fields of California, Australia, and South Africa. Hundreds of thousands more worked in the tin mines of British Malaya, and established merchant communities throughout South Asia.[3] While Qing laws prohibited such overseas migration, they could do little to stop the outflow. Instead, they became outraged when foreign governments tried to prohibit Chinese from arriving and engaged in acts of overt discrimination against the Chinese already in their territories. The poor treatment of overseas Chinese became a proxy for the weakness of the Chinese Empire, in the eyes of both Chinese officials and China's increasingly politicized urban population. To quote a Canton merchant in 1886, responding to widespread acts of mob violence against Chinese in the western United States, "I hope someday to see our fleets so powerful that we can point our guns at San Francisco, and demand of them the rights they have wrested from us, and reparation for the wrongs they have done us."[4]

Scholars of the history of images of the Chinese in American culture tend to agree that white Americans' fear and loathing of all things China preceded the first appearance of actual Chinese people on US soil. Accordingly, the wave of anti-Chinese prejudice and mob violence which culminated in the Chinese Restriction Act of 1882 and the Chinese Exclusion Act of 1888, the first US immigration laws to single out a specific ethnicity or nationality, were not solely a reaction to competition for low-wage jobs between Chinese and European immigrants in places like San Francisco. Instead, these acts were the sprouting of seeds which had been planted long ago and regularly reflected in American cultural products. According to Stanford Lyman, who in 1974 wrote one of the first general histories of the experiences of the Chinese in America, "by the time the Chinese made their appearance on American shores they had been preceded by a richly embellished but almost entirely negative stereotypy."[5] Stuart Creighton Miller, who in 1969 published the first study of early American images of the Chinese, concurred, writing that "the unfavorable image of the Chinese is discernible among American opinion makers long before the first Celestial gold seeker set foot upon California soil."[6] Politicians and journalists described China as "an unalloyed despotism," its people a "godless, immoral, and vice-ridden body of pagans."[7] Whereas colonial Americans frequently felt a sort of naïve and sentimental fondness for Chinese culture and civilization similar to that of contemporaneous Enlightenment-era Europe, the new republic viewed China as its mirror opposite, "singularly impervious to nineteenth-century ideals of progress, liberty, and civilization to which an emergent modern America was fervently committed."[8] This assessment ultimately served to "arouse fear and suspicion about Chinese immigration to America and to transfer the horror imputed to the Chinese polity onto individual Chinese immigrants."[9] Such sentiments were evident in newspapers and magazines throughout the United States, not merely on the West Coast where the Chinese arrived and settled in the largest numbers.

Other scholars have questioned this notion of ingrained and endemic anti-Chinese sentiment in the United States, focusing on how anti-Chinese movements took decades to gain support, and did so only after the number of Chinese in California and other parts of the American West became significant enough to pose a competitive threat to low-skilled white laborers. They point out that the peak of anti-Chinese sentiment occurred during the six-year depression which followed the Panic of 1873 when jobs became scarce. But the popularity of Harte's poem, which was published and popularized before this economic downturn, illustrates how primed the public was in this period. Its national popularity revealed that anti-Chinese animus extended well beyond places like San Francisco where the Chinese actually lived. Simply put, there were tens of millions of Americans who opposed additional Chinese immigration, and supported discrimination against those Chinese already present, who had never set eyes on a Chinese person.

In the "John Chinaman" minstrel songs which developed in the 1850s, Chinese men were presented as effeminate and unmanly. Many of the songs centered around failed pursuits of white women.[10] John Chinaman differed from Black minstrel stock characters like Jim Crow or Zip Coon through his feminine qualities. Whereas Black males were portrayed on stage and in song as hyper-masculine in their proclivities for violence and sex, the notion of a virile Chinese man was presented as ridiculous. White audiences laughed at the notion of a Chinese lothario the same way they laughed at that of a Black gentleman or a Black politician. Offstage, white men used the prevalence of Chinese-owned restaurants and laundries to further feminize them since cooking and cleaning were seen as traditionally female activities.[11] Chinese diets were also feminized, such as in American Federal of Labor leader Samuel Gompers's 1902 work *Meat vs. Rice: American Manhood Against Asiatic Coolieism*.[12] Irish immigrants, among whom minstrelsy was particularly popular, used these caricatures of the Chinese to emphasize their own whiteness, which among some native-born "Old Stock" descendants of English immigrants was occasionally called into question. Even African-

Americans, when they embraced the genre of minstrelsy after emancipation, created their own songs mocking the foreignness of the Chinese to emphasize their own credentials as genuine American citizens.[13]

Whether the motivations were economic, cultural, or racial, Chinese faced discrimination and (often violent) resistance to their presence in California from the moment of their arrival. Barely a year after the dockings of the first transport ships from Canton and Hong Kong, John Bigler became governor of the new state of California in 1851 by running on an explicitly anti-Chinese platform.[14] Bigler's appeals tapped into the anxieties of working-class antebellum Jacksonian Democrats migrating to the Golden State, while those of post-Civil War politicians drew on the Republican Party's "Free Labor" ideology, falsely depicting the Chinese as "coolies" who were effectively owned by their employers, as Black slaves had been. Opposing the laboring classes of both parties were employers who valued the Chinese as inexpensive immigrant labor and merchants who believed increased US trade with China was contingent upon good treatment of America's Chinese population.[15] When Chinese immigrants moved from gold mining in the 1850s to railroad construction in the 1860s to various commercial and manufacturing activities in the 1870s, the arguments against their presence relied less on "coolie" stereotypes than on fears of Chinese racial superiority. The leading newspaper in Tacoma, Washington, argued that if "millions of industrious hard-working sons and daughters of Confucius" were "given an equal chance with your people" they "would outdo them in the struggle for life and gain possession of the Pacific coast of America."[16] These stereotypes presaged future fears of an inevitably rising Chinese nation, the difference being that Chinese immigrants were an internal enemy and thus far more of a palpable and immediate threat.

Journalist Henry George is best known to posterity as the author of the 1879 book *Progress and Poverty*, a pioneering attack on American economic inequality during the Gilded Age period between the end of the Civil War in 1865 and the rise of the Progressive Movement around 1900. Its proposals for governments to take direct actions to redistribute wealth inspired both the Populist Movement and Franklin Roosevelt's New Deal. George's writings also provided the chief inspiration for Sun Yat-sen's program to modernize the Chinese economy, and his writings were still being praised by Chiang Kai-shek and his wife in the 1940s, long after they had been forgotten in the United States. That he was admired by the Chinese was particularly ironic because, a decade before producing his magnum opus, George first gained national prominence with his 1869 essay "The Chinese in California." Written in San Francisco, and quickly reprinted in newspapers across the nation, it argued for an end to Chinese immigration, lest their multitudes overrun the western United States. Acknowledging China's current state of weakness, George cautioned that the Chinese peoples' "mere numbers" would "make them a force of vast importance to the future of the rest of mankind." In that future, "China may wake from her sleep of ages, and learn from Western civilization." In the present, individual Chinese laborers were already doing so in California, due to their inherent "patience" and "economy."[17] Absent government action, with their patience, economy, and "endurance which countless ages of tyranny have ground into the character of the down-trodden peoples of the East," the Chinese "will crowd white labor to the wall," the result of which would ultimately be another civil war.[18]

George late admitted it was the eagerness of wealthy employers to hire Chinese workers which first inspired him to consider the dangers of monopolies and led to all his subsequent economic theories and proposals. The Panic of 1873 which nearly ruined George financially also increased political pressure for Chinese immigration restrictions, helping overcome opposition from the business interests who employed Chinese workers. It led to the 1877 formation of the Workingmen's Party in San Francisco by Dennis Kearny, an Irish immigrant and labor activist who coined the slogan "The Chinese Must Go!"[19] Soon to fuse with local Democrats, the Workingmen's Party shifted the focus of white working-class anger on the Pacific Coast away from their white employers and onto the Chinese workingmen those white employers hired. As the German Social Democratic Party's founder Auguste Bebel said of anti-Semitism in Europe, in the Gilded Age United States, anti-Chinese bigotry became "The Socialism of Fools."

This split between capital and labor was acutely reflected in the first novel to depict a Chinese invasion of the United States, P. W. Dooner's 1880 bestseller *Last Days of the Republic*. Set two decades in the future, Dooner depicts a rising China using its emigrants to establish an overseas empire and achieve global domination. Quickly learning from its European exploiters, the Chinese become the world's leading industrial exporter, building up a massive trade surplus the Qing Empire devotes to arms production. China's example inspires neighboring colonial peoples to cast off their European rulers and achieve independence under China's aegis.[20] Meanwhile, the other economic superpower across the Pacific Ocean transitions from a democratic republic of small producers into a plutocratic oligarchy. Rather than take care of its suffering multitudes, America's industrial titans choose instead to replace them with less expensive Chinese laborers. They take the places of European immigrants in the New England textile mills and Black sharecroppers in the southern cotton fields. Soon, some of these Chinese become wealthy themselves and are accepted into white high society as equals. They become both business and political leaders, gaining control of a number of state governments in partnership with white elites.[21]

Once effectively armed, the Qing Dynasty sends its state-of-the-art fleet to America's West Coast, carrying a sizeable invasion force. These soldiers are assisted by Chinese Americans, who arm themselves, form militias, and work with Chinese-American elites to seize power from whites around the country. Once in control, they create "the colossal fabric of barbaric splendor known as the Western Empire of his August Majesty the Emperor of China and Ruler of all lands."[22] Dooner set the standard for future works by depicting Chinese soldiers as "masses of mindless automata."[23] In his novel, Chinese immigrants were the "Trojan horse of Chinese imperial ambitions."[24] In addition, Dooner's portrait of an America beset by increasing income inequality and corrupt governing institutions anticipated both the arguments of the Populist Movement and their occasional ethnic scapegoating. America was conquered because its native-born elites allowed it to be conquered. Rather than take care of their own people, they collaborated with a foreign enemy for short-term profit.

Having been a mainstay of Democratic Party politics in California for a generation, opposition to the Chinese now became a nationwide bipartisan movement. In 1875, Congress passed the Page Act, which effectively stopped nearly all immigration by Chinese women by forcing them to undergo invasive and humiliating examinations upon entry to prove they were not sex workers. At the time, there were fewer than 5,000 women in the United States who had been born in China, comprising less than 5 percent of the total US Chinese-born population. The law ensured that the extremely skewed gender ratio in the Chinese-American community would persist well into the mid-twentieth century. Standing in the way of more sweeping action was the 1868 Burlingame Treaty between the United States and China, which theoretically prevented discrimination against Chinese immigrants to the United States. But diplomacy soon conformed to domestic politics, and the 1880 Angell Treaty with China reversed key portions of Burlingame's treaty to allow for restrictions of Chinese immigration.[25] This was followed in 1882 by the far more sweeping Chinese Restriction Act, which severely limited all Chinese immigration to the United States. What followed were several years of white mob violence against Chinese-Americans west of the Rocky Mountains, where nearly all of them lived. The attacks reached a crescendo in 1885 with the forced expulsion of the entire Chinese population of Tacoma, Washington, along with the Sand Creek massacre at a coal mine in Wyoming. The Tacoma expulsion inspired similar acts in numerous western cities and towns, forcing endangered Chinese to flee eastward and establish Chinatowns in cities like New York, or retreat to San Francisco for safety in numbers. Just as the lynchings of the 1890s spurred the segregation and disenfranchisement of African-Americans, these mob actions led Congress in 1888 to pass the Chinese Exclusion Act, which sought to bar all future Chinese immigration, prevent existing immigrants from becoming citizens, and forbid those who left the country from ever returning. These restrictions remained in effect until 1943.[26]

Chinese immigration to the United States continued, as evidenced by the fact that over the decades the Chinese-American population remained overwhelmingly young and of working-age. Immigration enforcement mechanisms remained rudimentary and underfunded well into the twentieth century. But these unauthorized entries constituted only a few thousand annual arrivals, allowing merely for the maintenance of a population of around 100,000. Thus, the population remained small enough not to be seen as a growing threat to national identity. The notion of the Chinese not as immigrants but as invaders was legally endorsed in the 1889 Supreme Court decision of "Chae Chan Ping v. United States," commonly referred to as the "Chinese Exclusion Case." The plaintiff had journeyed back to China and now wished to legally return to the United States in accordance with the Burlingame Treaty. The Court's unanimous decision affirmed legislative superiority in immigration law. In the opinion, the justices defended exclusion explicitly on national security grounds. The United States was apparently already at war with the Chinese people, referred to by the Court as "the vast hordes of its people crowding in upon us," and if "the government of the United States, through its legislative department, considers the presence of foreigners of a different race in this country, who will not assimilate with us, to be dangerous to its peace and security, their exclusion is not to be stayed because at the time there are no actual hostilities with the nation of which the foreigners are subjects."[27]

The Chinese were the first nationality specifically excluded from immigrating to and settling in the United States. While there had been intense localized opposition to Irish Catholic immigration in eastern cities such as Boston, New York, and Baltimore going back to the 1840s, and additional antipathy toward later waves of Italian and Russian-Jewish immigration in the late nineteenth century, these localized movements failed to successfully enlist national public opinion and Congress into their service during this period. This made anti-Chinese sentiment unique. Only after the rise of eugenics and Social Darwinism in the early decades of the twentieth century were immigrants from Eastern and Southern Europe feared even by those who lived among few if any of them, and only in the 1920s were severe legal restrictions put in place against them. While the Qing government acquiesced to this discrimination, politically active Chinese did not. In 1905, shortly after Congress made Chinese exclusion permanent, merchants in Shanghai organized a boycott of American imports. They publicized the boycott in newspapers in the port city and well beyond. Over the next year, US exports to China fell by nearly half.[28] However, this impacted Chinese sellers and distributors of American goods more than it did American manufacturers, and the boycott had fizzled by the end of 1906.

What happened in the United States in the 1880s sparked a transnational movement all along the Pacific Rim. In the western hemisphere, in addition to the more than 100,000 who had permanently settled in the United States, an estimated 35,000 made it to Canada, 23,000 to Cuba, 12,000 to Peru, and 12,000 to Mexico.[29] In neighboring Canada, the western coastal regions were far more sparsely populated than those in the United States. In 1885, the population of the province of British Columbia was only one-third white.[30] Most of the other two-thirds were comprised of First Nations peoples, but South Asians and Chinese were beginning to arrive aboard British steamships. The province placed a head tax of $50 on each immigrant arriving from China, an enormous financial impediment.[31] Canada would eventually ban Chinese immigration outright in 1923, in emulation of additional immigration restrictions being passed at that time in the United States.[32] Peru followed by banning Chinese immigration in the early 1930s, while Mexico expelled the Chinese businessmen residing in its northwestern states near the United States—where many of them had arrived from, fleeing discrimination—in 1931. Popular opposition to their presence had been growing for two decades since the start of the Mexican Revolution.[33]

The policy worked in Canada, with British Columbia's whites going from a minority in 1885 to 92 percent of the province's population in 1945, though its 8 percent proportion of non-whites was still quadruple that of Canada as a whole.[34] The apogee of the cross-border anti-immigrant movement on the North American Pacific Coast had occurred in the early 1900s. Founded in 1907 in San Francisco, the Asian Exclusion League swiftly gained members and influence in Seattle, Washington, and Vancouver, British Columbia. That year, whites on both sides of the border attacked Chinese, Japanese, and Indian immigrants.[35] Protesters marching in Vancouver chanted for "a white Canada and no cheap Asian labor." These agitations directly led to diplomatic agreements banning immigration from Japan to the United States and Canada in 1908.[36]

These events occurred during the global circumnavigation of the "Great White Fleet," sent by President Theodore Roosevelt as a symbol of America's rising global presence and power. Australians gave these ships a jubilant welcome when they arrived in 1907. Given the United States's relative geographical proximity, the Australians were increasingly looking to America, and not Britain, for protection from Japanese military aggression. Theodore Roosevelt himself called for a "White Pacific," which was music to the Aussies' ears.[37] Called "a tiny drop in a coloured ocean" by Prime Minister Billy Hughes, Sydney was as close to Canton as Liverpool was to New York City.[38] Geographically, empty Australia was crowded Asia's natural hinterland. As in the United States, this inspired fears of both invasions of immigrants and armies. Australian journalist Kennedy McKay's book *The Yellow Wave* imagined an attempt by a Russo-Chinese alliance to conquer Australia.[39] Australians saw themselves as pampered and verging on degeneracy due to how little they had to work to prosper. Intellectual leaders and politicians worried their young men were too devoted to frivolous sporting activities and insufficiently attentive to martial pursuits. What was more, Australia's tiny population was concentrated along its temperate southeast coast. The subtropical northeast coast closest to Asia was virtually empty. Many in Australia and England argued that this territory was better suited climatically to the "yellow" races from the far south of China or the "brown" races from South Asia. White Australians believed they were inadequate for the task of settling that vast region, whereas Asians could presumably thrive there.

In 1851, three years after the discovery of gold in northern California, another gold strike occurred in Australia. This drew in over a half million new arrivals over the next two decades to a continent whose non-indigenous population stood at only 170,000 in 1850.[40] A substantial portion was from China. By 1859, there were 50,000 Chinese working in the Australian gold fields in the interior of the state of Victoria, which had Melbourne as its capital. In five years, Victoria's Chinese population increased twentyfold, and by 1859 one in five of the state's residents was Chinese.[41] As in California, white

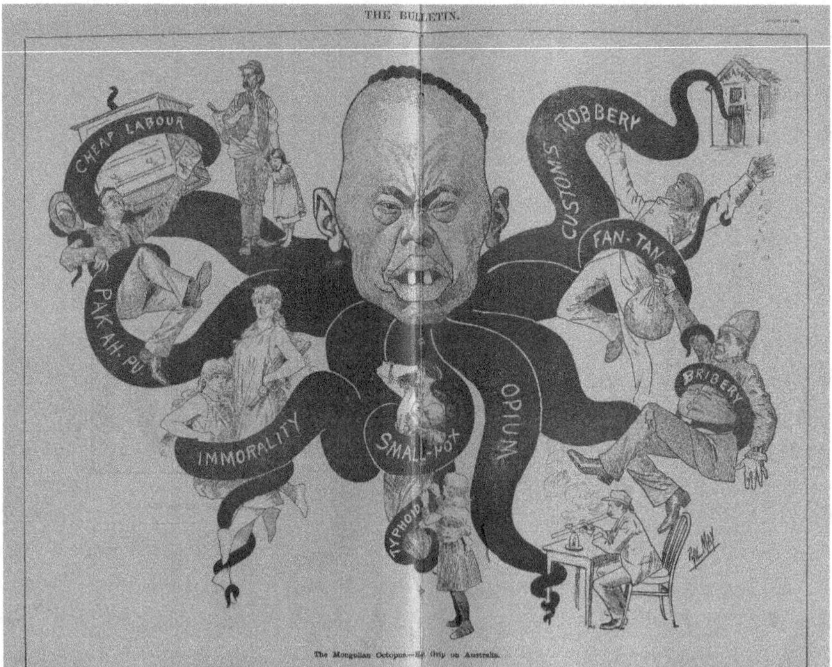

FIGURE 2 *"The Mongolian Octopus—Its Grip on Australia." In the 1880s, white Australians took inspiration from the Chinese exclusion laws recently passed by the US Congress and demanded similar actions. Cartoon by Phil May,* The Bulletin, *August 21, 1886. Courtesy of the National Library of Australia, nla.obj-507911285.*

laborers agitated against the white employers and landowners who eagerly employed Chinese. Efforts at restriction would long be hamstrung both by Australia's colonial status and its division into multiple colonies. Chinese in Victoria who faced violence and discrimination could move north to New South Wales and Sydney. Those attacked in Sydney could continue northward to Brisbane in Queensland and from there to the sparsely populated north coast. That region's isolation and tropical climate discouraged white immigration. By 1888, the non-native population of the area around Darwin—the north coast's largest town—was more than four-fifths Chinese.[42] With its urban Chinese businessmen and rural Chinese farm laborers, the area resembled the plantation colonies of the West Indies, not the white settler colonies of Canada and New Zealand. White Australians in the southern coastal regions became increasingly motivated to stop this influx to preserve their economic livelihoods and democratic political system. As one leading Australian wrote in 1899, unless white southern Australians "stand shoulder to shoulder" with northern Australian whites "in keeping out the Asiatic and other coloured aliens, the greater part of their magnificent patrimony will fall into the hands of the yellow races" (Figure 2).[43]

In 1901, Britain unified the continent politically as the Australian Federation and provided the new federation with a parliament and de facto home rule. Australians wasted no time in following the American example when it came to Chinese immigration. One of the first laws the new parliament passed was the Immigration Restriction Act, banning immigration from China. This established what became known as the "White Australia" policy which officially guided the nation's immigration policies until 1972, and still casts its cultural shadow in terms of the nation's treatment of refugees.[44] In the sixty years before federation, approximately 100,000 Chinese had entered Australia, though most did not settle there permanently, and women comprised less than 2 percent, an even more skewed gender balance than in the United States.[45] By 1939, the number of Chinese Australians stood at 15,000, illustrating the policy's success.[46] The northern Australian economy was intentionally left to languish rather than allow the region to be developed by non-whites.

The Boston-based *North American Review* celebrated Australia following in America's footsteps on this matter and provided an apt summary of the motivations in multiple nations. The article's author conceded that it "is admitted everywhere" they lived that the Chinese were "hard-working, frugal and, on the whole, fairly inoffensive and law-abiding people." In other words, they were everything anti-immigration forces in the United States claimed Irish, Italians, and other recent European immigrants were not. Still, unlike the Irish or the Italians, the presence of the industrious Chinese inevitably would lead to racial "deterioration" due to their having "wholly different ideas and traditions from their (Australians') own." The article concluded by declaring the hope for Australia remaining "a country of free men, possessed of equal right—which necessarily means of white men."[47] In the Australian parliament's 1901 debates, the White Australia policy was defended as representing "the instinct of self-preservation, quickened by experience," since "we know that coloured and white labour cannot exist side by side."[48]

Though Australia had followed America's path in rejecting Chinese labor, the British Empire persevered in encouraging Asian migration to its other colonies, particularly in southern Africa. The parliaments of Australia and New Zealand responded with an unprecedented rebuke of the mother country, with both passing symbolic resolutions in 1903 condemning Chinese immigration into the South African colonies. In 1906, four years after its victory in the Boer War created secured Britain's ability to fully exploit the region's gold mines, the mines' owners sought to recruit 60,000 skilled Chinese miners.[49] This sparked fierce reactions from white Afrikaans and British settlers alike, leading to the halting of Chinese immigration by the South African parliament in 1907, followed by discrimination against the Chinese already present as a small part of the incipient Apartheid system.[50] Like in Australia, Canada, and the United States, Chinese labor threatened the worth and dignity of white labor.

In the European-ruled lands on the Asian continent, the one place exposed to significant Chinese migration was the eastern Siberian region of the Russian Empire. By 1882, there were estimated to be 15,000 Chinese living north of the Amur River (which formed the border between the Russian and Qing Empires), compared to only about 40,000 Russians. As in other nations, Chinese were both needed for their labor and resented for their presence. At this time, the Russian government placed no legal restrictions on migration from China. It would institute a head tax in 1887 similar to the one recently established in Canada, and in 1892 ban foreigners from purchasing farmland, something else which would also occur in California around this time.[51] During the Boxer Rebellion, the New York newspaper *The Sun* wrote "the Chinese, it is predicted, will emigrate to Siberia and the 'yellow horde' will again precipitate itself toward European Russia, which will sink to the position of a second-rank power."[52] In the rebellion's aftermath, Russians drove thousands of Chinese south of the Amur and destroyed numerous Chinese settlements. The deadliest incident occurred in July 1900 in the border town of Blagoveshchenk, when Russians expelled 3,000 Chinese and proceeded to drown them in the river.[53] Still, fears of Chinese migrants remained prevalent. In 1908, Russian prime minister Petr Stolypin told the assembled parliamentarians in the Duma that "the foreigner will penetrate us unless the Russian comes before him, and this penetration has already begun."[54] By 1920, Soviet eastern Siberia contained an estimated 120,000 Chinese and Koreans, one in four residents of the region.[55]

The small Chinese communities remaining the aftermath of exclusion would be stigmatized in the United States and elsewhere as centers of vice: drugs (specifically opium), prostitution (specifically of white women hooked on opium), and gambling.[56] In Britain in the early 1900s, newspapers published sensational stories of life in Limehouse, the tiny Chinese enclave along the Thames River in East London, focusing particularly on the interaction of Chinese men and English women, along with describing Chinese predilections for gambling and opium smoking.[57] It was to appeal to the audience for such anti-Chinese tales that the small-time journalist and failed playwright Saxe Rohmer created his legendary character Fu Manchu, the most successful fictional personification of the Yellow Peril. Chinese men frequently traveled to Britain as sailors aboard ships from the Far East, and some stayed. Yet, in 1911, government records indicated that there were a total of 1,319 Chinese residing in all of England and Wales. The notorious neighborhood of Limehouse contained only 247 Chinese, barely enough to fill a few city blocks along the wharves.[58] Therefore, numbers were not necessary for fear to develop. A few hundred in a city of a few million was enough to create a threat of moral pollution.

As early as 1900, the British magazine *Outlook* railed against any Chinese immigration to Great Britain as a form of social corruption, arguing that "sanitation or its value is unknown to them" and that Chinese "breed and spread disease."[59] Three decades earlier, Henry George had termed the industrious Chinese immigrants "filthy in their habits" and called their neighborhoods "breeding-places for pestilence."[60] In the early 1900s, his left-wing compatriots in Britain followed his lead and latched onto the anti-Chinese cause for political gain. Around this time, similar sentiments led to the political rise of socialist parties in Australia to defend the interests of white workers. In Britain, it helped inspire the creation of the Labour Party.[61] As miniscule as it was, Chinese immigration became a central issue in both the Labour and Liberal Party platforms in the pivotal 1906 election. The victorious Liberals (in alliance with Labour) attacked "Chinese slavery," echoing the language of Kearny in 1870s California.[62] The Liberal government went on the pass the "People's Budget" of 1907, increasing the (admittedly miniscule) tax rate on the wealthy to fund rudimentary benefits for the poor. The Liberal Party's efforts ultimately proved insufficient to satisfy Britain's working classes who by the 1920s switched their loyalty to Labour and drove the once-dominant Liberals into permanent third-party obscurity. But the "New Jerusalem" of Clement Atlee's 1945 triumph might never have materialized without the by then long-forgotten anti-Chinese movements four decades previous. Anti-Chinese bigotry may have been the socialism of fools in the United States. But, in Britain, in Australia, and to a lesser though still significant extent in South Africa, it became a weapon for achieving socialist success.

The global movement to restrict future Chinese migration and discriminate against those migrants already abroad was the first concrete manifestation of the fears of Chinese power. The fantasy of a powerful Chinese nation setting forth beyond its borders became manifest in the reality of Chinese individuals settling in foreign lands, and thriving there. Chinese immigrants were stereotyped as the opposite of other undesirable migrants: never lazy, usually not criminal, and not destined to become a burden upon the state. Their purported superiority, rather than any inferiorities, was what made them a threat. Rather than degrade the nations in which they arrived, they would take control of them. The set of pernicious positive stereotypes attributed to the Chinese has striking parallels with the anti-Semitism of the period. Charles Pearson described the Chinese as being as "flexible as Jews" in terms of being able to thrive in diverse societies, but at the same time "more versatile than Jews" in excelling in a wide variety of professions and occupations.[63] This characterization was quoted approvingly by the later eugenicist and immigration restriction advocate Lothrop Stoddard, whose ideas on race significantly impacted Adolf Hitler and influenced Nazi Germany's racial classification laws. The crucial difference, of course, was that the Jews were few, whereas the Chinese were multitudinous. If a few million Chinese could thrive outside China, what might a few hundred million within China be capable of, if given the chance?

3

Warlords and Fu Manchu

1900–20

At the dawn of the twentieth century, in the immediate aftermath of the crushing of the Boxer Rebellion, China seemed to be as helpless and hapless as ever. Militarily humiliated, beset by domestic unrest, and saddled with an immense punitive indemnity, it was no one's idea of a threat. Rather, it was the "Sick Man of Asia." In a little over a decade, the Qing Dynasty, whose Manchu emperors had ruled China for more than a quarter of a millennium, would be overthrown, and China would become a republic led by ethnic Han Chinese politicians and generals. It quickly evolved into a military dictatorship that enjoyed substantial sympathy and support within the United States, before devolving into decentralized warlord fiefdoms. Its economy was either undeveloped or dominated by foreigners. Its military—or, rather, militaries—posed a threat only to the Chinese people. Meanwhile, countries across the Pacific had banned or severely limited immigration from China, effectively removing that perceived threat. The Yellow Peril fears and predictions of the late nineteenth century had all fizzled or been sidestepped for the time being. China seemed far away from fulfilling its potential.

Or so it should have seemed. Ironically, it was just when China was at its lowest ebb of power that foreigners saw national revival as imminent. During the twentieth century's first decade, there was a profusion of hope that the Chinese were finally turning a corner, that the latest humiliations would lead to the jettisoning of traditional beliefs, practices, and institutions, and that China would at last modernize and grow strong. These hopes mostly centered around the Qing Empire's belated attempts to reorganize its military forces. Few if any felt threatened by China's latest attempt at effective self-defense. On the economic front, the situation was different. A consensus formed in Europe and the United States highlights that the Chinese threat, when it came, would be predominantly economic in nature. This fed on existing stereotypes of the Chinese as an industrious yet docile people ideally suited for the modern factory, but out of place on the modern battlefield. Yet during this decade, China made even less progress in the economic realm than it did in military affairs.

Europe's devastating war dominated the century's second decade, placing East Asia on the backburner. The Japanese immediately sought to exploit Europeans' distraction, but its predatory behavior toward China failed to elicit much concern among the European powers. The Japanese threat remained as deflated as the Chinese threat was inflated. Meanwhile, the enormous success of Saxe Rohmer's first three Fu Manchu novels revealed the popular market for Chinese villains. These stories diverged from the invasion narratives which inspired them by making the geopolitical personal. Gone were great battles on land and sea. Now, the fight was for individual hearts and souls that were in constant danger of corruption. The author fused the fears of Chinese utilizing the tools of the West to bring about Europe's destruction with immigration-related worries about the polluting potential of an alien race. Such fears of spiritual and moral pollution carried on into the depictions of Chinese in early films. The threat at the time was less of conquest than of corruption.

This period featured three divergent trends. The first, "Awakening China," involved missionaries and their boosters in the press seeking to will into existence a China stable and strong enough to stand up to Russia and Japan. The second, "Industrious China," centered in the business community, whose members saw the Chinese as either an opportunity or a threat, depending upon one's vantage point. The third, "Corrupting China," was the most widespread among the European and American populaces. While the first two were largely elite conversations, the third fed into prevalent negative stereotypes whereby both Chinese strength and Chinese weakness could be threatening.

The concept of awakening has long been synonymous with China's path to modernization. Upon briefly assuming power in early 1912, Sun Yat-sen punctuated his first address to the citizens of the new Republic of China with the admonition "China, wake up!" Long before this concept of a slumbering China was attributed to Napoleon, it flowered in the early 1900s, expressing hope for a powerful China, rather than fear of it. Initiated among the missionary community, it had explicit spiritual and religious connotations. Its widespread appearance in newspapers and magazines in the immediate aftermath of the 1900 Boxer Rebellion, when Chinese fury placed the foreign missionary community in its greatest peril until the rise of the Communists, is especially puzzling. Following the conclusion of the Russo-Japanese War in 1905, the concept became secularized, acquiring the meaning of an "awakening China" as we would understand it today, albeit without the menace. President Theodore Roosevelt aptly summed up this movement in the title of his 1908 *Outlook* magazine article "China's Awakening One of the Great Events of the Age." He credited this awakening to the strenuous efforts of "our Christian missions," and hoped that it would provide "the remedy for the 'yellow peril,' whatever that may be."[1]

His placing of the phrase Yellow Peril in quotes was notable for two major reasons. First, it was extremely rare to do this at that time and would remain so for nearly four more decades, after which point such quotation marks became ubiquitous, indicating the supposedly antiquated nature of explicitly racialist thinking. Second, Roosevelt himself was no stranger to such racialism. As president, he signed the law which made Chinese exclusion permanent and negotiated an end to Japanese immigration. In addition, he coined the term "Race Suicide," called for a "White Pacific," and counted as one of his best friends the leading eugenics advocate Madison Grant, who was deeply prejudiced against Chinese—along with, it must be noted, nearly every other non-Anglo-Saxon race and ethnicity.

Roosevelt's surprising take was also rather belated in terms of its emphasis on missionary activities, which was a turn-of-the-century phenomenon. Missionary to China Judson Smith's 1899 essay in the *North American Review* typified the trend by declaring that "now, after the sleep of centuries, we look upon the awakening of China, the stir of new life among her rulers, the impact of new forces upon her social and intellectual institutions."[2] This was no doubt a reference to the proposed 1898 reforms during the "Hundred Days" period. The attempt at wholesale reform began when the young Guangxu emperor began favoring the ideas of political philosopher and government official Kang Youwei. Kang sought to abolish Confucian exams for government officials and replace the traditional Chinese educational system with universities teaching the social sciences, natural sciences, and engineering. He also favored the establishment of a constitutional monarchy with elections featuring a limited franchise to choose a representative assembly.[3] Such actions would help China construct railroads, industrialize, and build up its military strength. Yet they would have also alienated the traditional Mandarin elite whose entire status was bound up in the knowledge of the Confucian classics, to say nothing of the legions of young Chinese men who had spent years studying these materials in hopes of joining that elite. Before any such proposals could be enacted, the emperor's mother, Cixi, staged a palace coup, sidelining the emperor and reformers like Kang, and replacing them with conservative officials resistant to such reforms.[4]

Historians have termed this episode a lost last chance for the Qing, and proof of the power of institutional resistance to needed reforms in the China of that era.[5] In other words, it is a story of failure. Yet, in the immediate aftermath of that failure, as confirmed by the deposing of the leading reformers within the imperial government, foreign observers drew no such conclusion. The Chinese successfully progressed from failure to failure. A 1900 essay in *Outlook* credited the 1895 Japanese victory over the Chinese with providing "a rude shock to China's self-conceit" and forcing China to figuratively "rub her eyes."[6] While this came during the height of the Boxer violence, the author entirely avoided the subject and praised the very missionaries that Chinese rebels were then attacking for having sparked this national awakening. In a 1901 speech in New York City entitled "China's Awakening," China's Minister of Commerce and Railroads called the "Boxer trouble" a "blessing in disguise," assuring his American audience that "everything will come out all right after several years" now that China's latest defeat in a six-decade string of humiliations had finally provided the necessary wake-up call.[7]

But there was always another humiliation around the corner. In this case, it was the large-scale war Russia and Japan fought in 1904 and 1905 on territory in northern China and Manchuria that was technically still part of the Qing Empire, but which the opposing armies could effectively regard as unclaimed *terra nullius* due to the powerlessness of the Qing to defend it. As that war concluded, the *Atlanta Constitution* declared "the awakening of an entire empire" as evidenced by what the newspaper's editors saw as "the welding of a national spirit which has, up to this time, been lacking." Japanese and Russian aggression over the preceding decade had only succeeded in "resuscitating" Chinese power.[8] A month later, *Harper's Weekly* approvingly noted the training of "scores of thousands of Chinese soldiers" by Japanese officers, predicting that these forces would soon succeed in expelling "the foreign intruders from her soil."[9] Japan here was portrayed as China's friendly tutor rather than one of the "foreign intruders." In 1906, the *North American Review* declared that "the feeling of national unity in China, in lethargy for centuries, seems unmistakably aroused." The author, who was Japanese, credited Chinese General Yuan Shih-kai with this military awakening and held out the prospect of China embarking upon an "alliance and partnership" with the Japanese.[10] Regardless of whether China partnered with the Japanese, that nation's success would be an inspiration to China in particular, and all of Asia in general. The *Washington Post* declared in 1908 that Japan's rise "has shattered the old conception of Asia" and thereby increased the Yellow Peril.[11]

In nearly all these pieces, writers portrayed a strengthening China as an unalloyed good. Chinese power was to be praised, not feared. An exception was a 1907 *New York Times* editorial, which began with the sentence "China no longer sleeps," and concluded that the Yellow Peril "has dawned at last" due to the much belated "martial awakening of China."[12] Not all were so hyperbolic, the *Nation* magazine more soberly and accurately predicting it would "take more than two decades" for the Chinese to produce a powerful army.[13] As the provenance of these sources indicates, this boosterism was very much an American phenomenon. The *Times of London* rejected the notion of a China threat due to purported pacific nature of the "Chinese character."[14] Still, even the British could observe "the dormant potentiality of China," as put in a piece from that time in the magazine *Forum*. The author rehearsed the usual stereotypes of Chinese quantity and quality. Containing "an industrious and frugal population of 400,000,000 in number," when came to China, "no prophecy of future power can well seem overdrawn." This ominous and inevitable eventuality was still well in the future, though Japanese tutelage of the Chinese could accelerate the process and "give form and substance to the shadow now known as the 'Yellow Peril.'"[15] While deriding the Chinese as "a race of passive resisters" and "the unresisting victims of invasion and tyranny," British journalist and China expert J. O. P. Bland in 1912 took them very seriously as an economic threat.[16] In his opinion, "their ready adaptability to environment, untiring industry, skilled craftsmanship, and unconquerable power of passive resistance have never been equaled by any race of men, unless it be the Hebrews," yet another example of a comparison of the Chinese to Jews. Bland fretted about "the hopeless inferiority of white men against yellow in the grim struggle for life."[17] Like Henry George from the previous era, Bland believed whites could not withstand Chinese economic competition.

The Yellow Peril leapt from politics to popular culture in 1913 with the publication of Sax Rohmer's novel *The Mask of Fu Manchu*. Followed in 1916 by *The Devil Doctor* and in 1917 by *The Si-Fan Mysteries*, this trilogy of runaway bestsellers proved seminal. Described by one scholar as "the Osama Bin Laden of his day," Fu differed from the villains in invasion narratives by being a stateless actor. A part-time journalist and failed playwright and music hall songwriter, Rohmer capitalized on the popularity of sensational newspaper stories about the scandalous goings-on in the Limehouse district of East London.[18] Its scattering of gambling and opium dens had provided fodder for Edwardian-era Jeremiads about Britain's alleged moral decline, with the Chinese immigrants providing convenient scapegoats.[19] The First World War inflated these fears, causing Rohmer to set Fu Manchu's lair in Limehouse in the second novel, and also providing the setting for his friend Thomas Burke's bestselling collection of short stories *Limehouse Nights: Tales of Chinatown*, also published in 1916.[20]

Parts of *The Mystery of Fu Manchu* first appeared in magazine form in 1911. Asked about his inspiration, Rohmer at that time said "conditions for launching a Chinese villain on the market were ideal" because "the Boxer Rebellion had started off rumors of a Yellow Peril which had not yet died down."[21] To create his literary world, Rohmer borrowed from existing literary icons, particularly those from the 1890s. The "Fu Manchu" mustache comes from the cover of *The Yellow Claw*. He is tall, bald, and thin like Sherlock

Holmes's archnemesis Dr. Moriarty.[22] As an unnaturally powerful foreigner making London his base of operations, he recalls Bram Stoker's metaphor of reverse colonization in his *Dracula* novel. In turn, future generations of writers would borrow from Rohmer. The hero of the novels is the dashing Burmese Commissioner Sir Denis Nayland Smith, who bears a striking resemblance to Ian Fleming's James Bond. Early in the first novel, Rohmer provides this memorable description of his titular villain:

> Imagine a person, tall, lean and feline, high-shouldered, with a brow like Shakespeare and a face like Satan, a close-shaven skill, and long, magnetic eyes of true cat-green. Invest him with all the cruel cunning of an entire Eastern race, accumulated in one giant intellect, with all the resources of science past and present, with all the resources, if you will of a wealthy government—which, however, has denied all knowledge of his existence. Imagine that awful being, and you have a mental picture of Dr. Fu-Manchu, the yellow peril incarnate in one man.[23]

Though physically imposing, Fu Manchu was not physically aggressive. His great power was mind control, using his "magnificent, perverted brain" to manipulate people. His head was unusually large, long, and thin, like that of the ideal racially superior Aryan according to the then-current vogue of pseudoscientific phrenology.[24] In keeping with existing racial stereotypes, he was effeminate and asexual, with many readers assuming him to be homosexual.

Fu Manchu's frequent use of cutting-edge science, including innovations yet to exist in the real world, made Rohmer's early books a major influence on the emerging genre of science fiction. The Yellow Peril was present at the genre's creation. Hugo Gernsback, who coined the term "science fiction," published Philip Francis Nowlon's short story "Armageddon 2419 A.D." in his magazine *Amazing Stories* in 1928. That story featured its protagonist Anthony Rogers, who fights a "Mongol" invasion of the United States.[25] In 1929, Nowlon teamed up with the artist Dick Calkins, changed Anthony Rogers's first name to Buck, and began producing *The Adventures of Buck Rogers in the 25th Century*, the first science fiction comic strip. In 1934, Alex Raymond started the comic strip *Flash Gordon* to compete with Buck Rogers. Raymond created a world "dominated by the yellow peril," in which the hero battles "Ming the Merciless" from the planet Mongo.[26] Flash Gordon soon became the basis for a popular series of movie serials, which George Lucas later credited as the original inspiration for his "Star Wars" films. Fu Manchu himself appeared in multiple short silent films and was played by noted horror actor Boris Karloff in the 1932 feature-length adaptation of "The Mask of Fu Manchu," one year after the actor won accolades for his classic portrayal of Frankenstein's monster. Karloff would go on to play numerous Asian characters, including the Chinese detective hero Charlie Chan in multiple successful films. Intelligent, hardworking, and non-threatening, Chan was an early iteration of the Asian-American "Model Minority" stereotype. In contrast to Fu, he is short and plump, though the two of them share a feminine "feline" appearance and a pronounced asexuality.

Like Sherlock Holmes's creator Arthur Conan Doyle, Rohmer soon grew tired of his star creation and attempted to discontinue the novels and move on to other projects. But his works on other subjects failed to sell, and the author returned to Yellow Peril themes in a series of short stories in the 1920s. President Calvin Coolidge said he only read *Collier's* magazine for these stories, and "he just could not wait each week to learn whether the hero would foil Fu Manchu and how."[27] Coolidge was likely referring to Rohmer's series "The Emperor of China," which did not actually feature that character. In the 1930s, Rohmer finally revived him and would produce ten additional Fu Manchu novels before his death in 1959. He would heartily embrace his now-legendary creation, shaving his head and dressing in Chinese silk robes. New Fu Manchu films appeared in the 1960s attempting to capitalize on revived Yellow Peril fears sparked by the Chinese Communists. Rohmer's work also inspired numerous comic book villains in the Cold War era. Legendary Marvel Comics writer Jack Kirby created *The Yellow Claw* in 1956, named after the title of a 1915 Rohmer short story which was an early attempt by Rohmer at a Fu Manchu spinoff. As such overt racial stereotypes became less culturally acceptable, *The Yellow Claw*, defeated in 1968 by Nick Fury and his organization S.H.I.E.L.D., was revealed to be a robot. Around this time, Marvel purchased the comic book rights to the Fu Manchu character from Rohmer's estate and created Shang-chi, a hero who was the son of Fu Manchu (Figure 3).[28]

While serving as symbols of conquest in literary works of fantasy, the Chinese primarily appeared in early films as figures of corruption. This played upon the association of Chinese immigrants with opium dens, and the fear that the young white women drawn to these dens would be forced into prostitution. A noted exception to this stereotype was D.W. Griffith's popular 1919 film "Broken Blossoms," which was about opium addiction, and based on Burke's short story "The Chink and the Child," which had appeared in his popular 1916 *Limehouse Nights* collection.[29] Most famous for his technically groundbreaking, deeply racist, and hugely successful 1915 film "Birth of a Nation," Griffith imbued Burke's salacious tale with surprising sensitivity, portraying the Chinese protagonist with a humanity he failed to grant his Black characters. An opium addict who gambles, he is also hardworking and kind. He draws the attention of a poor white woman who is seeking to escape her physically abusive white husband. She soon falls in love with him, leading her husband to track her down and beat her to death. Upon

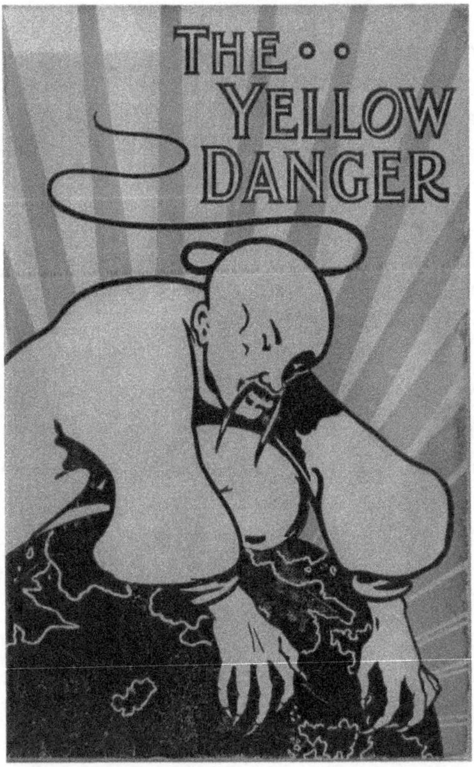

FIGURE 3 *Cover image,* The Yellow Danger, *1898, by Matthew Phipps Shiell. The book was an attempt to capitalize on the fears recently fanned by Kaiser Wilhelm II, and the image of a bald Chinese villain with a thin handlebar mustache plotting world domination would inspire Saxe Rohmer's Fu Manchu novels.*

discovering her corpse, her Chinese lover proceeds to murder the husband, then takes his own life. This was pathbreaking in two key aspects. First, the Chinese man was sexually desirable to an attractive white woman. Second, he was physically aggressive, not passive or weak. One can explain Griffith's seemingly anomalous racial sensitivity by his bleeding-heart romantic streak. In all his movies, Griffith dramatized the suffering of his heroes and heroines. It just so happened that in "Birth of a Nation," the victimized heroes were white and the victimizers black.

Western observers long looked for a single "Great Man" to be China's savior. Well before he assumed power, many Americans had cast Yuan Shih-kai in that role. Shortly before the signing of the Treaty of Shimonoseki ending the Sino-Japanese War in 1895, recent US Secretary of State John W. Foster tried to convince Yuan to launch a military coup and seize power from the tottering Qing in Beijing. During the early stages of the Russo-Japanese War in 1904, the *North American Review* termed Yuan "the leader for whom China has waited so long" who would "develop her unrivalled resources and maintain her independence" while opening up China's markets to American goods.[30] After Yuan seized power, an Indian observer called Yuan "the Lion of Asia," predicting he would make China united, strong, and unrivaled in the region.[31]

Less than three years after Yuan became the Chinese Republic's first president in 1912, the beginning of the First World War diverted the attention of the United States and the European powers from East Asia for most of the rest of the decade. This would have provided the infant Chinese Republic with a potential respite from exploitation were it not for Japan's emboldened predatory impulses. As a formal ally of the British, French, and Russians from the war's opening months, Japan was granted—against China's strenuous protests—the right to conquer and possess the German colony of Qingdao in Shantung Province, along with many of Germany's island colonies in the western Pacific. Japanese leaders were not bashful about exploiting these advantages, issuing to the Chinese government on January 18, 1915 the "Twenty-One Demands," intended to turn China into an economic colony of the Japanese. Lacking the military resources to resist, Yuan accepted most of the demands, including Japanese possession of Shantung Province. These concessions outraged the Chinese public and irreparably damaged his domestic prestige.[32] While attempting to crown himself as a new emperor in 1916, rebels bombed the presidential palace from the air, showing how little support Yuan had. He died shortly thereafter of natural causes, ending the possibility of a united China for the time being.

As China's nominal central government in Beijing rapidly lost control of the southern and western regions of the country, its officials grappled with how best to respond to the ongoing world war. They assumed the Allied Powers would prevail, and looked to earn postwar rewards for being on the winning side. Unable to deploy soldiers, the Chinese official Liang Shiyi came up in 1916 with a "labor plan," explained by his colleague Yigong Daibing as "laborers in the place of soldiers."[33] Arriving in France in 1917, 140,000 Chinese worked on the Western Front for the Allied Powers, with nearly 3,000 dying either at the front or from German submarine attacks on the ships bringing them to France.[34] About half the Chinese came by way of Canada, where during their journeys they were treated by Canadian authorities as unwanted refugees, kept under armed guard, and forbidden to leave their overcrowded train cars.[35] A largely overlooked 50,000 Chinese labored for the Russians on the Eastern Front.[36] An additional 150,000 Chinese labored in Russian factories, mined coal, and built roads and railroads for Russia.[37]

Those Chinese had a far stranger, and often tragic, fate. The Bolshevik Revolution of November 1917 both took Russia out of the war and left the Chinese in Russia stranded and unemployed. When Russia descended into civil war and famine, more than 40,000 of these Chinese laborers volunteered for the Red Army.[38] They were among the Bolsheviks' most loyal and trusted soldiers. Seventy of Vladimir Lenin's 200 bodyguards were Chinese. Hundreds served in the Cheka secret police due to their lack of compunction about executing Russians.[39] Most eventually found their way home along the railroads, though unknown numbers died of fighting, famine, and disease. Tens of thousands remained in Russia proper or settled in Siberia. Under Lenin's rule, the Soviet Union pledged to abrogate all the exploitative treaties the Tsarist Empire had forced upon Qing China, but this was never implemented.[40] The rise to power of Joseph Stalin after Lenin's death brought a swift shift in Soviet ethnic policy, with Russian chauvinism replacing acceptance of ethnic diversity. A 1926 Soviet census counted 100,000 ethnic Chinese, 70 percent of whom lived in the Soviet Far East, including 30,000 of Vladivostok's 100,000 residents. In the 1930s, Stalin killed or expelled these populations, leaving Vladivostok as the only large city along the Pacific Rim without a Chinatown.[41]

The war also witnessed the rising force of informed public opinion among educated urban Chinese, who expected Chinese assistance to be rewarded. When this failed to happen in the Treaty of Versailles, which allowed Japan to retain Shantung Province, in contravention of US President Woodrow Wilson's principle of national self-determination, it undercut this emerging elite's faith in Western liberalism.[42] Upon learning of the Chinese government's accession to Japan's possession of Shantung, on May 4, 1919, 3,000 students demonstrated in front of the Tian Gate (Tiananmen) in Peking. They proceeded to riot, and authorities arrested nearly forty of the demonstrators. This event birthed what came to be known as the May Fourth Movement, which embraced and advanced the already existing New Culture Movement among young intellectuals. That ongoing movement sought to jettison Chinese traditions and embrace European modernity.[43] Among other things, the May Fourth Movement led to the founding of the Chinese Communist Party in 1921.

American educator and pragmatist philosopher John Dewey happened to be touring Japan and China in 1919 with his wife to investigate institutions of higher education in those countries. They were in Shanghai that May, and in Peking during the summer as student unrest continued. The two of them recorded their first-hand impressions of these events in a series of letters to friends. Dewey dined with Sun Yat-sen in Shanghai on May 13 and said Sun blamed Confucianism for China's current backwardness. According to Dewey, Sun told him that "the Chinese were paralyzed by fear of making a mistake in action. So he (Sun) has written a book to prove to his people that action is really easier than knowledge."[44] Near the end of May, Dewey wrote that "the trouble among the students is daily getting worse," though at this stage he was more worried about endangered university faculty than the students' potential impact on Chinese politics and society.[45] Arriving in Peking at the beginning of June, Dewey reported the arrest of about one thousand striking students on June 5, though they were soon released when this sparked even larger demonstrations. He wrote that "no one can tell today what the students' strike will bring next; it may bring a revolution."[46] Shortly before departing in early July, he wrote the following:

> I find in reading books that the Awakening of China has been announced a dozen or more times by foreign travelers in the last ten years, so I hesitate to announce it again, but I think this is the first time the merchants and guilds have really been actively stirred to try to improve industrial methods. And if so, it is a real awakening—that and the combination with the students.[47]

Dewey was perceptive enough to realize informed opinion had been inflamed by the Versailles Treaty and united various elements of an emerging civil society—merchants, workers, students—in a manner which would have a lasting impact.

Others saw such developments in a less positive light. In 1921, the American publisher of *McClure's* magazine wrote about a revived Yellow Peril in the *Times of London*, noticing "a new ferment" in East Asia, and calling for a revival of white racial unity.[48] The previous year, Lothrop Stoddard made very similar and ominous arguments in his bestselling book *The Rising Tide of Color Against White World-Supremacy*. This bestseller is best known today due to it being referenced in F. Scott Fitzgerald's *The Great Gatsby* by the villainous Tom Buchanan, who says he's been reading a book by "Goddard" about how the white race will soon be "utterly submerged."[49] Stoddard's book contained an introduction by Madison Grant, whose 1916 work *The Passing of the Great Race* was an early entrant in this genre of Western decline. Grant's focus was the threat to "Nordics" from white immigration from Southern and Eastern Europe. He only mentioned the Chinese in passing in that work, in relation to their immigration to the United States in the previous century.

But in his introduction to Stoddard's book four years later, Grant wrote that "Asia, in the guise of Bolshevism with Semitic leadership and Chinese executioners, is organizing an assault upon western Europe." In such a situation, Grant argued "democratic ideals" are "suicide, pure and simple."[50] Drawing on Pearson's prophecies from a generation earlier, Stoddard captured postwar angst about a divided and weakened West no longer able to hold back the hordes of the East. In his forward, Grant had referred to the recent conflict in Europe as "the White Civil War," claiming it had weakened the race to a perhaps crippling degree.[51] Like Pearson, Stoddard argued conquest was fleeting, but settlement permanent, warning of "more enduring conquests like migrations which would swamp whole populations and turn countries now white into colored man's lands irretrievably lost to the white world."[52]

Stoddard's fears added a demographic tinge to the existing Social Darwinist worries about Chinese economic superiority.

In a chapter entitled "Yellow Man's Land," Stoddard claimed that "China was at last shaken awake" when foreign militaries crushed the Boxer Rebellion in 1900 and for the first time occupied the China's capital of Peking. He lauded the Chinese people's "extraordinary economic efficiency" while denigrating the Japanese peoples' lack of "adaptability to climatic variation" compared to Chinese, again another borrowing from Pearson.[53] Continuing with Pearson's arguments to the point of plagiarism, in a chapter entitled "The Outer Dikes," he began by informing his readers that "the white man will have to recognize that the practically absolute world-dominion which he exercised during the nineteenth century can no longer be maintained," while also jettisoning old prejudices that "Asiatics are necessarily 'inferior.'"[54] Europe and the United States could—and should—ban all Chinese immigration. With this in mind, he praised "the instinctive and instantaneous solidarity which binds together Australians and Afrikanders [*sic*], Californians and Canadians" in support of Chinese exclusion.[55] But that still left open the opportunity for them to migrate to Africa and Latin America, the regions which formed these "outer dikes." Thus, whites must prevent Asian migration to these regions as well.[56]

In his concluding chapter, entitled "The Inner Dikes," referring to the white homelands, Stoddard raised the possibility of "the industrial awakening of China," which would lead to the exclusion of European and American products from "Asiatic markets." Stoddard thus expanded upon Person's arguments by discussing the impact of Chinese industrialization and raising the possibility of Chinese influence replacing European domination of Africa and Latin America, which Mao Zedong would later refer to as the "First Intermediate Zone," where he sought to use China's status as a non-white power to compete with and supersede American and Soviet influence. But while Pearson proposed that white nations adopt socialism to strengthen themselves, Stoddard only proposed an expansion of immigration exclusion policies.

Two years later, the British intellectual Bertrand Russell published *The Problem of China*, a slim volume that sought to both explain how China could become powerful and hypothesize what its people might do with that power. He began by noting the "peculiar" position of China in the international system at that time, since "in population and potential strength China is the greatest nation in the world, while in actual strength at the moment it is one of the least." Addressing those who worried about China's potential military might, he stated that "a strong military China would be a disaster" for the Chinese people, they would then be following the erroneous path of Western European development.[57] But this was an unavoidable possibility since "China, by her resources and her population, is capable of being the greatest Power in the world after the United States," and that any nation of such immense strength would be tempted to become imperialist.[58] Russell put his faith in "Young China," specifically the students politically awakened by the May Fourth Movement, who constituted "the renaissance spirit now existing in China." Russell hoped these young Chinese would not be seduced by the examples of the European powers, and instead combine the elegance of traditional Chinese culture with modern science to produce "a better economic system" without exploitation of domestic labor or foreign peoples.[59] For him, this should be China's contribution to world civilization in the twentieth century.

Even during the anarchy and disunion of the warlord period between 1916 and 1928, Americans still recognized that "China's latent power is tremendous."[60] The hope was that the United States would offer China friendship rather than exploitation in its time of weakness and be repaid with kindness when China became strong. Still, Americans shared with Europeans a strong sense of racial and civilizational superiority and an urge to dominate those they viewed as outsiders, whether in their own lands or in distant colonies. Social Darwinist thinking maintained its grip on both international relations and domestic politics. This entailed continued discrimination against Chinese wherever they traveled, and continued exploitation of Chinese in their own country. Such behavior did not bode well for future relations between the United States and Europe on one side and a powerful China on the other. As one pessimistic American puts it, "racial antagonism resembles justice in one respect if in no other; it may sleep but it never dies."[61]

4

Hopes and Fears and Chiang Kai-shek

1920–37

Andre Malraux's 1927 debut novel *The Conquerors* began with the dateline "25 June 1925: A general strike has been declared at Canton."[1] This brief and popular work centered around a fictionalized account of the effects of the rise of the Guomindang to power in the Pearl River Delta region of China's far south on the eve of the Northern Expedition. The narrative alternates between depictions of Chinese nationalist militancy and representations of British imperial anxieties. Malraux portrayed the party's rise to local and eventually national prominence as the fruits of a grassroots anti-British uprising among the Chinese coast's urban masses. He claimed that "the British in Hong Kong live in fear of an insurrection, with authorities in Singapore nervously eyeing developments in China which they deemed a potentially grave threat to their position in the entire region."[2] Malraux summarized this fight as a "gigantic struggle being waged by the empire of disorder, hastily organizing itself, against a nation which stands above all others for strength, determination, and tenacity."[3] Yet, to Malraux, the motivations of the Chinese masses were less nationalistic than racial. This mirrored Britain's conception of itself not only as the leading world power but also as the leader of the white nations. Despite their internecine disputes leading to the spilling of the blood of millions in Europe in the previous decade, the white powers still were largely united in maintaining their privileged positions in China. British and Germans might shoot each other between the eyes in the fields of Flanders, but they saw eye-to-eye on the streets of Shanghai.

To Malraux, Hong Kong was the symbol and source of this privilege. Taken as a port during the First Opium War and expanded into genuine entrepot colony on the eve of the Boxer Rebellion, it would become the most successful and lucrative imperial acquisition from China during its "Century of Humiliation." Chinese Communists portrayed its return in 1997 as a key moment in the nation's rise to great power status. Seven decades earlier, Malraux warned that if "China, in her struggle against the white race," were able to "organize itself, in a manner hitherto impossible" and seize Hong Kong, then "there might be an end to European domination."[4] The eventual peaceful handover of control of Hong Kong from the British to the Chinese came long after the end of European domination of Asia. In 1997, it was more about confirming China's economic rise, as the neighboring city of Shenzhen and the nearby metropolis of Guangzhou (formerly Canton) at first emulated, and then surpassed, the prosperity of Hong Kong. Sino-British disputes were by then about political as opposed to racial conflicts. The British wished to preserve some semblance of the semi-democratic freedoms and political autonomy they had belatedly permitted in their colony. A quarter of a century on, that battle continues, though with foreigners merely as onlookers to an essentially domestic dispute.

The Guomindang, a political party formed by Sun Yat-sen and brought to power after Sun's death by his successor Chiang Kai-shek that is often referred to as the Nationalists to contrast it with the Communists, is remembered as fundamentally conservative in ideology and as a party viewed favorably by foreigners, particularly Americans. Its leaders became the mortal enemies of the country's genuine revolutionaries, the Chinese Communist Party. But, as Malraux's book illustrates, the benefit of hindsight distorts the actual initial impressions. Chiang could never have risen to power without the assistance and tutelage of the Soviet Union's Comintern and his alliance of convenience with the Chinese Communist Party. Combined with its members' skillful and intentional exploitation of anti-foreign sentiment, this made the Guomindang seem dangerously radical and decidedly militant, even to Chiang's later champions.

The Guomindang's takeover of China between 1926 and 1928 began what came to be known as the "Nanjing Decade," the ten-year period between their 1927 establishment of a national capital in that Yangtze Valley city and the Japanese capture of the city during its full-scale invasion of China in 1937. Attempts during this period to consolidate power domestically made China more domestically unified than it had been since the fall of the Qing and ended the era of warlord dominance which had begun with the death of Yuan Shih-kai in 1916. Efforts to eliminate foreign exploitation began the reversal of nearly ninety years of increasing European economic and military encroachment. This chapter details the motivations for and effects of the party's policies within China, and their impact on how outside powers in Europe, Asia, and the Americas viewed them. I argue that Chiang and his ruling party fostered a divergence of opinions between powers from the three regions.

The Europeans felt their position the most threatened and oscillated between describing China's supposed continued state of internal decay and postulating its future menace. In this case, the new Chinese regime menaced the privileged position of Europeans in China, particularly in their de facto shared colony of Shanghai. At no point did Chiang's forces appear to menace even adjacent European territories like French Indochina or British Burma. Meanwhile, the Americans quickly dispensed with their suspicions and began to see Chiang and his retinue as the harbingers of a new nation which could become both powerful and friendly. On the other hand, the neighboring Japanese shared the anxieties of the distant Europeans, while possessing the ready means to take preventive action and keep the Chinese in a supine state. For a time, the Guomindang pulled off the age-old Chinese imperial trick the Qing Dynasty could not, playing the barbarians against one another for China's own benefit. But, ultimately, diplomacy proved no match for brute force, and the Japanese plunged China into more than fifteen years of near-constant warfare.

While the dominant individual in this era was Chiang, the pivotal figure in the transition from warlord hegemony was Sun Yat-sen. Sun was not a military man, and military men had squelched his first attempt at assuming power in 1912. Appointed Prime Minister on January 1, 1912, he stepped down on February 15 under the pressure of General Yuan, who then declared himself President and sole ruler.[5] A self-styled revolutionary and erstwhile national savior, Sun's legacy was in the realm of ideas. His ideas reflected his peripatetic life. A Chinese national hero who spent the majority of his life outside China, he sought a synthesis between Chinese tradition and Western modernity, particularly in its American incarnation. To quote his leading biographer, Sun's legacy was inaugurating the process of "China moving toward modernity."[6] His famous Three Principles, which he spent the last two decades of his life defining, refining, and elaborating upon, were an attempt at ideological domestication, adopting what was new abroad without shattering native traditions. Ideology followed biography. Born in 1866 in the Pearl River Delta near his future political base in Canton, Sun relocated to then-independent Hawaii in 1880, where he attended an Anglican high school and was baptized as a Congregationalist.[7] In addition to his religious awakening, Hawaii was also the site of his political awakening. Along with other expatriates in that archipelago, he was a part of the Revive China Society. Soon after returning home, he participated in the failed Canton Uprising of 1895 and spent the next sixteen years in exile. Sun first settled in Japan, which within a decade would become home to over 10,000 Chinese students keen to learn from their neighbor's successful process of military, political, and economic modernization.[8]

Also in Japan at that time was the exiled reform-minded Qing bureaucrat Liang Qichao, who in 1906 originated the "People's Three Principles" which formed the framework for Sun's political philosophy.[9] While living abroad, Sun assisted multiple unsuccessful attempts at overthrowing China's Manchurian rulers and replacing them with a Han Chinese-led republic. In the end, it was the involvement of the military in one of these uprisings in October 1911 which toppled the Qing, leading to the abdication of the final emperor on February 12, 1912. Traveling by train from Denver to Kansas City at the time of this uprising on a fundraising tour for his cause, Sun quickly returned to China, where he served as the republic's first Prime Minister. During his forty-five-day tenure, Sun replaced China's traditional lunar calendar with the solar Gregorian Calendar, and the dragon emblem with a five-striped flag of red, yellow, blue, black, and white, representing the Five Races of China: Manchurians, Han Chinese, Mongolians, Tibetans, and Uighurs.[10] Yuan's death in Peking on June 6, 1916, eliminated whatever tenuous unity he had imposed upon China, and power swiftly devolved to his generals and other regional military leaders. Sun relocated from Nanjing—which he intended to make China's permanent capital—to Canton, near his birthplace and base of political support.

Sun's Three Principles are most commonly translated into English as "Nationalism, Democracy, and People's Livelihood." Of the three, only the first bears a strong resemblance to how Westerners would interpret the term. Respectively, they borrow liberally from Social Darwinism, the Progressive Movement, and Populism, all of which Sun was exposed to in his overseas travels. The overriding goal of the principles was to strengthen the Chinese nation-state, allowing it to first expel foreign influence and then obtain status as a great power. Thus, the second and third principles existed to serve the first. He would share these goals with Chiang and Mao Zedong. Xi Jinping's current articulation of "The Chinese Dream" is a twenty-first-century reframing of Sun's philosophy as filtered through Mao and Deng Xiaoping. Even the old Chinese Communist uniform of the "Mao Jacket" was a boxy knock-off of Sun's preferred attire, itself borrowed from the Japanese military dress of the period. For a man who never exercised significant political power, he cast a long shadow.

Sun's original book-length manuscript was destroyed by a 1922 fire in the Canton library where he had stored it while awaiting publication. The work we have today is based on transcriptions of a number of extemporaneous lectures he gave in 1924.[11] Therefore, the text is repetitive and poorly organized. It was condemned by a hostile British reader as an "inchoate mass of crude ideas."[12] Nationalism, the English translation of Sun's and Liang's *minzuzhuyi*, originally meant opposition to Manchu rule. The goal was to "restore Chinese sovereignty." After that had been achieved in 1912, Sun evolved the meaning to include anti-foreignism, which in the 1920s he reworked into anti-Westernism.[13] Sun coined and popularized the term "Unequal Treaties" to describe the agreements Western powers forced China to sign in the nineteenth century which opened the empire to foreign trade and Christian missionaries.[14] In his final formulation, presented in 1924 as the book *Three Principles of the People* (*Sanminzhuyi*), Sun embraced Asian cultural supremacy, separating a beneficent Japan from the malign Western powers.[15] Nationalism became racial nationalism. Declaring China to still be under foreign domination, Sun feared the "white peril" and warned of "racial extinction" (*meizhong*).[16] In this social Darwinist framework, where only force mattered, China must either strengthen or die. Sun fervently opposed a federal China modeled on the structure of the United States, which he claimed violated China's tradition of having a unitary state.[17]

These assumptions shaped his definition of "Democracy" (*minquanzhuyi*). Liang based his definition on the concept of the "General Will" as detailed in the writings of Jean-Jacques Rousseau, which stressed the power of the group over individual freedom. Traditional Chinese society featured too much individualism. Calling his people "a sheet of loose sand," Sun opined that "we must break down individual liberty and become pressed together into an unyielding body like the firm rock which is formed by the addition of cement to sand."[18] The state would be organized into "Five Powers": Executive, Legislative, Judicial, Examination, and Censure, fusing Confucian-inspired departments with the US Constitution's three branches of government, derived from Montesquieu's *The Spirit of the Laws*. Onto his top-down project of nation-building, Sun grafted recent Progressive Era reforms, borrowing from a movement where many of its members advocated elitist reform from above. The state's Five Powers would be complemented by the people's "Four Rights": Suffrage, Revocation, Initiation, and Referendum.[19] Sun's economic program focused on state-led economic development. Its socialist components were the equalization of land ownership and a single land tax based on the theories of Henry George.[20] This somewhat eccentric attachment to the writings of a Gilded Age journalist would persist in the economic rhetoric—though by no means the practices—of the Guomindang Party long after its leaders had jettisoned any tenuous attachments to left-wing policies. Even Chiang Kai-shek's wife would reference them when visiting the United States in 1943.

Sun knew he had to seize power by force, in which he was decidedly deficient, lacking even the support of the dominant warlord in Canton. He thus decided to seek foreign assistance. The United States, the Western Europeans, and the Japanese still recognized the official government in Beijing. But the Soviet Union showed interest through its Comintern office that sought to spread revolution across the globe. Having failed to bring about any successful revolutions in Europe, the Bolsheviks now looked to the colonial and quasi-colonial world for a breakthrough. Sun came to refer to Mikhail Borodin, the Soviet adviser who began assisting him in 1923, as his "Lafayette."[21] Borodin forged an alliance between the Guomindang and the then-miniscule

Chinese Communist Party. Sun hoped to exploit the organizational talents of the Chinese Communists and learn from the Soviet Communists how to instill organizational discipline in his own growing ranks.[22] Borodin and the Comintern recommended that Sun appeal to the Chinese masses.[23] Though at times embraced by the public, and able to intermittently harness mass enthusiasm, the Guomindang would throughout its history remain an elite organization without the widespread appeal of the Soviet Bolsheviks, Italian fascists, or German National Socialists and never attempted to develop the organizational structure to do so. This would prove a significant flaw, especially after its break with the Chinese Communists.

In addition to providing the party with a strong hierarchical structure based on the Bolsheviks' own organization, Borodin and his aides gave Sun much-needed military power by starting the Whampoa Academy in May 1924.[24] Located on its namesake island in the Pearl Delta, this officer training academy remained in operation for two years, and only provided between six and twelve months of training to each recruit, a woefully insignificant amount of training by the standards of professional armies of the day.[25] Nonetheless, it provided the party with a competitive military advantage over the even less professional warlord armies, while creating the nucleus of future military leadership for Nationalist armies. Chiang Kai-shek, who possessed some military training from his time in Japan, became the head of the Whampoa Academy, a position from which he began his swift rise to party leadership. By the time of full-scale war with Japan in 1937, a majority of Chinese divisions would be commanded by Whampoa graduates.[26] In addition, many leading Communist generals such as Lin Biao received their education at Whampoa, while Zhou Enlai was the academy's chief political officer. One could thus compare its influence to that of West Point upon the armies of the Union and the Confederacy during the American Civil War.

Sun died on March 12, 1925 at age fifty-eight while on a diplomatic mission to Peking.[27] Chiang quickly assumed party leadership and began preparations for putting his relatively small forces to use. Events would soon provide fruitful opportunities for exploitation by an ideologically motivated military force such as the Guomindang. On May 30, an estimated 2,000 Chinese students took to the streets in Shanghai to protest the recent killing of a Chinese worker at a Japanese-owned cotton mill during a strike for higher wages. At the time, Shanghai was a partial colony shared by the Europeans, Japanese, and Americans, with the British exercising the most control. The heart of the growing city was itself under complete foreign control. In the 1920s, it was the world's second busiest port, responsible for three-quarters of China's foreign commerce.[28] This made the city both the epicenter of China's interactions with the outside world and a site of nationalist tensions. In Shanghai's foreign zone rose China's first modern skyscraper. Shanghai's Chinese intellectuals were the first to coin a Chinese translation of modern—"modeng."[29] Its intellectuals learned from Western writers, and its workers earned their living from Western employers, but both chafed under foreign domination. This all came to a head on May 30, when British security forces fatally opened fire on the student demonstrators.[30] Anti-foreign demonstrations soon spread to other major cities in what came to be known as the May Thirtieth Movement.

Lasting more than two years, the movement both propelled the Guomindang to national hegemony and sparked explosive growth for China's Communist Party. From fewer than 1,000 members in May 1925, the Chinese Communists claimed over 57,000 members by 1927.[31] Domestic anti-foreign discontent allowed the Guomindang's leaders to set themselves apart from regionally based warlords as the lone potential entity which could unite China and enable the nation to finally stand up to powerful foreigners. Under the leadership of Chiang, the party brought this to fruition through a series of military offensives conducted in 1926, 1927, and 1928, collectively known as the Northern Expedition. Chiang's Soviet advisers initially opposed the campaign out of the well-founded fear that it would strengthen the rightist faction, which was strongest in the party's armed forces. However, once it became clear Chiang was going to attack with or without the Bukharin's approval, the Comintern offered their support, which proved to be essential for the operations' success. Launched from its base in Canton in July 1926, the main force moved northward and westward along the rail line to Wuhan, which they captured in September. Turning eastward, the army followed the railroad to the Yangtze Delta region, reaching Nanjing and Shanghai in February 1927.[32] The army's arrival in the region provided the inspiration for violent anti-foreign demonstrations in Nanjing. Also inflaming the populace was Britain's sending of 13,000 Royal Marines to Shanghai in late January as Guomindang forces approached.[33]

Enabling these hastily trained and inexperienced forces of fewer than 100,000 to achieve so much with such ease was the Comintern-directed indoctrination of soldiers and the party's political officers' organizing of civilian populations in advance of their armies' progress.[34] The promise of revising or even rescinding the "Unequal Treaties" with foreign powers carried special resonance in a city like Shanghai, with its substantial foreign presence. Guomindang forces entered Shanghai on March 26, 1927. Riding this popular enthusiasm, Chiang proclaimed the establishment of the Republic of China in Nanjing on April 18, 1927.[35] At this time, the Guomindang's leading general was viewed with suspicion by the outside powers both for his fanning of the flames of anti-foreign sentiment and his alliance with the Chinese Communist Party.

The Communists were the Guomindang's best organizers both ahead of and behind the lines. They had used their participation in the Northern Expedition to expand their support among laborers in Shanghai and were predominant in the provisional leftist government operating out of Wuhan. For these reasons, once he had consolidated control over the largest cities in southern China, Chiang moved quickly to smother this potential incubus within the party's big tent. What became known as the "Shanghai Coup" began in that city on April 12, 1927.[36] In close collaboration with that city's criminal "Green Gang," the Guomindang slaughtered thousands of Communists over the next several days, driving the rest of them either inland to the countryside or into hiding within Shanghai. This marked the beginning of the first Chinese civil war, pitting Chiang against the Communists in a war of attempted extermination. After repeated Communist defeats of Nationalist armies sent to destroy their base areas in the southern Chinese interior, Chiang's forces finally succeeded in encircling the Communists in 1935. The Communist armies broke out of this encirclement, and fled to safety in a 6,000-mile retreat known as the "Long March," their severely reduced forces finally setting up a new base in the isolated and desolate north-central Chinese region of Yenan. Still, even these actions did not fully allay foreign suspicions. The elevation of Chiang in American eyes into a Chinese George Washington would be a more gradual process than later events or memories would lead one to believe.

Western journalists viewed the Guomindang's ascendancy during the mid-twenties as the result of an upsurge of militant nationalism with radical political potential. It took several years for Chiang and his party to gain their trust and support. Outsiders viewed these events as the definitive end of the foreign domination of China, through a combination of robust Chinese action and indecisive Western reaction. As the initial Shanghai demonstrations of 1925 died down, the editors of the *New Republic* opined that "the Chinese situation has become less dangerous, but much more serious." In the view of this journal, which published more consistently on Chinese events during Nationalist rule than just about any other weekly publication, popular fervor would soon be turned into official action by the Chinese government, meaning that "western ascendancy" will be "challenged, if not gone." In retrospect, the interwar period can be viewed as one in which European imperialism was tottering and in crisis, though in most of Africa and Asia that was not how Europeans viewed matters at the time. The exception to this was the quasi-imperial situation within China. The essay concludes with the statement that "times have changed. The White Man's Burden refuses to be carried any longer at an exorbitant charge for freight."[37] As *The Nation* put it in September of that year, "China is self-conscious and determined and angry" and that what its people want "in general, is freedom" from foreign domination.[38] The Boxers were "Old China," while the Guomindang was the wave of the future. Chiang would soon force foreign powers to accept a newly powerful China and as their peer.[39]

The moment was ripe for government action. The question was, which government? China's internationally recognized leaders controlled little beyond the outskirts of Peking, and dozens of "Tuchun" warlords dominated the rest. Outsiders recognized something new was afoot. In April 1926, three months before the start of the Guomindang's triumphant Northern Expedition, a Chinese writer noted how there had been much talk for two decades within and beyond China about the nation's "awakening." But now the situation was different, for "the present outburst of xenophobia is unlike anything of the sort that has happened before."[40] A year before Chiang's armies marched northwards, the magazine *The Living* Age declared his party to be "the standard bearer of the movement behind the present antiforeign agitation in China."[41] At the start of Chiang's campaign, an American remarked that his supporters possessed "not the language of old China but of young Europe," believing that as the author believed was the case with European youth, the Chinese youth wanted "to be like us."[42]

This hope was countered by the fears of others who focused on the Soviet presence in the background. No publication is more associated with support for Chiang Kai-shek than Henry Luce's *Time* magazine. As a child of missionaries who spent much of his childhood in China, the Christian leader of China and his American-educated Christian wife would become his ideal embodiment of what many Americans had long dreamed that China could be. It is thus rather surprising that the magazine's first mention of Chiang, in October 1926, referred to him as "the Cantonese Communist Super-Tuchun Chang [*sic*] Kaishek."[43] For the time being, Luce made no distinction between Chiang and his Communist allies. He was seen as one of them.

In 1927, the United States joined British efforts to protect their nationals in China by deploying its Asiatic Fleet into the Yangtze River. But Guomindang propaganda remained focused on the British, while US public opinion pressured Congress and President Calvin Coolidge to eliminate US involvement in the "unequal" Treaty System.[44] Early in 1927, Congress passed the Porter Resolution, calling for Coolidge to take precisely these steps.[45] After spending the remainder of 1927 attempting to liquidate their Communist ex-allies, Chiang's forces pushed north of the Yangtze in 1928, entering the former capital of Peking in June 1928, effectively dethroning the nominal national government based there.[46] The United States quickly became the first power to recognize Chiang as the ruler of all of China and led the way in renegotiating the treaties in terms of how they governed China's tariff autonomy. The Guomindang soon gained far greater leeway than the Qing had possessed for setting tariff rates, allowing tariffs on imports to constitute 40 percent of China's government revenue over the ensuing decade.[47] Chiang further solidified his US connections by converting to Christianity and marrying the Wellesley-educated Soong Meiling in December 1927.[48] Meiling was the younger sister of both T. V. Soong, who attended Harvard and would become a leading Guomindang official, and Sun Yat-sen's widow. Into the 1940s, American journalists frequently and erroneously referred to Chiang's regime as the "Soong Dynasty."

But a star had yet to be born. The pages of *Time* in the late 1920s illustrated how gradual and halting this process was. In April 1927, after Chiang captured Shanghai, the magazine labeled him "thoroughly modern" and "businesslike," and approvingly noted that "he has publicly disavowed Bolshevism."[49] By that August, they championed his bloody purge of Chinese Communist allies, though the magazine also mentioned the defeats his armies suffered in their first attempt to take Peking from the warlord Chang Tso-lin.[50] The magazine's piece that December on his wedding to Soong Meiling reads like a frivolous society piece about a rising star-turned-has-been. The writers snidely observed that Chiang "once conquered half of holy China," but now had been defeated. They referred to his bride as "that intensely Westernized 'modern woman,'" but tellingly made no mention of her being a Christian. *Time* did however note that she was a graduate of Wellesley College, that her brother and government official T. V. Soong attended Harvard, and that one of her older sisters was the widow of Sun Yat-sen, while the other was the wife of powerful Guomindang official H. H. Kung.[51] Chiang was only incidental to a story about the apparently ascendant Soong family.

If Chiang's April 1927 break with the Communists was the first minor turning point with his eventual leading cheerleader, his June 1928 capture of Peking was the second. For the first time, *Time* compared "slender, modest, democratic Chiang Kaishek" to George Washington, and called his party "a Liberal entity."[52] Still, the magazine credited the victory to "Christian" warlord Feng Yu-hsiang's defection from Chang Tso-lin to Chiang.[53] Chang Tso-lin was called the superior general, and the magazine noted that he retreated with his forces intact into Manchuria, where he would be under the protection of the Japanese, who were rapidly filling the region with their "little brown colonists."[54] The third—and most decisive—turning point would be Chiang's own baptism as a Methodist in November 1930. Now the adulation could finally commence. *Time* compared Chiang to Roman Emperor Constantine I, and noted that his wife converted him—the first time the magazine mentioned either her religion or her influence over Chiang.[55] Reflecting six years later on how Chiang attempted to morally reform China as his wife had morally reformed him, the magazine claimed the US equivalent would be if "President Roosevelt should have become a Mohammedan and prefaced his New Deal with some such words as: 'Our American people seem to me a nation of jazz-loving gum-chewers, profligate installment-plan buyers, poltroon capitulators to racketeers, gasoline-wasters and coffee-addicts.'"[56] *Time* now portrayed Chiang as "a diligently prayerful Methodist and a tireless preacher of Spartan virtues to indulgent Chinese" (Figure 4).[57]

Chiang's brother-in-law T. V. Soong also developed a large following, but in the United States rather than in China. Termed the Alexander Hamilton to Chiang's George Washington, Soong was intermittently put in charge of Chinese government finances and tasked with stabilizing its currency.[58] Tellingly described by *Time* as both "the Chinese upon which so much of China's fate depended" and "as much like an American as an Asiatic could or would care to be," Soong was well known as a supporter of political liberalization and democratization.[59] This perennially put him at odds with the party's leadership, and his position within the government was inversely proportional to the faith America's political leaders had in Chiang. On multiple occasions, he was used as a sop to US complaints about creeping authoritarianism and the lack of reforms, only to be demoted once Chiang had regained the confidence of the Americans.

Chiang's successful reassertion of China's sovereignty in 1928 led to debates over how reflective China's increased international stature was of the regime's internal strength. On this matter, most foreign observers

FIGURE 4 *Cover,* Time, *April 4, 1927. The first appearance of Chiang Kai-shek on the cover of* Time *was decidedly less heroic than his later depictions in that magazine. It reflected the initial suspicions Chiang faced from foreigners who feared the effects of the militant nationalism his Guomindong Party had exploited in its rise to power.*

remained pessimistic. *Foreign Affairs* declared the "Nationalist Revolution" a success in shattering the position of the great powers in China, though it credited the weakness created by the destruction of the recent world war more than any strengthening on China's part.[60] In a debate in the pages of *Living Age*, an optimist about China noted the explosion of newspapers and political awareness in the 1920s, while a pessimist pointed out the lack of economic development or rule of law, and blamed US missionaries for creating an inaccurate positive picture of the situation.[61] China correspondent for the *New Republic* Nathaniel Peffer, who in the 1920s and 1930s taught at Columbia University and was one of America's leading China experts, viewed the Japanese evacuation of Shantung Province in 1929 as the final sign that "the Chinese have won."[62] Yet he predicted this victory would ultimately prove a hollow one, due to the character and composition of the Guomindang. In his perceptive opinion, "it is too inchoate, too lacking in cohesion, composed of too many irreconcilable elements, and too unstable in its policy and program."[63] China contained multitudes, and, unfortunately, so did its ruling clique. In this early period, liberals tended to express optimism and conservatives fear. While the English press "call the present crisis in China the gravest since the Boxer rebellion," the then-influential American weekly *Literary Digest* assured its readers that while the Boxers were "reactionary" in nature, the Nationalists were "modern China."[64] On the other hand, British journalist J. O. P. Bland condemned Anglo-American policies of conciliation based upon the principles of "racial equality" and "self-determination" as naïve.[65]

In the meantime, English-language publishers produced books with titles such as *A Bolshevised China: The World's Greatest Peril?*, *What's Wrong with China?* and *Is China Mad?*[66] Lionel Curtis's 1932 study *The Capital Question of China* conveyed both optimism and concern about China's potential, predicting that "this isolated people resembles a vast body of ore ready to yield metals that are useful, precious and beautiful, when metallurgists learn how to treat its refractory qualities."[67] Curtis concluded by reminding readers "the spectre which haunts Europe is fear—not of France, but of Germany. The nightmare which troubles the Far East is not fear of Japan, but fear of China."[68] Ultimately, it would in part be fears of a China united under Chiang which helped inspire Japan's wanton aggression against Chiang's China.

The book which best encapsulated the early Western perceptions of the early Guomindang era was Floyd Gibbons's 1929 novel *The Red Napoleon*. His pathbreaking work was the first invasion narrative to fuse fears of communism with the Yellow Peril. Still, race remained front-and-center, with communism merely acting as a catalyst for increased military mobilization. The imagined war remained one of racial annihilation and amalgamation. Gibbons's chosen agent of conquest was a Cossack of Mongol descent named Karakhan of Kazan, who as a teenager became a Soviet general during the Russian Civil

War. At Joseph Stalin's side when the Soviet leader is assassinated by a Polish Nationalist in 1932, Karakhan quickly assumes control of the Soviet Union and merges it with a "slowly awakening China," fresh off its defeat of the Japanese and expulsion of the French and British from South Asia. China's rise also sparks anti-imperialist revolts throughout North Africa. The author called all of this "the natural result of the unification of China," implying European imperialism was contingent upon a weakened China.[69] Slim, over six feet tall, and with "long-fingered, well-manicured hands," Karakhan sounds the spitting image of Fu Manchu.[70] Karakhan and Roemer's arch-villain share an obsession with white women, though the former decidedly lacks Fu Manchu's asexuality. He soon leads a multiethnic non-white army dominated by Chinese infantry across Europe, overrunning the continent in five months under banners reading "Conquer and Breed" and a "rainbow-like" flag "of miscegenation" with stripes of red, yellow, white, brown, and black.[71]

The key to Karakhan's success is the swiftness of attack he achieves with a combination of horse cavalry and tactical fighter aircraft. While this near-future fiction made no mention of tanks or motorized infantry, it featured all manner of aircraft, utilized in both close ground support and long-distance strategic bombing, as well as plentiful aircraft carriers. After sweeping through Europe in 1933, annihilating Australia's white inhabitants, gobbling up Latin America, and overpowering Canada, Karakhan sets his sights on the United States. With an army of eight million—mostly Chinese—he pushes through New England in 1934, only to become bogged down outside New York City. The turning point comes when the American navy destroys the Chinese fleet off Kingston, Jamaica, in a daring sneak attack early in 1936. The loss of naval superiority dooms his land forces, though not before they have obliterated New York and bombed Washington, D.C. to rubble. Karakhan is then captured and imprisoned in Bermuda, where he warns his captors "a comparative handful of white skins cannot continue to crowd their brothers of coloured skin out of a place in the sun."[72]

Despite the "Red" of the title, there are only two references to class conflict. The first is a socialist revolution taking Britain out of the fighting in 1933. The second is the claim the United States successfully fought off conquest because "it was the first time the yellow horde had encountered a nation free from internal class dissension."[73] The narrative of his European conquests credits superior numbers, mobility, and weaponry as opposed to any internal tensions among his adversaries. Nor does the protagonist make appeals along class lines. Instead, the focus is almost entirely upon race—specifically Karakhan's perverse commitment to racial equality, which the author defines as a form of white genocide. The origin of this obsession was "defiant pride in his coloured skin" and the "impacts of white dominance" on the world. In response, Karakhan takes a series of willing white female lovers and encourages his non-white soldiers to do likewise in order to bring about the extinction of pure whiteness. The author makes much of the voluntary nature of these sexual couplings, to the shame and horror of European and American white men. When one white man asks another how "these American women submitted to him willingly," he is told, "because they love him."[74]

The sexual element in *The Red Napoleon* was noteworthy, having only appeared before in *The Yellow Danger*. One can make a direct connection to Wilhelm's racialized civilizational fears from more than three decades previous, and the implication that a powerful China would destroy global white supremacy. The Guomindang were the first modernizers to have a chance to unite and strengthen the country. It was this promise which engendered initial domestic popularity and some foreign fears. Though its leaders almost immediately made clear their opposition to communism in China, they could not have risen to power without Soviet assistance. At first, the regime's appeal to foreign powers was not rooted in a specific ideology. It was created by Russian Communists, embraced by the democratic United States, and strengthened by significant military assistance by first Weimar and then Nazi Germany. Its leaders earned the hostility of the British and the Japanese. Thus, the diplomatic breakdown could best be characterized as support from weaker and dissatisfied players in China who saw something to gain and opposition from the dominant powers who had the most to lose from a revived China.

As Soviet Comintern adviser Mikhail Borodin recognized from early on, the Guomindang's great weakness was its lack of a mass social base of support. At times, when seen as defenders of the Chinese nation, it could galvanize domestic public opinion. But it lacked the institutional structure to systematically harness this intermittent enthusiasm. The problem of ruling China has always been the problem of scale. From the comparative failures of the Qin and successes of the Han Dynasties more than two millennia earlier, China's leaders have oscillated between tightening and loosening their control over the immense numbers of Chinese living across a continent-sized territory. Excessive tightening and centralization—as under the short-lived Qin and Sui Dynasties—led to revolt. Excessive loosening and decentralization—as occurred in the later periods of the Han, Tang, and Qing Dynasties, allowed centrifugal forces to pull the nation apart. Modern transportation and communications technologies presented the Guomindang with an opportunity to combat the causes of decentralization as never before. But they never seized the opportunity to do so.

Part of the reason was a series of circumstances beyond the party's control: an ongoing Communist insurgency and more than two dozen other localized revolts in its first decade in power, followed by a massive Japanese invasion.[75] But another contributing was its own innate structural weaknesses. Ideologically, the Guomindang was incoherent. It had a leftist intellectual reformist faction which enabled the temporary alliance with the Communists, as well as urban middle-class supporters of democracy and industrialization. But its commanding heights were rightist and authoritarian. In the cities it was the party of businessmen. In the countryside, it was the party of landlords. This built-in commitment to the status quo was anathema to transforming Chinese society. Also, the rightists were strongest in the military, upon which Chiang's power most depended. Therefore, it was only natural that its yearning for modernization would draw its leadership to seek inspiration not from communism, socialism, or liberalism, but from fascism.

In 1932, Chiang created the Blue Shirts Movement. The group was led by a group of young officers, and centered within the army's officer corps. These officers had been exposed to fascism through the German military advisers who trained Chiang's best divisions. For instance, Lieutenant Colonel Herman Kriebel, who arrived in China in 1929, participated in the 1923 Munich Beer Hall Putsch and briefly shared a prison cell with Adolf Hitler. In a letter sent to Nazi Party headquarters in August 1932, Chiang inquired into how the National Socialists "maintain such strict discipline among followers" and "take such harsh measures" against their opponents. Just as the Soviet Comintern shaped the Guomindang's early party structure because no other foreigners came calling, Germany enjoyed strong economic connections to Nanjing Decade China by default. They were by far China's leading source of foreign investment during this period.[76] With economic and military assistance came the introduction of new ideas.

In Chinese, there were two translations of the word fascism. The first was the simple transliteration *fan-hsi*, but the second was *pang-ho*, which literally meant "to arouse a person from his stupid ways as if hitting him with a club."[77] This accurately reflected how the Guomindang thought they could put the concept to good use. In a 1935 speech, Chiang argued that "fascism is a stimulant for a declining society" and that "fascism is what China now most needs."[78] Blue Shirt rhetoric stressed the two defining pillars of fascism: contempt for liberal democracy and the exaltation of violence. Chiang advocated "the principle of fighting violence with violence," declaring "there must be a determination to shed blood—that is, there must be a kind of unprecedented violence to eliminate all enemies of the people." Blue Shirts called for a "permanent purge" of the bureaucracy, which they correctly saw as a wellspring of corruption, and believed the only way to do so was to "create a mass violence organization." They hoped to reach the youth through militarizing the educational system, which the Guomindang had done much to expand. Their slogan was "Nationalize, Militarize, Productivize."[79]

The Blue Shirts differed from their Italian Blackshirt and German Brownshirt inspirations by being an elite, and not a mass, organization. Its membership peaked at 10,000 in 1935.[80] While the Blue Shirts increased militarization among educated young Chinese men in the early-to-mid thirties, they lacked the reach to live up to their boastful rhetoric of remaking society. Their impact was largely superficial, and in this way typified Chiang's rule, which little affected the lives of the uneducated rural Chinese who represented the vast bulk of the nation's populace. Blue Shirt cultural ideology did bleed into the broader New Life Movement, which Chiang began in 1934 in an attempt to reform Chinese society. Followers of the movement attacked examples of what they believed to be sinful Western decadence, raiding dance halls and movie theaters and pouring acid on Chinese clothed in Western attire.[81]

This reflected the regime's focus on the influence of popular culture on Chinese youth. In 1936 and 1937, the government banned the showings of one in ten films the Hollywood studios attempted to distribute in China due to what the government perceived as these films' demeaning portrayals of Chinese people and Chinese culture. In recent years, much has been made of the Chinese Communist Party's leverage over US filmmakers, and how Hollywood has taken to self-censorship to protect the distribution in China of the superhero blockbusters that provide so much of the studios' current earnings. But this was not a Communist innovation. Like China's current government, Chiang's government sought to glorify Chinese civilization through acts of cultural and educational diplomacy, most notably in a 1935 exhibition of Chinese artifacts at the Royal Academy in London. Known as the Burlington House show, it was well-received by a vast audience in Britain and beyond, which Chiang hoped would boost China's international status.[82]

The period of Guomindang rule before Japan's invasion of China—often called the "Nanking Decade" after the regime's capital—was also an unprecedented era of foreign assistance, particularly from American technical experts who sought to improve Chinese agriculture, medical care, and education, among other areas of focus. One of these experts in the field of agriculture was Pearl Buck's husband. The couple's lengthy period of residence in China's rural interior provided the material for Buck's novel *The Good Earth*. Released in 1931, it was the bestselling work of fiction in the United States over the next two years. American readers who were suffering through the harshest period of the Great Depression identified with the struggles of the family of peasant Wang Lung, who persisted through natural disasters and human predation. This was among the earliest of a wave of bestsellers about struggling farming families, the most famous of which would be John Steinbeck's *The Grapes of Wrath*.[83]

Buck's genius was in making white Americans identify with Chinese characters. By doing so, Buck inaugurated a brief period of American hope for and belief in a benevolent China, one that could be, as Time-Life publisher Henry Luce saw it, "an Asian equivalent of America."[84] Luce and Buck formed the two poles of informed American opinion toward China. Luce was a conservative idealist who taught Americans to believe in a friendly China on the path to modernization and ripe for conversion to Christianity. Buck had leftist leanings and was skeptical both of Chiang's leadership and other missionaries' hopes. While Luce wrote of an "American Century," Buck had a 300-page file with the Federal Bureau of Investigation.[85] But during the 1930s, they were the twin apostles of a kinder, gentler China that should be loved rather than feared.

Still, Chiang had to wait for disaster to strike China before he would be fully lionized by the likes of Henry Luce. Even during the later years of the Nanking Decade, when Chiang strove mightily to eliminate the Chinese Communists, his press was far from worshipful. This changed almost immediately after Japan's Kwantung Army headed south from Manchuria following the Marco Polo Bridge incident on July 7, 1937. By this point, the Japanese had occupied Manchuria for over five years and many leading Chinese figures—including in Chiang's own military, believed he should cease attacking the Communists to focus on the Japanese. Matters came to a head with the kidnapping of Chiang in December 1936 in Xian by units within his own forces that were exiles from Japanese-occupied Manchuria.[86] At that moment, he was preparing a final offensive to annihilate Mao's forces in Yenan. But Chiang could only secure his release by pledging to form a united Chinese front against Japanese aggression, technically turning the Communists in Yenan overnight from mortal enemies into vital allies. Chiang legalized the Red Army, authorizing the Eighth Route Army centered in the CCP's northwestern base area, and the New Fourth Army among the Communist remnants in southeastern China.[87] Chiang had defined the Communists a "disease of the heart," while the Japanese were merely "a disease of the skin."[88] Now, he would have to put aside the civil war for an interstate—and later international—war. It would prove to be his regime's defining test.

PART TWO

The Dragon Roars: 1937–76

5

The Communists' Path to Power 1937–53

It was only supposed to last one month.[1] The Japanese army would march into Peking—which was no longer the Chinese government's capital city—then push aside the ill-trained warlord armies in control of northern China. After Japan added the North China Plain to its Manchurian territories, Chiang's rump state would quickly fall in line and negotiate peace conditions under which southern China would retain nominal sovereignty but effectively become an economic colony of Japan. According to Theodore White, one of the leading American war correspondents in China, "the Japanese hoped to fight in the north and to negotiate in the south."[2] By the fall of 1937, the Japanese would be unchallenged masters of East Asia. European and American colonies in the region would remain unmolested, but only upon Japan's sufferance. Victory would be swift, the rewards immense, and the costs minimal.

Japan had good reason to expect this result. Since easily conquering Manchuria in 1931, Japanese forces had been gradually nibbling their way into North China, until by the summer of 1937 they were at the northern approaches to Peking. Chiang had done little to resist Japan's encroachments. *The New Republic* in 1935 described Chiang as "the tool through which Japan's military and diplomatic leaders have been enforcing Japanese primacy in China."[3] Furthermore, certain Westerners viewed Japan's presence in China as the strongest bulwark against Soviet expansion into East Asia.[4] Yet nothing would go according to plan. Not for the Japanese. Not for the Chinese. Not for the Europeans, and not for the Americans. Japan's estimation that Chiang's government lacked the ability to defend Chinese territory proved correct. But its assumption that the Guomindang would therefore not offer determined resistance proved woefully off-the-mark. Japanese forces became sucked into a conflict they could not win against an adversary that could not defeat them. While successfully seizing the bulk of China's industrial capacity, occupying most of China's major cities, controlling the bulk of its population, and rarely losing a battle, over the course of the following eight years, Japan's occupation of China would cost it 50,000 military fatalities each year, along with an additional annual toll of 200,000 wounded. Meanwhile, Chinese forces sustained at least 1.3 million battle deaths, and well upward of ten million civilian casualties.[5] Consistent Japanese tactical triumphs failed to yield strategic success in the face of what one observer aptly referred to as China's "contradiction of determined weakness."[6]

Given the fact that Japan took it upon itself to attempt to devour a far larger neighbor it could not hope to successfully digest, the temptation is to compare the 1937 invasion of China to Nazi Germany's 1941 invasion of the Soviet Union. A more apt analogy would be Napoleon's 1808 invasion of Spain. In both cases, immense forces which could have been deployed against enemies elsewhere remained tied down, and needed to be continually reinforced to make up for the steady and unavoidable casualties occasioned by a fiercely resented occupation. Japan's need to stanch its "Chinese Ulcer" led to desperate attempts to isolate China from outside assistance through additional acts of military aggression. Japan's army conquered all of China's southern neighbors to cut it off from imperial Britain, while its navy pushed deep into the Pacific Ocean to keep the United States at bay while using the resources of the region to maintain its military forces. When fighting finally stopped—not in 1945 but in 1953—the regional situation was utterly transformed in ways the Japanese in 1937 could hardly have envisioned.

This sixteen-year period of nearly continuous war for the Chinese people can be divided into four periods of approximately equal length: Japan's invasion and attempted conquest, China's involvement as a US ally in the Second World War, the Chinese Civil War, and the Korean War. In the first two phases, a weak China fought foreign invasion. In the third, the divided Chinese fought each other. In the fourth, China fought beyond its borders on a significant scale for the first time in three-and-a-half centuries.[7] This occasioned the most extreme fluctuations in foreign opinions of China in modern history. The Northern Expedition had made Chiang powerful. Conversion to Christianity made him acceptable. But fighting the Japanese made him heroic, and even, in the eyes of some in the United States, quasi-messianic. But the war that made his international reputation also destroyed his domestic power. While the Japanese overran China's southeastern economic heartland, Mao Zedong's Communists, safely ensconced in the economically backward northwest, spread their control throughout the northern Chinese countryside wherever Japanese garrisons were absent. After the Japanese returned to their own devastated homeland, the waxing Communists expelled the waning

Nationalists, then purged all Western influence. At the wars' conclusion, the fears of multiple generations of foreigners seemed well on their way to fruition, the Yellow Peril having merged with the red menace.

This chapter takes a look at these pivotal events through the eyes of foreign observers. Fear that Chiang's Guomindang might eventually succeed in creating a strong and united China helped drive Japan's sense of urgency when it came to their own acts of aggression in 1937.[8] Serene in the face of foreign onslaught, Chiang plotted China's future, displaying a confidence which struck fear in certain foreigners but hope in others. His wartime lionization by American pundits and politicians led to vicious scapegoating upon his eventual defeat. With the Communists' ascent to power, the United States and its allies faced a strategic and psychological nightmare: a foe they could not vanquish but only hope to contain as it eagerly fished in the troubled waters of the collapsing colonial empires all around China. With the Century of Humiliation ended, the question became when—and if—a Chinese Century would arrive.

The Japanese military had coveted territory in northern China since the final decades of the Qing Dynasty. In the early Republican period, the Twenty-One Demands made clear Japan's desire to economically dominate China. Under British and American pressure, the Japanese adopted a more restrained attitude in the 1920s, but the onset of the Great Depression decimated Japan's export industries, leading to calls for renewed imperialism to attain economic self-sufficiency. Japanese army officers, and then naval officers, proceeded to intimidate and marginalize civilian politicians before feuding with each other over the best path to take. The army gained the initial upper hand and prioritized capturing Manchuria to exploit its grain, metals, and industrial capacity. After the brief Sino-Soviet War of 1929 established Soviet hegemony over the region, Japan also felt compelled in 1931 to deny its resources to the Soviets. Similar fears occasioned the southward lunge into China proper in 1937. The Japanese had long feared the establishment of a formal Sino-Soviet alliance, which Chiang's newly sealed united front with the Chinese Communists seemed to presage.[9]

Japan's 1931 capture of Manchuria by the Kwantung Army had been little more than a mere matter of marching, and its commanders no doubt expected something similar in 1937. Instead, the poorly trained Chinese warlord armies put up unexpectedly spirited fights. Resistance only stiffened as the Japanese approached the Yangtze River Valley and the territory directly controlled by the Guomindang. Chiang concentrated his best-trained forces north of Shanghai, intending to make a heroic stand that would impress the large foreign community in the city. In this he succeeded, albeit at the cost of 300,000 of his best troops. On November 20, Chiang retreated 500 miles inland to Wuhan and relocated his capital to Chungking a further 500 miles to the west in Sichuan province, effectively abandoning Nanjing, which was less than 100 miles upriver from Shanghai.[10] In a manner which would become characteristic of their behavior in all theatres of operations, Japanese soldiers ran amok in the defenseless city after entering it on December 13 and continued with their outrages into February 1938.[11] During this six-week orgy of atrocities, Japanese soldiers—aided and abetted by their commanding officers—killed hundreds of thousands in what became known to history as the Rape of Nanking. The juxtaposition of Chinese heroism in Shanghai and Japanese savagery in Nanjing created an unprecedented wellspring of international goodwill toward the Chinese people and their government. *Time* named Chiang and his wife 1937's "Man and Woman of the Year," and its publisher Henry Luce became his most influential foreign booster. But Luce was far from alone. After Hitler's Wehrmacht conquered Western Europe in only six weeks in 1940, US publications marveled at China's perseverance, fighting on with fewer weapons while absorbing far more casualties than Germany's European adversaries.[12]

Belatedly adjusting to the reality of Chinese noncompliance with national dismemberment, the Japanese regrouped and pushed inland along the major rail lines. After a few tactical Chinese triumphs against isolated Japanese forces, the Chinese abandoned Wuhan by the end of October 1938.[13] After over a year of large-scale conventional warfare, Chiang, his armies, and their supporting personnel retreated upriver and along rail lines to Chungking. Joining them were nearly a million civilians—government employees, students, factory workers, and their families. The Guomindang managed to relocate fully 80 percent of their weapons factories, as much a testament to their ingenuity as to the paucity of their munitions manufacturing capacity.[14] The population of the sleepy inland provincial city at a bend along the upper Yangtze quintupled from its prewar total of 200,000, straining its infrastructure far beyond the breaking point. Japanese planes bombed Chungking 268 times in 1939, 1940, and 1941.[15] These attacks created a rallying effect similar to Britain's "Dunkirk Spirit" during the German Luftwaffe's "Blitz" attacks in late 1940 and early 1941. Residents dug tunnels and caves into the cliffs which hemmed in Chungking as makeshift bomb shelters. Paradoxically, the reprieve offered by the US entry into the war against Japan led to a resurgence of private selfishness and public corruption, destroying the wartime capital's morale by 1945, a harbinger of the Nationalists' exhaustion.

Before 1941, the Chinese received little more than sympathy from the United States. Then Lend-Lease provided the Chinese forces with trickles of supplies, and in May former Army Air Corps Colonel Claire Chennault arrived in Chungking as the leader of the "Flying Tigers" volunteer force, in which approximately 100 American aviators would initially serve.[16] Madame Chiang greeted the Louisianan with a southern drawl, and he was immediately smitten. The airman would later rank her husband as "one of the two or three greatest military and political leaders in the world today."[17] Chiang polarized the opinions of American observers. Something about the Generalissimo's presence seemed to suck the nuance out of any space he entered. Whatever first impression he created tended to be lasting. Journalist Theodore White proved an exception, later on calling China's wartime leader "a man I learned first to respect and admire, then to pity, then to despise," indicating that even those capable of shifting their views still could only conceive of the man in caricature form, rather than as a multifaceted human being with a mix of strengths and weaknesses.[18]

For such a divisive figure, Chiang's approach to fighting and winning his war was decidedly moderate and pragmatic. His main forces would prevent the Japanese from advancing westward upon his government-in-semi-exile, while the Americans advanced westward across the Pacific Ocean and defeated Japan. He believed the Japanese bombing of Pearl Harbor in December 1941 assured him of victory. His best course of action now was to wait for others to win the war while conserving his resources for the inevitable showdown with the Communists. Like any canny aspirant to the power of a Chinese emperor, he rated domestic foes above foreign ones. This caution frustrated American commanders in China, who wanted no part of a mere holding operation.

Chiang's goals were better received in Washington. The Chinese merely needed to stay in the war, and tie down a million Japanese, for US efforts to be counted as a success. Also, China proved useful for rallying Asian public opinion. As the lone non-white ally fighting the Axis Powers, its participation helped mitigate the appearance that the fight against Japan was a race war. The most pressing concern regarding China in Washington—and, for that matter, in London—was its postwar fate. Roosevelt envisioned a united China led by Chiang Kai-shek that could act as one of his "Four Policemen." Along with the United States, the USSR, and Great Britain, China would preserve order along its periphery and guard against any resurgence of Japanese aggression. Believing possession of its Asian imperial territories depended upon a weak China, the British felt quite differently. A British ambassador in Chungking informed his American counterpart "the American policy to unify China was detrimental if not destructive to the position of the white man in Asia." In addition to not wanting a strong China, the British also believed such predictions of a powerful China by Americans were delusional. Churchill ridiculed American affection for China as "strangely out of proportion." Foreign Secretary Anthony Eden tried to rationalize these delusions by hypothesizing that "it is through their feeling for China that the President is seeking to lead his people to accept international responsibilities."[19]

English anthropologist Geoffrey Gorer once remarked that "Asia is the one continent about which Americans are emotionally attached." Franklin Roosevelt claimed to feel a connection to China because his great-grandfather had been involved in the China trade in the early 1800s. What Roosevelt failed to mention, and might not have even known, was that the primary product his great-grandfather sold to Chinese customers was opium.[20] This aptly reflects the divide between American ideals and Chinese realities. During the early 1940s, the idealistic streak regarding China was at its apex. Fueling such sentiments was former Republican presidential candidate Wendell Willkie. In 1942, he traveled around the globe in forty-nine days on a plane he christened *Gulliver*. Roosevelt had sent Willkie abroad both as a show of bipartisan comity and as a way to exploit the man's showmanship to encourage Americans to care about the distant lands where their sons were now being sent to fight.[21]

Willkie recounted his travels in the 1943 runaway bestseller *One World*. China was his final stop, and his impressions of that nation take up the final quarter of the book. Even more than most American dignitaries, Chiang and his wife charmed Willkie, who provided a glowing portrait of them. According to Willkie, "possibly no other country on our side in this war is so dominated by the personality of one man as China." In fact, "both as a man and as a leader," the Chinese leader was "even bigger than his legendary reputation."[22] The sole negative aspect Willkie reported was China's economic problems, particularly with inflation.[23] Ultimately, this would sap civilian support for the Nationalists and help pave the way for the Communists' victory. Willkie did meet with Communist official Zhou Enlai, who was in Chungking at the time. He assured his readers that the Chinese Communists were "more a national and agrarian awakening than an international or proletarian conspiracy."[24] All told, he provided Americans with an optimistic portrait of China and its future.

Willkie was far from alone in expressing such optimism during these years. Nathaniel Peffer called the invasion "a catalytic agent" for China's national development, and British leader Sir Frederick Whyte believed China was becoming "a National State of the first order of importance."[25] The peak of US and Chinese optimism occurred in November 1943 at the Cairo Conference, where Chiang sat with Roosevelt and Churchill as a nominal equal. The was also the year the US Congress repealed the nation's Chinese exclusion laws, and the US and Great Britain agreed to undo all "Unequal Treaties" still in effect.[26] Wellington Koo, the Columbia-educated Chinese diplomat who played a major role in the latter achievement, warned his colleagues about letting these successes go to their heads, lest they "think they were real heroes" and became overconfident "in estimating their position of influence in international politics."[27] Koo became a diplomat because of his admiration of Count Cavour, the mid-nineteenth-century Italian government official who did much to garner support in France and Britain for Italian unification and briefly served as the Kingdom of Italy's first prime minister. The parallel proved more apt than Koo might have intended.[28] During the period of Italian unification from 1859 to 1871, known as the Risorgimento, the Piedmontese kingdom which came to rule the peninsula achieved more at the conference table than on the battlefield, and had to rely always on the kindness of allies for its successes. Even if all went well, and the Guomindang succeeded in uniting China, a similar fate seemed to beckon for Chiang's regime.

One would not know this from how the regime presented itself on the world stage in the early 1940s. Chiang styled himself the leader of Asia's colonized non-white peoples, just as Mao would after he assumed power. One of his chief propagandists Lin Yutang published *China's Destiny*, which predicted China would soon become a regional hegemon.[29] American journalists who had knowledge of its contents during the Second World War referred to it as "an Oriental version of *Mein Kampf*," while Harvard Sociologist Barrington Moore, in his landmark 1966 book on the sources of modernization *Social Origins of Dictatorship and Democracy*, compared Chiang's ideas to those of European fascists.[30] Just as Sun had popularized the phrase "Unequal Treaties," Chiang coined the slogan "Never Forget National Humiliation," which Mao and his successors would eagerly adopt.[31] But news of the book's content became known in the region, leading British officials to predict a postwar China would prove to be its greatest regional threat. Even some Americans were taken aback. Roosevelt's envoy to Chungking, Lauchlin Currie, warned Chiang that many Americans were disturbed by his pan-Asian stylings and wondered whether a liberated China would become militaristic and imperialist like Japan.[32]

The next year provided a cruel reality check. The construction of US bomber bases in Chinese territory prompted the Japanese to launch the Ichigo Offensive, their largest in China since 1938.[33] By 1944, Chennault had 900 planes at his disposal—more than the Japanese had in China.[34] Following the inland rail lines which paralleled the front lines, between April and October the Japanese headed first south, then west, in a J-shaped path. Fifteen Japanese divisions killed, captured, or otherwise eliminated 700,000 Guomindang soldiers and advanced to within 200 miles of Chungking. In the offensive's first month, 100,000 Japanese destroyed a force of 300,000 Chinese soldiers while incurring only 1,000 fatalities. Swept up in the pell-mell retreat, the Americans abandoned seventeen of the air bases they have just finished constructing. In the end, the US forces flew a grand total of twenty bombing missions against Japan from Chinese soil.[35]

The spectacle of massively outnumbered Japanese routing Chinese forces at will damaged the Roosevelt administration's image of Chiang and the Guomindang beyond repair. Also, since the Japanese conducted the offensive by stripping divisions from occupation duties in the north, the Communists had an opportunity to significantly expand their reach into the heavily populated northeastern Chinese countryside.[36] This decisively shifted the balance of power within China, which the Soviets would soon exploit with

American acquiescence. Roosevelt wrote to his Secretary of State Edward Stettinius that his assumptions about China as a great power were "based on the belief" that "450 million Chinese would someday become united and modernized" and therefore "assume the leadership" of East Asia.[37] But at this point, he was uncertain that Chiang would be the one to achieve this. Roosevelt now concluded that "three generations of education and training would be required before China could become a serious factor" in world affairs.[38] At Yalta in early 1945, Roosevelt chose to prioritize a swift end to the war against Japan, readily acceding to Stalin's requests for a Soviet invasion of Manchuria, along with other concessions that would compromise China's postwar sovereignty and hobble that nation's future standing as a great power and viable US partner in the region.

Lurking in the background, like Fortinbras off Elsinore, were Mao and his Communist forces. Communism's potential to strengthen China had appealed to a young Mao. He claimed in a 1937 interview that upon learning of Japan's victory over China in 1895, "I felt depressed about the future of my country and began to realize that it was my duty of all people to help save it."[39] In 1919, two years before the founding of the Chinese Communist Party, Mao wrote "The Great Unity of the People," arguing that China's traditions of collective action had made it strong before, and could do so again.[40] Mao, therefore, was asking the same questions that Sun had, but arriving at slightly different answers, in large part because he was doing so a generation—and a Bolshevik Revolution—later.

Nearly all foreign journalists in China during the Second World War based themselves in Chungking, where familiarity with the Guomindang invariably bred contempt. The Communists, nestled in distant, isolated Yenan, retained an air of positive mystery. The Communists could control access in ways the Nationalists could never hope to. The few Western journalists who encountered the Communists were invited by them, and presented with elaborately stage-managed depictions of their realm. Paradoxically, the personal informality of Communist leaders had a special appeal for Americans who felt alienated by the stifling protocol observed by officials in Chungking, who followed the traditional ritualist modes of Chinese statecraft. Decades later, Henry Kissinger and Richard Nixon would note the magnetic charisma of Mao and the seductive charm of Zhou Enlai, so it is easy to imagine lowly journalists being taken in by their charms. The trickle of press reports from Yenan sharply contrasted Communist-ruled lands with Nationalist territory. The former's towns were clean, whereas the latter's were filthy. Peasants and soldiers in Communist territory were healthy and happy, not starving and miserable. The Guomindang enforced "a rigid censorship," whereas in Yenan there supposedly was press freedom.[41] This third set of contrasts—to us the most bewildering—can be chalked up to the posture of casual forthrightness adopted by Mao and Zhou, as well as Communist generals like Zhu De. Future Marine General Evans Carlson, who commanded the Second Ranger Battalion during the Second World War, spent time in Yenan in 1937, and based his unit's famous "Gung Ho!" battle cry on one used by the Chinese Communists, which roughly translated as "working together."[42]

Edgar Snow had been the first foreign reporter allowed to speak to Mao in his recently established base area in 1937. From his observations and interviews, he produced *Red Star Over China*, which glamorized the rag-tag Communists to audiences the world over, lending what would become Maoism a glamorous appeal Leninism or Stalinism never enjoyed.[43] His book quickly became the bestselling non-fiction work in America on East Asia ever published.[44] Snow called Mao "a man of considerable depth of feeling," and believed he had "been a moderating influence in the Communist movement" when it came to its amount of killing and levels of brutality.[45] Snow also introduced the notion that Maoism and communism were not necessarily one and the same. He argued that Chinese communism "might more accurately be called rural equalitarianism than anything Marx would have found acceptable as a model child of his own."[46] Snow was proved most accurate in his book's conclusion, which proved astoundingly prophetic:

> The movement for social revolution in China might suffer defeats, might temporarily retreat, might for a time seem to languish, might make wide changes in tactics to fit immediate necessities and aims, might even for a period be submerged, be forced underground, but it would not only continue to mature; in one mutation or another it would eventually win, simply because (as this book proves, if it proves anything) the basic conditions which had given it birth carried within themselves the dynamic necessity for its triumph.[47]

In failing to understand the true nature of Mao's movement, Snow was hardly alone. Freda Utley's 1939 book *China at War* also argued that the Chinese Communists were not Leninists.[48] She would later recant, and by the late 1940s had become one of the leading journalists on the American right blaming left-leaning American journalists, academics, and diplomats for contributing to Mao's triumph by denying his movement's true nature. University of Washington professor George Edward Taylor, who would become the most esteemed right-leaning China studies academic during the early Cold War, argued in the early 1940s that the Chinese Communists were moving toward "an institutional basis for democracy."[49] Senator Michael Mansfield (D-MT), a one-time professor of Asian history, said of the Communists after a tour of China in late 1944 that "there is more democracy in their territory than in the rest of China."[50] Thus, most of Mao's early American admirers were anything but fellow travelers. Even *Time* magazine took the Chinese Communists' "United Front" rhetoric seriously in the war's early stages, referring the Mao's leading general Zhu De as Chiang's "best aide" in defeating the Japanese and "China's #1 Guerrilla Fighter."[51] The magazine only changed its tune quite belatedly during the war's final year, largely under the influence of editor and repentant former American Communist Party member Whittaker Chambers.

Chambers clashed with Theodore White, who was the magazine's Chinese correspondent. Frustrated by his editor, White chose to speak his mind in the 1946 book *Thunder Out of China*, which he co-wrote with Annalee Jacoby. The handful of guerrilla fighters that Snow encountered might have still resided in caves, but they now ruled a state-within-a-state, commanding an army of well over 500,000 and controlling a population larger than that of any nation in Europe besides the Soviet Union. White and Jacoby visited the Communist-run areas in 1944 when Mao embarked upon a brief but intense charm offensive toward the US government and public. White took the long-term approach to history when telling the story of the Second World War in China. As destructive as it was, the Japanese invasion was but a fleeting event in the historical trajectory of China and Asia. What mattered more were the powerful social undercurrents that he defined as "the greatest revolution in the history of mankind, the revolution of Asia."[52]

The "tragedy of Chiang Kei-shek" was his failure to harness this power and instead squandering the initial revolutionary appeal of the Guomindang to the Chinese peasantry. The peasants' foes were "the ancient trinity of landlord, land shark, and merchant," precisely the authority figures Chiang allied himself with to cement his hold on power.[53] Mao had not made this mistake and was thus destined to rule China. Interestingly, by this point the Communists were aware of their own flattering American press, some of which they did not find especially flattering. According to White and Jacoby, "the Chinese Communists flatly deny the assumption of many American friends that they are merely agrarian reformers, not Communists at all. They insist they are Communists in the full sense of the word, and they are proud of it."[54]

For a long time, there existed the notion of a "Lost Opportunity" for Sino-American relations in the brief window between the founding of the People's Republic of China in October 1949 and the beginning of the Korean War in June 1950. For instance, in 1982, former Columbia University professor Arthur Doak Barnett, for a long time considered the nation's leading expert on contemporary China, wrote that had the Korean War not happened, US recognition of the PRC would have occurred within two years, and "the Chinese would have become more flexible."[55] Over the past twenty years, access to Chinese archives has disproven the "Lost Chance" theory. White and Jacoby presented their own version of this argument even before the Communists had triumphed. They argued that Americans had squandered an opportunity for friendly relations with the Chinese Communists in 1944 by making it clear the US sided with Chiang, forcing Mao in 1945 "back to an alliance and dependence on Russia."[56] They compared the divisions between Communist-ruled and Nationalist-ruled provinces in China to different US states being controlled by Democrats or Republicans, an analogy that would also be embraced by General George Marshall when he tried to broker peace between Chiang and Mao in 1946.[57] This ignored the Nationalists' nearly two-decade-long war of extermination against the Communists, as well as the fact that each "party" controlled a massive and independent military force, something that was not the case with political parties in the United States.

War was inevitable, but its result wasn't. China could become all Nationalist. It could become all Communist. But it could also become divided between the two groups for an extended period of time. White and Jacoby, who expected a Communist victory, assumed it would take at least a decade. Mao appeared to be operating along a similarly extended timeline. But Chiang was in a hurry. The US military transported a half million of his soldiers from the rural interior to China's coastal cities in what became the largest ever US military airlift.[58] American officers warned Chiang about the dangers of spreading his forces too thin, but he was willing to take that risk in order to extend his control to all areas of China, especially its industrial base in Manchuria. After the breakdown of Marshall's negotiations near the end of 1946, the Chinese Civil War began in earnest. Chiang went on the offensive first, capturing Mao's base area in Yenan by March 1947.[59] Mao retreated with his primary armies to Manchuria. By the end of that year his forces, mostly led by General Lin Biao, had bottled Nationalist forces within the region's cities and cut off their communications and supply lines, thereby slowly but surely starving them into surrender. Chiang's disposition of forces proved a fatal blunder and cost him hundreds of thousands of his best-trained and most loyal soldiers and commanders.

By early 1948, the Truman administration saw Chiang as more of a liability than an asset.[60] The notion of cutting Chiang loose without significant domestic political costs seemed feasible at the time. White and Jacoby's book, so laudatory to the Communists and dismissive of the Nationalists, sold 450,000 copies in the United States in 1946 and was a Book-Of-The-Month Club selection.[61] This indicated that its arguments were not yet terribly controversial. There was a chance the administration could sell the notion of Chiang as an unworthy ally who was too incompetent for the United States to save at any cost. Furthermore, the Republicans' attempts to turn what they saw as Truman's half-hearted financial and military support for Chiang into a major issue in the 1948 presidential campaign failed to prevent a Democratic victory. In 1949, as Mao's forces crossed the Yangtze River unopposed and overran southern China while facing little organized opposition and Chiang fled to Taiwan, it became clear that Truman had miscalculated politically. Faced with the reality of a hostile Communist China, Americans became enraged. Pearl Buck's stoic peasants had turned red. The world's most populous nation, which for more than a century the United States had sought to help and aid in so many ways, was now an enemy. Even during a period when, in short order, the Germans and Japanese went from monsters to friends, and the Soviet Russians from allies to enemies, this instance of geopolitical whiplash proved particularly disorienting.

Truman attempted to absolve his administration of any culpability and place the blame for defeat purely on Chiang's and the Nationalists' shoulders. In March 1949, George Kennan, at that time director of the Policy Planning Staff at the State Department, proposed producing a lengthy report documenting the Guomindang's weaknesses. Truman initially resisted but relented in May 1949 in the face of escalating Republican criticism of Truman's inability to stave off Chiang's loss of the civil war.[62] On August 5, 1949, the administration released a 1,000-page report entitled "United States Relations with China, With Special Reference to the Period 1944-1949." Commonly known as the "White Paper," this massive collection of narrative, analysis, and documents assigned sole culpability for the Communist victory in the Chinese Civil War to Chiang and his regime. The preface, written by Secretary of State Dean Acheson, argued that the Guomindang "had lost the confidence its own troops and its own people," and that the war's result "was beyond the control of the government of the United States."[63] The White Paper's criticisms of Chiang and his Nationalist forces inflamed Truman's Republican opponents, and swung US public opinion to their side, isolating the president domestically. It also outraged Mao, who proceeded to write five lengthy responses to the White Paper in August alone, further solidifying Sino-American hostility. Mao asked why Truman provided so much financial and military support to forces he believed to be "demoralized and unpopular." Mao could only conclude such irrational behavior was solely based on imperialist intentions toward China and Truman's sadistic desire "to slaughter the Chinese people" by needlessly prolonging the war.[64]

Republicans in Congress responded to the White Paper's attacks on Chiang with the argument that US policy during the Civil War had been fatally compromised by State Department officials in China who presented a misleading and sanitized picture of Mao's movement as not being fully aligned with Soviet communism and capable of evolving in a less threatening direction. Speaking in Tiananmen Square on October 1, 1949, Mao formally announced the existence of the People's Republic of China. In that speech, he announced that "the Chinese people, comprising one quarter of humanity, have now stood up," adding that "ours will no longer be a nation subject to insult and humiliation."[65] He explained that "the Chinese have always been a courageous and industrious nation," with the previous 110 years being an anomaly "that was due entirely to oppression and exploitation by foreign imperialism and domestic reactionary governments."[66] Now, China could resume its rightful role as the Middle Kingdom.

What the future held, for China, the United States, and the world, still seemed up in the air. On the one hand, Winston Churchill termed the result of the Chinese Civil War "the worst disaster suffered by the West since the war."[67] On the other, the editors of *Business Week* predicted the US government would quickly grant Mao's regime formal diplomatic recognition to get a share of China's market, while Edgar Snow predicted the Chinese would reach out because of their economic need for trade with the United States.[68] Snow predicted the People's Republic of China "would become a kind of Asiatic Moscow, an Eastern Rome preaching Asiatic Marxism."[69] China would be both resolutely Communist at home and eager to export revolution abroad.

With its pronounced sympathies for the Chinese Communists, Jack Belden's book of reportage *China Shakes the World*, released in 1949 at the conclusion of the civil war, formed a sort of bookend to Theodore White's effort at the conflict's start. Alluding to Napoleon's supposed quote, this book and its title played a crucial role in popularizing that quotation. Yet, curiously, Belden only predicted the Communists would shake China, making no mention of the potential effects of Mao's triumph on the region or the world. He noted how, with every stage of China's revolutionary period, from the last Qing emperor to the warlord period to Chiang and on to Mao—the central government had grown ever stronger. This seemed to fit a historical pattern. It had been the case in England with Oliver Cromwell, in France with Napoleon Bonaparte, and in Russia with Joseph Stalin.[70] Unmentioned was how all of these leaders led their nations' armies beyond their borders after significantly militarizing the state. Mao's China would not embark on wars of conquest to bolster the leader's power and prestige, as Cromwell and Napoleon had, or establish neo-imperial spheres of influence as Stalin had. But thousands of Chinese military advisers soon headed across China's southern border to assist the Communist Vietminh insurgents in their efforts to expel the French from Indochina, and millions crossed the Yalu River along China's northern border to push back—and perhaps expel—American forces from the Korean peninsula.

North Korea's attempt in June 1950 to conquer South Korea began the first "hot war" of the Cold War era. After North Korea succeeded in occupying nearly all of the Korean peninsula that summer, in September US forces counterattacked, quickly recapturing South Korea's capital of Seoul before sweeping into North Korea, capturing its capital of Pyongyang, and pressing forward to the Chinese border at the Yalu River, hoping to conclude the war by Christmas. But devastating Chinese attacks in the winter of 1950–1 drove American, South Korean, and other allied forces 400 miles south, the longest retreat in American military history. Isolating opposing units and striking them with overwhelming numbers, they seemed a terrifyingly literal manifestation of the mythical Eastern Horde. It also humbled the US military, whose leaders like Douglas McArthur had discounted the fighting prowess of a people who had not defeated a foreign foe in centuries (Figure 5). Since the First Opium War of 1839, the Chinese had been the anvil upon which white warriors hammered. Now, that Chinese anvil was falling onto their heads.

By the spring of 1951, American forces had retaken Seoul from exhausted, overextended, and undersupplied Chinese armies, and repelled the fifth and final major Chinese offensive. The war then settled down into trench warfare. Fighting continued for an additional two years, costing American forces nearly half of its 38,000 war fatalities. During this bloody stalemate, Chinese, American, North Korean, and South Korean negotiators haggled over the drawing of borders and the fates of prisoners of war. Lurid stories had already appeared in numerous media outlets of Chinese attempts at "brainwashing" American prisoners. The term first appeared in an article by the journalist Edward Hunter in an article in the *Miami Daily News* in September 1950, two months before the first combat between Chinese and American forces. The article was entitled "Brain-Washing Tactics for Chinese into Ranks of Communist Party."[71] Hunter's subsequent reportage on the psychological

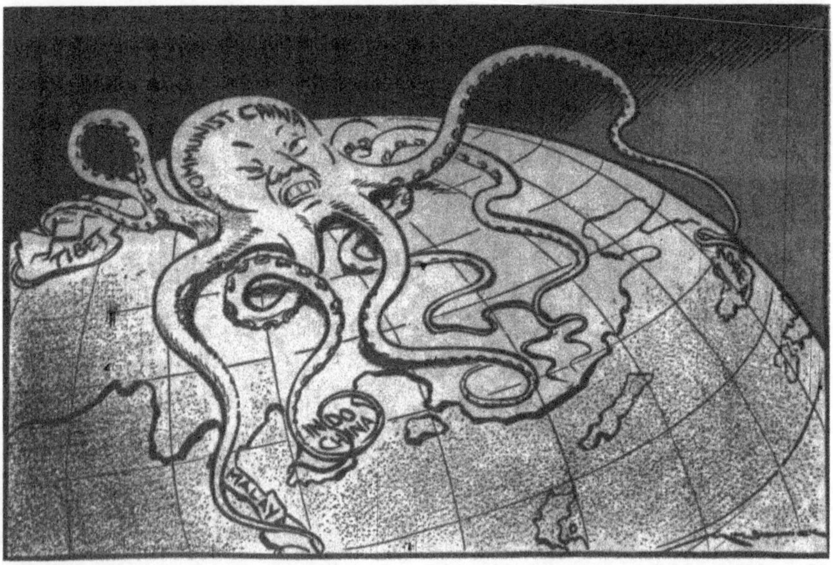

FIGURE 5 *"The Octopus of Chinese Communism," November 1950, Gordon Minhinnick,* New Zealand Herald. *Published as Chinese soldiers began attacking United Nations forces in the Korean peninsula, this cartoon revealed worries about Communist expansion beyond China's historic borders. Note how the cartoon depicts Tibet as non-Chinese territory, on par with Korea, French Indochina, and British Malaya.*

manipulation of prisoners soon drew the attention of future director of the Central Intelligence Agency Allen Dulles, as well as the American military.[72] It also penetrated popular culture in films such as 1956's "Invasion of the Body Snatchers" and 1962's "The Manchurian Candidate."[73]

Hunter summarized his findings in a popular 1956 book. Comparing brainwashing to witchcraft, he explained that his preferred term for the practice would be "brain warfare."[74] His book contained uplifting stories such as those of African-American prisoners who refused to succumb to their captors' exploitation of grievances based upon racial oppression in the United States.[75] Overall, Hunter's lesson appeared to be that so long as the targets possessed hope, they would be immune from brainwashing, which preyed on feelings of "hopelessness" and "inevitability." Such conditions were most often present in totalitarian societies like Communist China or the Soviet Union.[76] Unlike many who were inspired by his writings, Hunter did not single out the Chinese as expert brainwashers, or otherwise employ racialized stereotypes. His brief attempt at producing a "history" of the development of brainwashing began with Pavlov's experiments in Tsarist Russia, which the Soviets supposedly based their methods on, and these methods were then borrowed by the Chinese.[77]

More than two million Chinese served in Korea, and more than 152,000 Chinese (perhaps many times more) died in battle.[78] China's human and financial exertions set back its economic development and poisoned already fractious relations with the United States, but also confirmed China's new status as a regional power. During the war, journalist Hanson Baldwin addressed the question of whether the West was "beginning to witness the transmutation into fact of that old bogey of 50 years ago—'the Yellow Peril'?" Baldwin's answer was no—for now. First, the Chinese economy needed to be far more industrialized and developed, which would require decades.[79] But, in the present era, "the Chinese Army, little regarded in the past, is now a major political factor in the Orient."[80] It was notable that Baldwin put the phrase Yellow Peril in quotation marks, as if it was only alleged, and not actual. This also created a distance between the writer and the term, indicating Baldwin knew it was a pejorative phrase.

In that way, the Second World War proved a dividing line on views of the Chinese threat. Before 1945, journalists wrote of the Yellow Peril. After 1945, it was almost always the "Yellow Peril." The use of quotations became as ubiquitous after that date as it had been absent beforehand. This indicated that pure racialization was no longer acceptable. The Chinese now were a threat for reasons of ideology, or military and economic prowess, not race or color. Still, the old stereotypes of the supposedly bygone racialist era persisted. Baldwin praised Chinese soldiers for—unlike their North Korean allies—not being "quick to surrender." But he attributed this bravery to their gullibility, declaring them "easily controlled through false propaganda." He approvingly cited a US Army Field Forces report that stated "the inherently fatalistic attitude of the Chinese makes them seemingly fearless as long as their leadership does not falter."[81] Here once again appeared the Oriental automaton, docile on his own, but ferocious when under the spell of a charismatic leader. It was a characterization right out of *The Yellow Danger* or *The Red Napoleon*. But those were fiction. Invasion tales were invented nightmares. The Korean War was reality. The question then became what additional nightmares could come true.

6

Mao Zedong Confronts the World

1953–66

Dean Rusk was trying to warn Americans about a dangerous future, not remind them of a disgraceful past. He thought the sentiments he expressed were purely anti-Communist—about ideology, not race. The ensuing controversy took him, and the Johnson administration, very much by surprise. When asked by a reporter in October 1967 what was "at stake in Vietnam" for the United States, the Secretary of State responded that "within the next decade or two, there will be a billion Chinese on the mainland, armed with nuclear weapons, with no certainty about what their attitude toward the rest of Asia will be."[1] Rusk's comments framed the ongoing war in Vietnam as an attempt to contain an expansionist China. In addition, he was attempting to disagree with newly prominent Chinese studies academics over what he claimed were their attempts to downplay China's menace.

The ensuing media outrage was swift and widespread. Leading pundit James Reston—who supported the efforts of academics to encourage US diplomatic outreach to the Chinese Communists—accused Rusk of reviving "The Yellow Peril," and countered that like the Soviets, the Chinese understood "the necessity of restraint."[2] Liberal antiwar Senator Eugene McCarthy (D-MN) claimed Rusk's remarks were "the ancient fear of the yellow peril presented to us now in a new image."[3] Legendary journalist Joseph Kraft—who had informally advised presidents going back to Franklin Roosevelt—termed Rusk's words reckless, worrying about "a direct eyeball-to-eyeball confrontation between Washington and Peking."[4] Kraft also criticized similar remarks by Vice-President Hubert Humphrey. This was a telling pairing, since the previous year Rusk and

Humphrey had publicly clashed over China policy, with Humphrey advocating outreach while Rusk demanded continuing the existing policy of isolation.

President Lyndon Johnson soon felt compelled to deny and denounce any belief in the "yellow peril," telling reporters "we have utterly repudiated the racist nonsense of an earlier era."[5] The *Baltimore Afro-American* praised Johnson's remarks while absolving Rusk of any racial prejudice because the Georgian had recently consented to his daughter marrying a non-white man. The *Afro-American* also condemned "the false outcry that the Vietnam conflict for some unexplainable reason was a race war."[6] Carl T. Rowan, who had worked in Kennedy's and Johnson's State Departments as the first black head of the United States Information Agency, argued China was dangerous, but purely because it was Communist and not for any racial reasons. While terming the PRC "aggressive, belligerent, and reckless," he reminded readers of its numerous recent foreign policy setbacks, arguing the regime was weaker than the alarmists claimed. But at the same time, Rowan warned that "no one can afford to take China and 700,000,000 people lightly, especially when the leadership seems to be psychotic."[7]

This episode illustrated what had changed over the previous two decades, particularly in terms of what was considered acceptable discourse regarding China and the Chinese. Any notion of a "yellow peril" had fallen into official disrepute, a relic of a bygone era of phrenology, eugenics, and scientific racism. However, as with other prejudices, while the old phrases disappeared, the beliefs and behaviors persisted. They simply assumed new, more palatable forms.

This chapter documents and analyzes views about Chinese economic power and military intentions beginning with the end of the Korean War in 1953 and extending into the early stages of direct US involvement in the Vietnam War in 1966. During these thirteen years, the United States and its allies in Asia struggled to adapt to a unified and assertive Communist China, while the Soviet Union grew increasingly irritated with its most powerful and disobedient ally. For the United States, the crucial question became how durable was the Communist Chinese regime. Nearly all found China fearsome. But if it was fearsome yet fragile, the best approach would be isolating Communist China to hasten its demise. However, if that regime was destined to remain in power for the foreseeable future, then a different approach was called for. That approach would be a combination of continued containment and escalating levels of outreach in the hope that as Chinese power increased, its threat would decrease as it reciprocated the friendly postures of the United States and its allies. By the mid-1960s, proponents of outreach would begin to gain the upper hand over the advocates of isolation in the United States, Western Europe, and Eastern Asia, paving the way for the rapprochement of the early 1970s.

Historian Warren Cohen referred to the period of Sino-American relations from 1949 until 1971 as "The Great Aberration" because of the paucity of contact between the two nations' governments and their respective peoples. The US government enforced bans on Americans traveling to China and on American companies trading with China. Also, the United States did not accord Communist China diplomatic recognition, and did everything within its power to ensure United Nations membership—along with China's permanent seat on the UN Security Council—remained with the Taiwan-based Republic of China. But this period of official diplomatic isolation was also one of increasing military contact. It saw both the emergence of US hegemony in East Asia and the reemergence of China as a regional power capable of threatening that hegemony. Edgar Snow aptly summarized this paradox in 1961 when he wrote "never before had China received so much recognition and so much respect from the United States."[8] The return of a strong and centralized Chinese state for the first time in America's history as a nation sparked predictions about China's inevitable rise to becoming a global great power with an industrialized economy and a modern military. But those developments were contingent on the new Chinese regime staying in power. So long as policymakers believed its failure to be a strong possibility, the logical policy was to isolate China and strive to maintain the international pariah status it had achieved upon attacking United Nations forces in Korea. This was the approach taken by the Eisenhower administration from 1953 until 1961.

Though perceived as fragile, the People's Republic was a threat to its neighbors because those regimes were equally—if not more—fragile. According to a 1952 Eisenhower campaign memo, any further Communist advances in Asia would result in a crippling "psychological" blow to the US strategic position.[9] This fear guided Eisenhower's policies toward China, as well as the rhetoric of those who served him. In 1953, the new Secretary of State John Foster Dulles predicted any sign of US retreat would "set up a chain reaction," an early enunciation of the famous Domino Theory, whereby one US ally in Asia succumbing to Communist subversion would spark similar revolutions in all neighboring states. In a 1955 speech, Dulles discussed the "great danger" which would result if the "non-Communist peoples" of Asia came to doubt United States resolve to halt any and all additional Communist expansion in the region.[10]

General James Van Fleet, the former commander of United Nations forces in Korea, traveled for over three months in 1954 around China's periphery on behalf of Eisenhower. His report to the president labeled China "a greater menace to the Free World than the Soviet Union itself."[11] In an article published in *U.S. News* upon returning, Van Fleet cautioned Americans that "I don't think that time is on our side."[12] A few months later, that same magazine argued that while "acting tough," the Chinese "are leading from appalling weakness."[13] A continued policy of isolation was the best way to keep the Chinese in that state of weakness. Leading China scholar Richard "Dixie" Walker of the University of South Carolina called China "a major power on the world scene" in 1958, but that only strengthened his support for a policy designed to "exploit the weaknesses of the country, to make him (Mao) fail."[14]

Eisenhower remarked in a 1955 meeting of the National Security Council that he "was not afraid of Communist China—not in this decade at least."[15] Many, including his Secretary of State, wondered if the regime would survive into the next decade. Only months after the establishment of the People's Republic of China, Dulles claimed the Communists in China "will find it very difficult to establish its uncontested rule unless we help that by seeming, ourselves, to accept that result." Provided that did not occur, "the Communist offensive in the East will be checked on the rocks of internal difficulties within China."[16] In 1954, he wrote Representative Clare Boothe Luce (R-CT) that "despotisms always look formidable and impregnable from the outside," but "they are usually rotten on the inside."[17] In a similar vein, a 1954 article in the *Saturday Evening Post* by leading foreign policy pundit and Chinese cultural enthusiast Joseph Alsop situated the regime's strengths and weaknesses within the context of distant Chinese history, comparing Mao's rule to the short-lived Qin and Sui dynasties which collapsed after trying to change too much too quickly.[18]

The administration outlined this strategy in three policy papers produced by the National Security Council in 1953. NSC 148 proposed "fostering and supporting anti-communist Chinese elements both outside and within China," with the ultimate goal being "to bring about changes in China which will eliminate the threat from that country to Free World security."[19] In terms of the scope of US actions to help achieve this goal, NSC 146 proposed backing not only Nationalist "raids against the Communist mainland and seaborne commerce with Communist China," but ensure Republic of China forces were able to conduct "large-scale amphibious operations," clearly with an eye toward an eventual invasion and reconquest of the mainland if an opportunity were to present itself.[20] These arguments reached their logical culmination in NSC 166, which called for the policy goal of "reorientation of the Chinese Communist regime or its ultimate replacement."[21] Concessions by the United States would only strengthen the regime, as well as lessen the chance of a rivalry developing between it and the Soviets. Furthermore, the United States should work toward "denying the Chinese Communist regime full status in the international community."[22] The administration mapped out a plan of not only containment and isolation but also subversion. Assistant Secretary of State for Far Eastern Affairs Walter Robertson made this clear in his January 1954 testimony before Congress, where he stated the administration hoped to solve "the problem of China" by engaging in "action which will promote disintegration from within."[23]

Mao put Eisenhower's determination to halt the spread of communism in East Asia to the test twice in the Taiwan Straits: first in 1954, then in 1958. Known as the First and Second Straits Crises, they were the most notable examples of what came to be called Eisenhower's tactics of "Brinksmanship" and "Massive Retaliation." In both instances, the tactics succeeded, but at the cost of rendering them inoperable from then onward. At stake was control of Quemoy and Matsu, two clusters of barely populated islands a few miles off the coast of Fujian Province that were held by 100,000 of Chiang's soldiers—fully one-third of his entire army. China initiated the crisis shortly after the announcement of the formation of the US-led alliance the Southeast Asian Treaty Organization (SEATO) along China's borders, as well the imminent establishment of a formal US security alliance with the Republic of China. The Communists wished to demonstrate the dangers of making security guarantees with their opponents. After the Communists began intensively shelling the islands in the fall of 1954, Eisenhower threatened to use tactical nuclear weapons against military targets in Fujian should the Communists attempt to seize the islands.

The reason for laying down the nuclear gauntlet over a few rocks was the belief that the fate of Taiwan, and of the entire US strategic position in the Western Pacific, were at risk. The loss of these islands would both embolden the Communists and dishearten the Nationalists.[24] These barren rocks represented the Nationalists' last existing link to the mainland, and according to Eisenhower, their army was "held together by a conviction that someday they will go back."[25] As he explained to a supporter, "internal disillusionment" and "despair" on Taiwan would lead to the fall of the non-Communist government.[26] If Quemoy went, so would Taiwan, and with it "the whole US security position" in the region.[27] Dulles declared in a February 1955 televised speech that regional allies would conclude "that the United has no real intention of standing firmly behind them."[28] Eisenhower emphasized the "psychological" effect of losing Quemoy and Matsu.[29] In the past six years, the Chinese mainland had been conquered by Communists, North Korea had survived the Korean War, and the Vietminh had driven the French out of Indochina and established a Communist regime in North Vietnam. The United States could not afford another such defeat. On a visit to Bangkok, Dulles wrote to Eisenhower that the loss of Formosa would even "convince Japan communism (was the) wave of (the) future."[30]

Though in retrospect it is clear neither the Chinese nor the Americans seriously considered risking war, that was far from apparent to outside observers at the time. In a televised address in January 1955, the president argued that threatening nuclear attack "would decrease the risk of war" as well as "halt the dangerous drift" in East Asian security policy since 1949.[31] The press applauded Eisenhower's firmness, with the *New York Times* calling it a "tour de force."[32] However, the public seemed less than enthused, with mail to the White House running 3-to-1 against the president's approach.[33] This was a preview of popular reaction to the Second Straits Crisis in September and October of 1958, which once again began with intense Chinese shelling of the island chains with the dual goals of rallying the Chinese public in the early stages of the Great Leap Forward and demonstrating Mao's contempt for Soviet Premier Nikita Khrushchev's goal of "Peaceful Coexistence" with the United States and its allies. Once again, Mao threatened invasion, and once again Eisenhower threatened nuclear strikes. US public reaction this time conclusively demonstrated the non-replicability of brinksmanship as a tactic in a democracy. The press shared the public's fears. Editorial opinion ran heavily against Eisenhower in September, the *Minneapolis Morning Tribune* expressing the thoughts of many when its editors wrote "if there ever was a war that would be fought at the wrong place, at the wrong time and for the wrong reason, it would be a war with Communist China over the islands off the coast of the mainland of China."[34] The president noted the criticism, remarking to Dulles his belief that "as much as two-thirds of the world, and 50% of U.S. opinion opposes the course we have been following."[35]

In addition, Eisenhower's nuclear brinksmanship inspired the Chinese to fast-track its nuclear weapons program. Mao decided to pursue the development of nuclear capabilities at a January 15, 1955 meeting of the Central Committee Secretariat, shortly after Eisenhower threatened nuclear strikes during the First Straits Crisis. Meanwhile, publicly, Mao insisted he remained unimpressed by these weapons, explaining in 1957 that if nuclear war killed half the human population, the result would be the destruction of Western "imperialism," the triumph of "socialism in the entire world," and the repopulation of the planet within fifty years. This comment implied the Chinese leader was not afraid of—and might even welcome—nuclear Armageddon, buttressing the notion of Mao as an irrational global actor. By the end of 1960, China's program had progressed to the stage where the CIA predicted the Chinese would successfully detonate an atomic device by the end of 1963.[36]

Meanwhile, the faintest cracks began to appear in the consensus of isolating the Chinese Communists. During the Second Straits Crisis in 1958, the *Kansas City Star* argued that since "we cannot overthrow" the Chinese Communists, diplomatic recognition and UN admission should be "dispassionately and hard-headedly" examined to pave the way for their future implementation.[37] This would remain an isolated opinion for the next half-decade, but in the mid-1960s it swiftly became the media consensus on China policy, paving the way for strong support of Nixon's actions in the early 1970s. Keeping dissent from the policy status quo muted were lingering bitterness over China's involvement in the Korean War as well as McCarthy-era attacks on those who had seemed too friendly to the Chinese Communists during the Chinese Civil War. Before Eisenhower took office, John Stewart Service, John Carter Vincent, and Oliver Edmund Clubb were forced to leave their positions at the State Department due to questions surrounding their previous service in China. John Paton Davies joined their ranks upon his dismissal in 1954.[38] Leaders and scholars of modern China such as Owen Lattimore of Johns Hopkins, Knight Biggerstaff of Cornell, and John Fairbank of Harvard also faced government investigations. These events had a chilling effect on East Asia experts both in Washington and academia, discouraging the public from questioning existing policies toward China until well into the next decade.

Despite Eisenhower's best efforts to suggest otherwise, and the utter lack of evidence to support it, the media repeatedly predicted an imminent opening to China during his presidency. Shortly after the president secured a second term in 1956, everyone from the *Washington Post* to noted psychic Jeane Dixon predicted change was around the corner.[39] At the same time, beginning with Zhou Enlai's speech at the Bandung Conference in April 1955, the Chinese strove to present a less belligerent and more welcoming image to the world. At the very least, people expected relaxation of the travel and trade bans in 1957. To quell such speculation, and reassure conservatives that the administration's hardline position on China was not being abandoned, Secretary of State Dulles gave an address in June at a Lions Club meeting in San Francisco. The speech's enduring passage came near its end when Dulles declared that "we can confidently assume that international communism's rule of strict conformity is, in China as elsewhere, a passing and not a perpetual phase. We owe it to ourselves, our allies, and the Chinese people to do all we can to contribute to that passing."[40]

Taiwanese diplomat George Yeh congratulated Dulles on the address, noting how when Chiang read a translation of the text he "was particularly impressed by your reference to the rule of international Communism in China as a 'passing and not a perpetual phase.'"[41] For those who wished to change policy, the notion that Chinese Communist rule was no passing phase would become a weapon to wield against hardliners the longer the PRC existed. On the Chinese side, Mao avidly read translations of Dulles's speeches, and remarked in 1959 that "Dulles wants to change countries like ours. He wants to subvert and change us to follow his ideas."[42] This conditioned Mao's suspicious responses to early attempts by officials within the Kennedy and Johnson administrations to reduce hostilities and attempt to construct some semblance of a friendly rapport.

Hovering in the background until the early 1970s was the question of whether the Chinese—while militarily and economically vastly inferior to the Soviets—were the greater threat, and if so, why that was the case. For those answering in the affirmative, the reasons were intentions, culture, and, if usually not explicitly expressed, race. Dulles cited the first two in 1955 when he argued that the Chinese were both "more belligerent" than the Soviets and enjoyed "a cultural prestige in Asia not enjoyed by Russia in Europe."[43] That same year, journalist Harrison Forman touched on the first and the third, claiming that "China's Yellow Communism is far more dangerous than the Red Communist of Moscow" because the Soviet leadership was more reasonable and could be negotiated with.[44] Writing in Britain, journalist Vincent Purcell echoed Forman by predicting "a stiffening attitude of Communist China towards foreigners, approaching arrogance, and of a programme of expansion which may amount in time to a 'Yellow Peril.'"[45]

Purcell wrote in 1958 at the moment Mao abruptly ceased China's accommodating international posture and reverted to belligerence. The reasons for this reversal were largely internal. By allowing the public expression of criticism, Mao's short-lived "One Hundred Flowers Campaign" in 1957 exposed the fact that Mao's domestic backing—particularly among intellectuals—was shaky at best. Mao followed this realization with the "Anti-Rightist Campaign," punishing those who had spoken out, and many who had not for good measure, before transitioning in 1958 to the Great Leap Forward, China's catastrophic attempt at rapid grassroots industrialization. The Second Straits Crisis, along with increasing estrangement from the Soviet leadership under Khrushchev, were the outward expressions of this internal shift.

Yet even those who feared the Chinese most did not anticipate conventional military action on its part. Dulles argued the Chinese would encourage aggression and subversion "by all means short of open invasion."[46] International relations scholar Hans Morgenthau agreed, writing in 1962 that "what threatens the United States in Asia is not primarily military aggression but political aggression and, more particularly, a slow and insidious shift of the allegiance of hundreds of millions of people to Russian and Chinese Communism."[47] In terms of targets, the head of the Central Intelligence Agency and brother of the Secretary of State Allen Dulles predicted that China was setting its sights on Southeast Asia, where it faced the least resistance. Massachusetts Institute of Technology professor Walt Rostow claimed the greatest point of weakness was South Vietnam, but also argued that so long as that nation held, China would not seek to expand its influence anywhere else.[48]

America's allies often faced a quandary of balancing their own national interests with US policy. Great Britain was one of the first non-Communist states to accord diplomatic recognition upon the PRC in January 1950. This was because of the extensive existing British financial interests inside China as well as concern about any threat to its Hong Kong colony. The beginning of the Korean War in June 1950 combined with unacceptable Chinese demands to delay the actual exchanging of ambassadors until 1972, though British Foreign Minister Anthony Eden and China's Zhou Enlai reached an agreement in 1954 to exchange *charges d'affaires*.[49] Winston Churchill defended Britain's approach by explaining that "the reason for having diplomatic relations is not to confer a compliment, but to secure a convenience."[50] A more exposed Australia criticized what they viewed as British fence-sitting, with Prime Minister R.G. Casey urging Britain to join a regional defense organization to hold back "the black clouds of Communist China."[51]

Australia experienced its own bout of red-baiting in the early 1950s, with Liberal Party leaders like Robert Menzies accusing Labor politicians of being insufficiently tough on the Communist Chinese. The arrival of China as a regional power occasioned renewed anxieties. In 1964, noted Australian journalist Donald Horne published his bestselling work *The Lucky Country*. He claimed the intention of his book was to portray "what the huge continent was like in those early days in the 1960s before it was peopled from all over Asia."[52] He reported Australians across the political spectrum had told him they saw Chinese becoming a superpower as "destiny," though there was disagreement over whether to accept or fight this inevitability.[53] Horne's work differed from similar works by Australians in the late nineteenth century due to the absence of polemic and his insouciant tone when describing future Chinese power and Asian migration.

Having only recently conquered and occupied large swathes of China, the Japanese took more time to accept the changed regional power structure. While Prime Minister Shigeru Yoshida told American diplomats in 1954 that "Japan always had one eye on China," the notion that the former East Asian whipping boy had transformed itself almost overnight into a regional giant was a tough pill to swallow.[54] Only China's 1964 detonation of an atomic weapon forced the Japanese to fully face facts.[55]

In Western Europe, where public figures had greater opportunities to object to the American project of containing communism, there developed what University of California-Berkeley professor Conrad Brandt described as a polarized dichotomy of "cries of alarm" and "cries of masochistic glee."[56] Rightists adhered to "the yellow peril," while leftists trumpeted "the decline of the West." Brandt believed both to be mistaken. He particularly took to task leftist French intellectual Simone de Beauvoir, who spent six weeks touring China in 1955, which formed the basis for her 1957 travelogue *The Long March*. Unsurprisingly, given that she was the author of the proto-feminist 1949 bestseller *The Second Sex*, Beauvoir praised the Communists for achieving "the emancipation of women." She also argued that China's "leaders lead the masses only upon condition they lead them where they have a mind to go," denying the existence of brutality or compulsion.[57] Brandt's example of renewed "yellow peril" fears was Frenchman Robert Guillain's

1957 travelogue *600 Million Chinese*, which portrayed the Chinese people as brainwashed automatons. This work was notable for its enumeration of China's population in its title, something one would not do in the title of a book on the United States or the USSR. Brandt saw both de Beauvoir and Guillain's arguments as rooted in the same stereotypical fetishization of a "Chinese giant aslumber through two millennia," with one side viewing the processing of awakening with terror, and the other with glee.[58] Both books were part of an emerging genre among European writers seeking to inform American readers of what was occurring behind the "Bamboo Curtain." Other books in this genre included *The Anthill, The Endless Hours, Ten Years of Storm* and *Diary from Red China*.[59]

Coupled with curiosity was increased fear of the Chinese Communists as more than mere tools of the Soviets. In March of 1961, Gallup asked a sample of Americans "Looking ahead to 1970, which country do you think will be the greater threat to world peace—Russia or Communist China?" Around 32 percent answered China, compared to 49 percent who responded Russia. According to George Gallup, most of those who chose China cited its "huge population" and "war-like policy." He concluded that China remained the "lesser evil" in the eyes of most Americans, but led with the statement that China "has yet to displace Russia as our chief opponent in the cold war struggle."[60] Two years later, in March 1963, when Gallup asked another sample the same question, 46 percent chose China, and 33 percent Russia.[61] President Kennedy seemed to concur, declaring at a press conference on August 1, 1963, that China was "menacing" and "Stalinist," while the Soviet Union was now a status quo power.[62]

"Red Chinese Battle Plan," a 1967 film produced by the Department of Defense to educate incoming military personnel about the geopolitical threats they were fighting against in Vietnam, was both stylistically and substantively a product of these fears from a half-decade earlier. The 25-minute film's black-and-white newsreel images and ominous narration harken back to 1950s Cold War cultural products. It opens by declaring that China's goal was to "divide and conquer; encircle and enslave." After a ten-minute overview of modern Chinese history, from the decline of the Qing through the rise of communism, it focuses on Mao's outreach to Third World nations in what today is called the "Global South," an international version of Mao infiltrating the "countryside" of the developing world to encircle the industrialized "cities" of Europe and North America. Quotes from Mao's writings reveal China's strategy, while images "Peking's apostle of world revolution" Zhou Enlai visiting Albania, Ghana, Pakistan, and Indonesia show its diplomatic tactics. When it could not charm a nation's leaders, China sponsored insurgencies, the most salient of which to these soldiers was in South Vietnam. Only in the film's final minute, after explaining in great detail why China was currently a much greater threat to the United States than the Soviet Union, does the narrator note that within the previous two years, the pro-Chinese leaders of Ghana and Indonesia had been overthrown, hinting at the film's possible obsolescence.[63]

Driving this sense of China as an independent actor was the ongoing divorce between the one-time close Communist powers. An important premise for isolating China was the notion that it was part of a Communist "monolith," and thus the PRC always acted in the service of the Soviets as a sort of Asian viceroy. But in the January 1962 words of Kennedy staffer Mose Harvey, "the monolith no longer exists."[64] In the background of this alliance breakdown were Soviet suspicions of Chinese power, as well as racialist thinking. In the foreground were changes in Soviet Cold War tactics. This is what began to break the Soviets and the Chinese apart.[65] Khrushchev's pursuit of "Peaceful Coexistence" with the United States irked the Chinese, while Mao's militancy estranged the Soviets.[66] During the mid-1950s, the Soviets devoted significant resources to developing China's industrial economy, building hundreds of factories and sending thousands of technical advisers to help the Chinese make use of them. All told, 20,000 advisers from the USSR and Eastern Europe worked in China between 1949 and 1960, while Soviet financial aid to China averaged 1 percent of the USSR's annual GDP over that period.[67] This was a far greater European presence in China than at the peak of missionary activity. Yet Mao feared party elites who favored Soviet-style economic development and bureaucratic structure were of dubious loyalty to him. The more estranged underlings like Zhou Enlai, Deng Xiaoping, and Liu Shaoqi were from Moscow, the closer they would have to cling to Mao in Beijing.

In retrospect, it is clear that this alliance had always been shot through with mutual distrust. The Chinese resented Moscow's often high-handed flaunting of its superior position. On the Soviet side existed, even before Mao began the process of estrangement in 1960, barely sublimated Yellow Peril-style fears. In his diary from the Geneva summit in 1954 that brought an end to the French war in Indochina, British Foreign Minister Harold Macmillan noted that the Soviet diplomats he interacted with on that occasion "are not keen on their Chinese connection," since the Chinese absorbed Soviet resources while growing stronger, perhaps one day strong enough to challenge the Soviets for primacy within the Communist Bloc. He recounted a Swiss diplomat telling him that one day Russia would seek "a situation of peace with the West" and "friendship with other Asiatic peoples" to contain the rising Chinese colossus.[68] In 1955, Khrushchev pleaded with West German Chancellor Konrad Adenauer—a staunch US ally, and therefore his country's enemy—"help us cope with Red China!"[69] In these fears, the Soviets shared common ground with Americans. Writing in the US journal *Commentary* as the fissures widened, Richard Lowenthal identified the "growth of Communist China into a great power" as "the beginning of the end of the single-centered

Communist movement."[70] Even the *Nation*, a strong supporter of diplomatic recognition of Communist China long before that idea had elite respectability, wrote in July 1961 that "when she (China) is strong, she is an incubus of massive proportions."[71]

The old stereotype that life was cheap in China was also a common belief in Communist Europe. After a fractious 1960 meeting of Communist leaders from across the globe, Czechoslovakian Premier Antonin Novotny remarked that the "Chinese delegates' total Asiatic disregard for the value of human life and material well-being came as a shock even to the Russians."[72] In his memoirs, transcribed in the late 1960s after he had been out of power for several years, Khrushchev declared that "Mao Tse-tung has played politics with Asiatic cunning."[73] Historian Sergey Radchenko has noted the prevalence of "cultural and implicitly racist notions of supposed Chinese expansionist designs, perfidiously concealed by cunning."[74] The Soviets in 1963 accused the Chinese of believing that the "leading role in world history belongs to the yellow race." The *Christian Science Monitor* approvingly cited this quote.[75] Americans that year began claiming that Chinese agents were shifting from class-based to race-based appeals in the rapidly decolonizing African continent, that their limited presence there was growing, and that the Chinese expected their presence on that continent to become permanent.[76]

Western observers viewed prejudice as an almost exclusively Chinese characteristic, absolving European Communists of racism. The influential liberal Catholic journal *Commonweal* declared in 1960 that "the [Chinese] regime is at once dogmatically Communist and unequivocally racist."[77] In 1963, the same magazine noted "the inescapable touch of racism in Chinese tradition." Yet in the same article, the author approvingly reported that Charles de Gaulle proposed outreach to the Russians in order to "combat the Yellow Peril."[78] The Protestant magazine *Christian Century* claimed Mao's calls for a "worldwide racial war" revealed him to be "psychotic," while the *Wall Street Journal* argued in July 1963 that "racial overtones have bulked larger in the recent rivalry as the Chinese bid openly for yellow, brown and black support against 'Europe oriented' (white) doctrine."[79] Mao was seeking "the solidarity of all the non-white races, against the whites, from Jakarta to Jacksonville."[80] In a September 1963 speech before the Massachusetts State Legislature on Sino-Soviet tensions, Assistant Secretary of State Averell Harriman argued the "racial issue" had been "injected by the Chinese" into its dispute with the Soviets.[81]

Politically and diplomatically, it made more sense for the United States to reach out to the Soviets and increase China's isolation. With that in mind, the Kennedy administration in July 1963 signed the Limited Nuclear Test Ban Treaty with the Soviet Union, which Chinese Marshal Chen Yi pointedly declared "is targeted against us."[82] Mao responded to this apparent anti-Chinese diplomatic realignment in September by enunciating his theory of "Two Intermediate Zones," the first being America's wealthy allies in Europe, and the second the less developed and largely non-aligned nations in Africa and Latin America. China would seek to court these countries and their populations, competing not only with its American adversaries but with the Soviets as well.[83] China was on its own, and for the time being, welcomed its isolation and status as the world's lone remaining truly revolutionary regime.

But first, to cite Tom Lehrer's 1965 song about nuclear proliferation "Who's Next," they better get a bomb. By 1963, China's nuclear program was well advanced, and apparently on the edge of success at a time when neither superpower welcomed such a development. The use of force to prevent the Communist Chinese from acquiring nuclear weapons was intermittently considered by both the United States and the USSR, but neither country ever came close to undertaking such an operation, on the US side because of the belief that possession of such weapons would not embolden the Chinese or significantly alter their foreign policy. The most fanciful proposal was for two planes—one Soviet, and one American—to fly together over China's nuclear facility in the deserts of Xinjiang Province. Both would drop a bomb capable of destroying the facility, but one would be a dud, so that neither the United States nor the USSR would know who did the deed. More peaceful means of suasion appeared fruitless, with Hong Kong Consul General Edward Rice informing Harriman in June 1963 that "it appears very unlikely that Communist China will be deterred from exploding a nuclear device merely because of a US-USSR test-ban agreement" (Figure 6).[84]

While in retrospect of significant importance, China's successful explosion of a nuclear weapon in October 1964 was something of a non-event at the time. It would take China's development of hydrogen bombs in 1967 and intercontinental ballistic missiles in the early 1970s for the superpowers to become alarmed. Hints of what would eventually happen came from Edward Rice in Hong Kong, who argued that the recent nuclear explosion could lead to greater acceptance abroad "of China as a permanent and major factor on the world scene."[85]

To say that China's nuclear advances in the early 1960s contrasted markedly with its economic performance during that period would be a gross understatement. These years saw the cresting of the great famine caused by Mao's initiation in 1958 of the Great Leap Forward. Emboldened by the Soviets' launch of Sputnik, and concerned about revolutionary complacency within his own regime, Mao announced his program of crash agricultural reform and industrial development in November 1957, confidently declaring "the east wind prevails over the west wind," meaning socialism had decisively gained the upper hand over capitalism. By the end of 1958, his regime had reorganized Chinese agricultural life into 26,000 giant communes. A combination of poor

FIGURE 6 *Herblock, "Mushrooming Cloud,"* Washington Post, *April 1, 1965. China's successful detonation of an atomic bomb in October 1965—the first by a non-white nation—demonstrated that despite severe economic setbacks, Mao's regime remained a menace, not only to the United States but also to its former Soviet ally.*

weather, the departure of Soviet technicians in October 1960, diversion of agricultural labor to fruitless attempts at small-scale metallurgy, and the colossal irrationality and callousness of the overall plan quickly led to severe food shortages. General Peng Dehuai, the leading Chinese hero of the Korean War and head of the People's Liberation Army, confronted Mao at the August 1959 Lushan Conference, only to be abandoned by his colleagues and soon purged by Mao. The disastrously poor harvests continued for two additional years before Mao quietly retreated, with his second-in-command Liu Shaoqi admitting to a "man-made disaster" in January 1962.[86]

Killing anywhere between 30 and 45 million people, the famine significantly set back China's economic development. However, the fact that the regime could not only survive such an immense self-inflicted calamity, but in fact face little open resistance, and no examples of actual rebellion, seemed to prove that the PRC was no passing phase. If the regime could survive the Great

Leap Forward, perhaps it could survive anything. After 1962, far fewer argued that its rule was a passing phase, making this an important turning point.

Additional proof that even a famine-stricken China needed to be feared was its decisive victory in the Sino-Indian War of 1962. Relations between the world's two most populous nations had been quite friendly for most of the 1950s, with Mao declaring in 1954 during his first meeting with Nehru that the Chinese and the Indians, as fellow "people(s) of the East," had "instinctive feelings of solidarity."[87] This would all change in 1959 when the Dalai Lama fled Tibet for India after the Chinese crushed a US-sponsored Tibetan revolt. That year, soldiers from both nations clashed for the first time, in October in Ladakh along India's far northwestern frontier, near where Tibet meets Xinjiang, and in August along the border of India's North East Frontier Agency, on Tibet's eastern border near Bhutan.[88] Tensions escalated over the next three years, with India keen to protect its territorial integrity, and China worried about Indian meddling in Tibet. In October 1962, Nehru ordered Indian soldiers to establish outposts on territory claimed by China in both these border regions, sparking a swift and devastating attack by the Chinese.

Along India's western border, the better-armed and trained Chinese quickly brushed aside Indian strongpoints in the Ladakh region and proceeded to occupy the desolate wasteland of Aksai Chin, where the Chinese remain to the present day.[89] Far more intense fighting occurred on India's northeastern border, where about 30,000 of its soldiers clashed with a similar number of Chinese in heavily forested mountain terrain. On November 18, Chinese forces annihilated the three Indian divisions facing them and advanced to the border of Assam province, which produced the bulk of India's petroleum and tea. Nehru declared a state of "total war" and asked Kennedy for 12 US-piloted fighter squadrons to halt the advance—over 300 planes in total.[90] Before Kennedy could respond, China announced a unilateral withdrawal from the disputed territory in India's northeast on November 20, formally annexed the Aksai Chin region in India's northwest, and declared a unilateral cease-fire.

China's restraint shocked both the American press and the Kennedy administration. *Time* opened its cover story on the war with the line "Red China behaved in so inscrutably Oriental a manner last week that even Asians were baffled." In its own cover story that week, *U.S. News* told its readers that "Mao Tse-tung caught the whole world by surprise when he pulled back from what looked like total victory."[91] Paul Nitze, the Pentagon's lead analyst of the war at the time, admitted in his memoirs that "the Chinese Communists surprised us all," while US ambassador to India John Kenneth Galbraith relayed Indian laments that "at the moment CHICOMS look reasonable and this advantage had to be taken away from them."[92] The war's conclusion demonstrated that Mao could behave in a rational manner—at least in matters of foreign relations. It also proved that even when laid low domestically by an unprecedented humanitarian catastrophe, China remained by far the most powerful nation on the Asian mainland.

Assuming the presidency after Kennedy's November 1963 assassination, Lyndon Johnson continued Eisenhower's and Kennedy's China policy, but rhetorically favored conciliation, whereas Kennedy often indulged in confrontational rhetoric. Johnson retained Kennedy's foreign policy team, led by Secretary of State Dean Rusk, who remained intransigently opposed to any policy changes. Johnson would largely defer to him and National Security Advisor McGeorge Bundy on this and other matters. The foreign policy of his administration soon came to be dominated by US involvement in the Vietnam War, the motivation for which was in large part the containment of Communist China. Assistant National Security Advisor Walt Rostow wrote to Rusk in January 1964—when US military personnel were still in an advisery role—to emphasize the need to prove the Chinese hope for "Wars of National Liberation is not viable," lest they be encouraged to undertake future adventurism in the region.[93] The press presented similar arguments, *U.S. News* reminding its readers in 1964 that in Vietnam "Red China is the real enemy," while Adlai Stevenson wrote in *Newsweek* in 1965 that Johnson's goal in Vietnam was to contain "Chinese expansionism."[94]

In the summer of 1965, just as the United States was pouring military personnel into South Vietnam to fight a Chinese-backed guerrilla war, People's Liberation Army leader Lin Biao published the manifesto "Long Live the Victory of the People's War!" The title sounded alarming enough for Dean Rusk and Robert McNamara to compare it to Adolf Hitler's *Mein Kampf*.[95] The press largely concurred, with the liberal-leaning *Newsweek* terming it "China's blueprint for the conquest of the world."[96] Yet even a cursory reading of the document indicated that it was actually a declaration of delegation. China wished the world's revolutionaries well and might offer them some training and possibly small amounts of arms, but they would have to take the fight to their capitalist and imperialist enemies on their own. The Rand Corporation recognized this, and believed it actually disheartened North Vietnam's leaders by displaying the limits of China's commitment to their success, creating "sharp differences between Peking and Hanoi."[97]

At the same time, fear of a repeat of the Korean War led to self-imposed restraints on US action, most notably a refusal to invade North Vietnamese territory. For their part, the Chinese refrained from introducing combat soldiers into North Vietnam, though over 100,000 Chinese served as laborers and engineers in that country during the late 1960s, and over 1,000 of them died from US bombing. The US military's inability to conclusively defeat Communist forces in South Vietnam in the face of a seemingly endless stream of reinforcements from North Vietnam, along with the extensive military equipment provided by the Chinese and the Soviets to the North

Vietnamese, ultimately led the United States to seek a compromise peace, try to improve relations with the Soviets, and establish relations with the Chinese Communists. Thus, while increasing tensions and the risk of Sino-American War in the short term, the Vietnam War hastened the path to rapprochement by dramatically illustrating the necessity of a different approach to containment in East Asia. In a memo sent to McGeorge Bundy in November 1964, National Security Council official Robert Komer called for a display of US strength toward Hanoi to open doors to Beijing. As Komer put it, the United States was "escalating to negotiate," not only with North Vietnam but with China as well.[98]

Nonetheless, it would be incorrect to give the Vietnam War sole credit for this development. Even before the introduction of US combat forces in 1965, there were strong signs of a shift in both elite and mass opinion in the United States and abroad. The first of these signs was France's announcement on January 15, 1964 of its decision to accord the People's Republic of China diplomatic recognition.[99] France thus became the first US ally to recognize the PRC in fourteen years.[100] French President Charles de Gaulle was no dove when it came to China, telling author Andre Malraux in 1965 "every time China becomes China again, she becomes imperialist."[101] But De Gaulle argued that isolating China only made it more of a threat by increasing its potential for aggression. Diplomatic contact could encourage moderation.[102]

In a similar vein, in early 1965 State Department official Lindsey Grant worried that showing "hostility for its own sake" could lead to a situation where the United States would "someday face a China both strong and deeply hostile."[103] To prevent this, "we must be prepared to accord her a degree of dignity," to be conveyed by a softening of US opposition to UN admission.[104] Around the same time, US ambassador to the UN Adlai Stevenson expressed hope for "an accommodation with Communist China" to bring about "peaceful coexistence" between the United States and the PRC.[105] Stevenson based his own proposal on foreign opinion, particularly in non-aligned nations where the United States was seeking to curry favor.

A similar dynamic was developing in domestic opinion. A focus group convened by Samuel Lubell Associates questioned 169 Americans the previous fall. This unscientific sample seemed to confirm recent polling that a sizeable majority of Americans viewed China "as a bigger threat to the United States than Soviet Russia." More tellingly, support for gestures of outreach toward China, such as allowing China to join the UN, strongly correlated with greater fear of China. Those who feared the Soviet Union more were almost unanimous in their opposition to changes in China policy, while those who feared China were evenly divided. This was despite the fact that participants who feared China expressed that fear in racial terms and described its leaders as "irrational" and "Oriental." The faction most afraid of China also expressed the belief that "China is here to stay and can't be ignored."[106]

Fear, not hope, appeared to be driving support for policy change among the general public. In a more scientific survey by Gallup in November 1964, three times as many Americans viewed China as a greater threat to world peace than Russia.[107] A Council of Foreign Relations survey conducted in the spring of 1964 discovered "a widespread fear among Americans that Communist China may attack the United States or may try to rule the world."[108] Typifying how this fear of rising Chinese power could lead some to calls for rapprochement was a June 1964 commencement address at St. John's University by congresswoman Claire Boothe Luce, the wife of *Time-Life* publisher Henry Luce. In her address, Luce expressed her fear that a rising China, if isolated, "might turn desperately aggressive," telling the students that if this occurred "your generation will know nothing but endless war in the Orient."[109]

Her comments were both a break from her husband's longtime approach to the Chinese Communists and represented the opening wedge in what became a bipartisan movement for an end to the policy of isolation. By the mid-1960s, few in any position of power or influence still made the "passing phase" argument about Mao's regime. The Chinese Communists had become a fact of geopolitical life, however unpleasant acceptance of this fact could be. The frustrations occasioned by the course of the Vietnam War hastened this process, but they did not cause it. Nixon would complete it, but he did not start it. Rather, when the time came, he would be riding a wave of public sentiment. By 1969, most of the US public, and the vast majority of their elected leaders, were ready to reopen the door to China. But from 1966 until 1969, the path to rapprochement would be anything but smooth and by no means assured.

7

China in Early Cold War Popular Culture

On December 17, 1962, the Kennedy White House hosted a Nobel Laureate. She had not come to receive an award, attend a banquet, or discuss the arts. She was there to plead for peace with China. She believed the people of Taiwan lived under grave danger from Mao Zedong's Communists. But rather than support Chiang Kai-shek, Pearl Buck was willing to offer him, and the island he ruled, as a sacrifice for peace among the Chinese, and between Communist China and the Western world. According to Michael Forrestal, "Miss Buck expounded at length on her fear that unless something was done in the very near future, the people of mainland China would become the permanent enemies of the Western world. She felt it was essential for the United States to attempt to reach a modus vivendi with Red China before the death of Chiang Kai-shek." Buck predicted Chiang's death would bring about "a collapse of the Taiwanese political and economic structure, leading to war." To prevent this catastrophe for the sake of all involved, "Miss Buck proposed that we make a discreet but very strong effort to convince the Generalissimo that his place in history can only be assured by a reunion under the auspices of the Formosa Chinese with their Mainland brothers." The method of this reunion would involve the preservation of the "de facto independence of Formosa for a 10-to-25-year period with an agreement at the end of the period for a negotiated settlement based upon a plebiscite or some other device."[1]

Buck maintained the United States would not be acting alone on this matter, insisting "throughout the conversation" that there was "communication and a basis for accommodation between Mao and Chou En-lai on the one hand and the Gimo (Chiang) and his followers on the other." What was needed to reach an agreement and preserve peace in East Asia was American leadership. At that moment, she believed Kennedy was the man to provide it. According to Forrestal, Miss Buck said that she had been "convinced by the President's handling of the Cuban crisis that it might be possible in his Administration for this problem to be tackled, and that was why she had come to Washington with her proposal."[2]

Buck still wrote novels in the early 1960s, but no longer about China, a land she had not visited in nearly three decades. Plenty of other Americans produced works of fiction involving the Chinese, but these works had little in common with her past output. Rather, they were much more reminiscent of the works of Sax Rohmer a generation before Buck's heyday. What had changed from the early twentieth-century and the 1960s was a newfound acceptance of Chinese-Americans. A notable example was C. Y. Lee's 1957 novel *Flower Drum Song.* In 1958, Richard Rodgers and Oscar Hammerstein transformed Lee's nuanced and often pessimistic portrayal of the lives of Chinese immigrants in San Francisco into a lighthearted musical comedy about immigrant assimilation. The 1961 film version of the musical was the first Hollywood production with an all-Asian cast, and the only such film until 1993's "The Joy Luck Club." A mild success, critics took issue with its lack of realism, noting how the lead characters all seemed unusually wealthy, as well as the fact that while the cast was entirely Asian, all but one of the leads were played by Japanese-Americans, while most of the dancers were Filipino-Americans. *Time*'s film critic joked, "honest fellows, they don't all look alike."[3]

Negative depictions were thus saved for Chinese Communists from China itself. With the friendly China of the Second World War in history's ashbin, the early Cold War witnessed an evolving depiction of Chinese villainy in US media, particularly film. At first, during and after the Korean War, familiar tropes of Asiatic hordes reminiscent of scenes from late nineteenth-century invasion novels dominated. Yet these multitudes were in the service of white Russian masters. In the early 1960s, as the Korean conflict faded from memory, Chinese villains were individualized and updated as Communist Fu Manchus. Reflecting increasing fears of Communist China, these villains became increasingly autonomous from the Russians. As the sixties progressed, Russian Communists became sympathetic characters as depictions of Chinese villainy mixed the stereotypes of the horde, the Fu Manchu supervillain, and the coolie interchangeably. By the late sixties, the emphasis was less on their communism than on their ethnicity. Yet just when depictions of Chinese reached their racialized peak, diplomatic relations began to improve, and the Chinese villain quickly vanished.

The start of this period was during the Korean War when Americans and Chinese were killing each other in large numbers. It was thus no surprise to see the Chinese being presented in a negative light. However, they were not yet front-and-center. The 1954 prisoner-of-war film *The Bamboo Prison* presented Chinese Communists as veritable slaves to their Russian masters.

When a Chinese interrogator attempts to turn a black American prisoner against his nation by reminding him of his degraded status back home, the black soldier retorts that his Chinese interrogator is no better off compared to his de facto Russian masters.[4] Gradually, this began to change. On television, Communist Chinese villains appeared on the show *Adventures of the Falcon*, which ran in 1955 and 1956, while Fu Manchu reappeared between 1956 and 1958 on the syndicated program *The Adventures of Fu Manchu*.[5]

Hollywood's Korean War films came in two varieties: standard combat films and prisoner-of-war pictures. The earliest combats films appeared during the war itself and tended to be low-budget productions like 1952's "Retreat, Hell!," set during the Changjin Reservoir battle, an early Chinese offensive against overextended US forces in Korea's far north. The Chinese in such films appear as faceless hordes seeking to overwhelm the supposedly underdog Americans by sheer force of numbers. There were only two big-budget battle films about the war: 1955's "The Bridges at Toko Ri" about Navy pilots and 1959's "Pork Chop Hill," by far the most interesting specimen of this subgenre. Starring Gregory Peck, the eponymous hill is the site of intense battles between Americans and Chinese soldiers on the eve of the 1953 cease-fire. Soldiers on both sides act bravely, displaying utter contempt for danger. Peck plays a sympathetic lieutenant who objects to the cynical orders of his superiors, whom he knows are pointlessly risking lives for no discernibly strategic purpose. In its depictions of trench warfare, and derision toward callous senior officers, the film recalls portrayals of the First World War.

The treatment of thousands of US prisoners of war by their North Korean and Chinese captors became an important issue as the war dragged on, and drew substantial media coverage. The attempts to turn US prisoners against their nation ultimately succeeded in convincing about two dozen Americans to remain in China and North Korea after the war's end. These defections gave birth to the concept of brainwashing. Hollywood explored this topic in a trio of mid-1950s films. The first, "Prisoner of War" from 1954, starred Ronald Reagan, in one of his final film roles, as an intelligence officer who volunteers to infiltrate a prisoner-of-war camp to document the prisoners' ill-treatment. The second, 1955's "The Bamboo Prison," depicts an escape from a prison camp. Most complex in its message was 1957's "Time Limit." This film dramatized the fictional court martial of an Army Major for collaboration with the enemy while he was a prisoner. Revealingly, between 1955 and 1960, Korean War films were outnumbered by films about Americans in Vietnam, where the United States had yet to begin its next war. Korea became a forgotten war almost from the moment it ended. This, in turn, limited the opportunities to depict Chinese in a negative way during the 1950s.

Though not about Korea, that war clearly inspired Robert Heinlein's hit 1959 science fiction novel *Starship Troopers*. The book depicted a future society quite different from that of his own time. The differences were as much political as technological, and the former were brought about in large part by the rise of China. In Heinlein's imagined future, by the 1980s the Cold War had become a thing of the past, and a world war was fought "between the Russo-Anglo-American Alliance and the Chinese Hegemony." The war ended inconclusively with "the negotiated treaty of New Delhi," which notably failed to achieve the return of 60,000 Alliance prisoners of war from Chinese custody. This would seem to indicate that the Chinese, though fighting alone, got the better of their combined adversaries, as would the fact that shortly after the war's end the societies and governments of their opponents quickly collapsed. Jobless and bitter, the veterans from what had been Britain, Russia, and the United States stepped up to "fill the vacuum" in national leadership. They may have "lost a war" abroad, but they would win the peace at home.[6]

The veterans established praetorian democracies in which only those few who had served in the armed forces possessed the franchise. Armies were numerically small, the mass conscription forces of the past having been discredited as ineffectual mobs from the first stalemated war against China in Korea until the last failed effort against that nation in the 1980s. China's position at the pinnacle of power would itself prove fleeting, as evidenced by the soldiers reading "Tsing's classic *Collapse of the Golden Hegemony*."[7] Government by military veterans soon became a global phenomenon, enabling a unified planet to successfully defeat giant communistic alien insects who threaten the planet. Left unsaid, but heavily implied, was that such a post-democratic polity might have been the only way to defeat the Chinese. Either way, the rise of China meant the death not only of Western supremacy but of Western liberal democracy. The novel's text made clear the model for the bug villains was Communist China. For instance, the Filipino hero Johnnie Rico observes, in a transparent allusion to Chinese human wave attacks during the Korean War, that "the Bug commissars didn't care anymore about expending soldiers than we cared about expending ammo. Perhaps we could have figured this out about the Bugs by noting the grief the Chinese Hegemony gave the Russo-Anglo-American Alliance."[8] The global alliance triumphed over Chinese stand-ins, a new army successfully re-fighting an old war.

Heinlein was not the first American author to envision a war between the united white nations of the world and an expansionist China, nor was he the first to predict a Chinese victory. But he was the first to have done so in over a generation, and the first to forecast a Chinese victory unaided by allies or local collaborators. Coming only six years after the end of the Korean War, Heinlein's vision of the near future had a certain plausibility, one that would be echoed four years later by the British historian Arnold Toynbee.[9] In a September 1963 essay entitled "Is a 'Race War' Shaping Up?," Toynbee came down on the negative side. The article was a sequel to one he had published in the

Times three years earlier entitled "A War of the Races? 'No'." In that article, he argued the "mental sickness" of nationalism was currently far more powerful than the "mental sickness" of racism in determining the actions of nations.[10] Evaluating recent claims by the Soviets that the Chinese were now pushing race—as opposed the class—conflict in an attempt to win influence in the developing world, the historian maintained that states follow their national interest, specifically defending their borders.

This meant that China's non-white neighbors to the south actually feared Chinese expansion, as evidenced by the multi-racial Southeast Asian Treaty Organization (SEATO). Only Pakistan might ally with China, and that was because of that nation's antagonism toward its racial brethren in India.[11] Toynbee accused China of a racial chauvinism similar to Europeans, and argued that "as the Chinese see it, the mandate to rule is China's birthright."[12] Any world war started by the Chinese would array the Chinese against just about everyone else, regardless of color. However, he ominously predicted that "by the year 2000, China may be strong enough to impose her domination on the rest of the world, even in the teeth of a worldwide coalition against her."[13] Even after the Great Leap Forward's failure, Heinlein's science fiction was being treated as future history. The only way to prevent this eventuality in Toynbee's view was for the United States and the Soviet Union to reach a modus vivendi and bury their mutual animosity. Were this not to occur, the world's people would lose faith in the two white superpowers, opening the door to Chinese domination. This notion of a superpower rapprochement would come to pass as the decade progressed, albeit only on US television and movie screens.

Following trends in American public opinion, Hollywood's depictions of the Chinese at home and abroad during the Kennedy years began to noticeably change. Russians were still bad guys, though their role was becoming more that of advisers, with their nominal Chinese underlings moving to the fore and showing increased initiative. In contrast to Heinlein's faceless hordes, Chinese villainy assumed individual form in the movies "The Manchurian Candidate" and "Dr. No," released in 1962 and 1963 respectively. Both were based on bestselling books written in the late 1950s, Richard Condon's *The Manchurian Candidate* having been published in 1959 and Ian Fleming's *Dr. No* a year earlier. Both drew upon the original lone Chinese villain, Fu Manchu.[14]

Released in October 1962, *The Manchurian Candidate* was immediately recognized as a cultural watershed. Critics took that film very seriously, as historians and cultural analysts still do today, although they viewed the film far less favorably than future generations would. One gets the distinct sense that few would have predicted it would one day be seen, according to the historian Christina Klein, as "one of the definitive works of Cold War filmmaking," a work which would warrant an entire book of academic essays analyzing its many facets, and what each of them said about Cold War culture.[15] Both the movie and Condon's source novel revolve around the brainwashing of US soldier Raymond Shaw in Korea by Chinese psychiatrist Yen Lo, whom the film's hero Captain Bennett Marco, played by Frank Sinatra, helpfully describes as "that Chinese cat standing there smiling like Fu Manchu."[16] Though Yen Lo works on behalf of the Russians, serving as director of the "Pavlov Institute" in Moscow, Condon makes clear in the novel that all but two of his technicians and assistants who help administer the brainwashing are Chinese.[17] Condon's novel refers to Marco's desire to "unlock all of the great jade doors" and liberate Raymond's mind from its Chinese captors.[18]

Presciently anticipating the Sino-Soviet split, as well as pinpointing one of its causes, Condon notes how the audience for the brainwashing, a mix in both the book and the film of Chinese and Russian Communists, was "divided, physically and by prejudice."[19] Screenwriter George Axelrod has Yen Lo tell the Russians who are impatient to witness the brainwashed Raymond murder a member of his squad, "I apologize to my dear Dmitri. I keep forgetting that you're a young country, and your attention span is limited." On another occasion, however, Yen appears to identify with the Russians, insisting he does not mean to insult "our brave Chinese allies" with the cover story that Raymond and his squad annihilated an entire company of Chinese soldiers.[20] While the details of Yen Lo's loyalties and personal identifications are ambiguous, the broad brushstrokes of his characterization are entirely Asian.

The secondary villain is Korean interpreter Chunjin, who betrayed the squad to the Communists and later comes to the United States to be Raymond's "houseboy." He seems to be a prototype of a new kind of Asian villain, what scholar Robert Lee called the "gook," meaning a deceitful young Asian male who pretends to be meek and friendly toward whites in order to betray them.[21] This type of Asian villain came into its own in the 1980s in works about the Vietnam War such as the film "Good Morning Vietnam" and the television show "Tour of Duty." Characteristic of Hollywood during the 1960s, neither Asian villain in "The Manchurian Candidate" was played by an Asian actor. Khigh Dhiegh, a New Jersey native of North African descent, played Yen Lo. Henry Silva, born and raised in Brooklyn by parents from Puerto Rico, portrayed Chunjin. Silva made a career out of portraying "ethnic" villains, East Asians as well as Native Americans, Mexicans, and Italians.[22] Dhiegh went on to be cast as other Cold War updates of Fu Manchu, most famously the recurring Communist Chinese villain Wo Fat on the television show "Hawaii Five-O" from 1968 until 1980. Later, he retired to his home state and embraced his fictional Asian identity by founding an institute for the study of Taoism.[23]

In his review of "The Manchurian Candidate," Arthur Knight of the *Saturday Review* wrote that he quickly came to the realization that "this was not Yen

Lo, the Red superman, but our old childhood friend, the insidious Dr. Fu Manchu." The connection made the film "a good deal more enjoyable" for him.[24] In a 1988 conversation between the film's director John Frankenheimer, its writer George Axelrod, and its star Frank Sinatra, which was included as part of the original VHS release of the film, Axelrod recalled expressing to Sinatra his worry that "when the picture is released, if Kennedy is just about to have some sort of rapport with the Russians, it's going to embarrass him." Sinatra remembered reassuring Axelrod by reporting that he had just visited Hyannisport, where President Kennedy asked him what his next film project was going to be. Sinatra replied that it would be an adaptation of *The Manchurian Candidate*, to which Kennedy responded "great—who's going to play the mother?"[25] That dispelled any concerns Axelrod had about possible negative geopolitical ramifications.

Ian Fleming's 1958 novel *Doctor No* and the 1963 film of the same title both begin outside of the Queen's Club on Richmond Road in Kingston. Fleming lovingly describes this thoroughfare as the most exclusive street in Jamaica's capital city and a bastion of colonial privilege before adding ruefully that "such stubborn retreats will not long survive in modern Jamaica. One day Queen's Club will have its windows smashed and perhaps be burned to the ground."[26] This sense of late colonial foreboding is absent from the film, which was released one year after Jamaica became independent, and which presents the island as a sunny, sexy vacation spot, albeit a particularly dangerous one for British secret agents. The danger emanates from the henchmen of the title character, the half-Chinese son of a German Methodist missionary whom Stanley Kauffmann of *The New Republic*, in his lukewarm review of the film, described as "a kind of space-age Fu Manchu."[27] In the book, No is very tall, thin, and bald, just like Rohmer's villain.[28] Played in the film by the white Canadian actor Joseph Wiseman, he is a debonair evil mastermind, sporting slicked-back hair, and attired in Nehru jackets, which his dark-skinned assassins also favor.[29] The novel chooses to accentuate the German side of No's character. When conversing with Bond in his underground lair, No quotes Clausewitz on strategy, paraphrases Freudian theory to explain why he is evil, and praises the Nazis for conducting sadistic scientific experiments on human subjects.[30]

This is not to imply Fleming completely downplayed Chinese villainy. In fact, every Chinese—or even part Chinese—character in the novel is a villain. After several close calls, Bond instructs Quarrel, his faithful local Black Jamaican guide and confidant, to "watch out particularly for any Chinese near you."[31] The assassins who massacre the staff of the local British intelligence office, prompting Bond's trip to Jamaica, are all "Chigroes—Chinese negroes," with "yellowish skin and slanting eyes."[32] Fleming has the Colonial Secretary, in a panoramic description of the numerous foreign merchant clans who dominate the island's commerce, describe the Chinese as "the most powerful clique in Jamaica."[33] In both the book and the film, No defends his lair on the island of Crab Key with an armored flame-throwing tractor costumed to look like a dragon. The tractor quickly incinerates the unlucky Quarrel.

The higher one moves up No's organization, the more Chinese it becomes. In the film, Chinese soldiers in vaguely Maoist uniforms capture Bond and defend their leader's lair, while Chinese technicians keep his nuclear reactor running.[34] In the book, No is working on a freelance basis for the Russians, endeavoring to jam the guidance systems on American nuclear missiles near the Caribbean basin, but would be willing to help the Chinese if the price was right.[35] In the film, he seeks to sabotage the US space program, had his services refused by both the United States and the USSR, and says of the Cold War "east, west, just points of the compass, each as stupid as the other."[36] The movie set a trend for the rest of the decade for espionage thrillers on both the big and the small screen by seeking to move beyond the Cold War while vaguely acknowledging its continued existence.

Two other films about China released during the early 1960s were set in China and touched heavily upon the potential threat posed by China. They have escaped scholarly attention, and perhaps for good reason. "55 Days at Peking," released in the summer of 1963, was produced by Samuel Bronston, the self-styled "King of the Epics," who had found box-office success in 1961 with both "El Cid" and "King of Kings." As its title indicates, the film focuses on the siege of the foreign legations in the Qing capital during the Boxer Rebellion in 1900. Charlton Heston, who starred in "El Cid," plays the Marine Major Matt Lewis, who leads the defense of the legations. David Niven plays British diplomat Sir Arthur Robinson, who seeks at first to conciliate the Boxers, ingratiate himself with China's rulers, and stoically endure their humiliations. Early in the film, his wife asks him "you remember what Napoleon said about China?," to which Robinson replies "I'll never forget it. Let China sleep—for when she wakes, the world will tremble." Robinson tells the Dowager Empress "China's greatest virtue is her patience, and if she will exercise that now, she will achieve everything," advice neither the Dowager then nor Mao in the film's own time heeded. Meanwhile, Robinson warns Lewis "you're not in the Wild West now, you know. You don't go around shooting Chinese like you do red Indians." Though a man of action, Heston's Lewis is introduced to the audience as a sort of "non-ugly" American, instructing his men as they march to Peking "this is an ancient and highly cultured civilization, so don't get the idea you're any better than these people just because they can't speak English."[37]

Before long, all attempts at cultural sensitivity and conciliation are cast to the winds when the empress's duplicitous advisers convince her to unite with the bloodthirsty Boxers and unleash their hordes upon every white person they can get their hands on. The Boxer Rebellion was the last time before the movie's own period that the European powers were united as one against the Chinese, and the film both celebrates this multinational coalition and hints and its fragility. It would, however, be stretching matters to find much intentional political symbolism in this particular movie. Its writer, Philip Yordan, declared that "it's pictures we're making, not history" in reply to criticisms of the considerable liberties his scripts for Bronston took with the historical record.[38] As with "Dr. No," critics' low expectations were largely met. They praised the film's high production values, particularly the lavish sets Bronston had constructed on the plains of Spain.[39]

The ethnic stereotypes and use of white actors to play the main Chinese characters were noted but not disapproved of, *Time* joking that "Prince Tuan, complete with jeweled-gold fingernail scabbards" appeared "about as welcome as Dr. Fu Manchu at a meeting of the A.M.A.," and Moira Walsh of *America* observing that British actors "oddly, but not ineffectively," played all the Chinese officials.[40] The critic from the *National Review* claimed to enjoy watching "thousands of evil-eyed Chinese villains" being mowed down by modern Western weaponry.[41] *Newsweek* did take note of the fact that Heston's on-screen love interest, the Russian Baroness Natalie Ivanoff, played by Ava Gardner, was killed off with a half-hour remaining in the film. Finding this odd, the critic surmised that "after all, Ava *is* a Russian, and she *has* an affair with a Chinese general, so for her to live and marry Heston would have been controversial" (italics in original).[42] Thus Cold War politics and racial anxieties might have intruded into even this confection.

The Cold War is ostensibly at the heart of "Satan Never Sleeps," such as that 1962 film can be said to have one. Director Leo McCarey, whose career had been on the decline since the commercial and critical triumphs of "Going My Way" in 1944 and "The Bells of St Mary's" in 1945, returned to the subject of the Catholic priesthood, albeit in southwestern China rather than midwestern America. William Holden stars as Father O'Banion, a former Marine and newly minted Chinese missionary, who is followed to his new assignment by the smitten Siu Lan, played by Vietnamese actress Frances Nguyen. O'Banion intends to replace the wise old Father Bovard, who worries about abandoning his local converts to both the new priest and the advancing Communist forces. O'Banion arrives in China in late 1949, a most unpropitious moment to begin a missionary career in China. Leading the oncoming Red Chinese forces is Colonel Ho San, a former parishioner of Bovard's, played by Weaver Lee. To mock Christian non-violence, Ho San repeatedly slaps O'Banion, yelling out "he's a paper tiger!" which inspires the former Marine to thrash the Communist, much to Bovard's disapproval and Siu Lan's delight.[43] Ho San goes on to vandalize and loot the church, rape and impregnate Siu Lan, and imprison Bovard and O'Banion. But he is then purged by a visiting Soviet official for treating the priests and their congregants with insufficient brutality. The Russian has Bovard tortured in order to extract a public confession. Yet the priest remains defiant, inspiring the villagers to rise up in revolt. The loyal Christians, including Ho San's parents, are promptly massacred by Chinese soldiers, inspiring his reconversion. Ho leads Siu Lan and O'Banion across the border—presumably to Burma—and eventually to Hong Kong, Bovard sacrificing himself to ensure the escape's success.

The film, a commercial failure, is essentially a screwball comedy set during an apocalypse. Critics noted this "unfortunate mixture" of "pseudo-romantic fun-and-games and the extremely serious Red oppression."[44] The strained relationship between the older and younger priest was dismissed as a tired retread of "Going My Way."[45] The redemption of the rapist, and his marriage to his victim, was universally condemned as offensive. "The colonel, it turns out, isn't really a nasty, Red rapist after all, see? He's a nice Christian rapist," *Time* rancidly concluded.[46] Of Ho San's transformation into a "comic hero," *Newsweek* responded "Aw. McC'mon."[47] Moira Walsh concluded that "it takes real talent to produce a film that everybody will hate, but this may be it."[48] Still, the making of the film indicated that a famous director believed the time was right for him to revive his career by exploiting anti-Chinese sentiment.

In his attempt to capitalize from Communist China villainy, McCrary was onto something. The remainder of the decade would feature, among other attractions, the Chinese assassin Odd Job in "Goldfinger" and no less than five "Fu Manchu" remakes.[49] In popular music, Barry Maguire sang "Look at all the hate there is in Red China" in "Eve of Destruction," a facsimile of a Dylan-style protest song that went to #1 on the charts. On television, beginning in 1964 an American and a Russian secret agent joined forces on "The Man from U.N.C.L.E." to battle mostly Asian villains in a distant post-Cold War future. The *Wall Street Journal* reported in October 1966 that the Chinese had not only displaced the Russians as the leading villains in Hollywood but that Russians were beginning to be "cast as good guys helping American heroes outwit the Orientals." In the article, Mort Fine, a producer of the television show "I Spy," said Russians were no longer "acceptable as villains anymore" to the general public. In one of that show's episodes, after defeating an Asian villain, the American protagonists played by Bill Cosby and Robert Culp were decorated in the Kremlin by Soviet officials for their efforts. "Get Smart," which premiered in 1965, featured an assortment of predominately Asian henchmen.[50] Khigh Dhiegh was quoted saying "we're getting back to the era of the 'Yellow Menace.'"[51] He added that and added, "I don't think this contributes anything to prospects for world peace."[52]

This shift was also reflected in comic books which, for the first time since "Buck Rogers" and "Flash Gordon" in the 1930s, embraced yellow peril stereotypes. The first of many examples was the character of

Radioactive Man, who made his debut in the June 1963 edition of "The Mighty Thor" series, entitled "The Mysterious Radio-Active Man!," On the comic's opening page, Thor, disguised as his alter ego Dr. Don Blake, cares for injured Indian soldiers fighting the Chinese in the Himalayas. Sounding like one of Kennedy's more hawkish advisers, he declares "if the Indians are to turn back the Red Chinese invaders in this border war they'll need more American arms and military advisers!"[53] Thor proceeds to single-handedly defeat and capture a Chinese armored column, which naturally incites Mao's anger back in Beijing. With his arm around Mao's shoulders, Zhou Enlai declares "sooner or later we must fight the democracies, and we must prepare for it now by shaking their morale! We must make free men tremble by destroying their hero-protector, Thor!"[54] Mao orders the scientist Chen Lu to devise a solution or die trying. Chen absorbs massive doses of radiation to turn himself into Radioactive Man, travels to New York City aboard a Chinese submarine, uses mind control to hypnotize Thor in Times Square, then begins raining down destruction upon midtown Manhattan. The use of hypnosis, in a tradition extending from Fu Manchu to 1962's "The Manchurian Candidate," wedded traditional Chinese stereotypes to its emerging nuclear program. In the comic, Thor sends Radioactive Man back to China with a tornado, causing him to land in western China with the force of a nuclear explosion. In real life, the Chinese would detonate their own atomic bomb in western China a little over sixteen months after the comic hit newsstands.

Such modern capabilities could be read as even more menacing than the human wave assaults of the Korean War. Technological prowess added a new facet to the Chinese menace. This was seized upon with gusto by Marvel Comics. By 1963, it was clear to the general public that a successful Chinese test of an atomic weapon was imminent. With this in mind, Marvel produced two Ironman issues with plots revolving around Chinese scientists trying to procure atomic secrets in the service of Mao's efforts to acquire a nuclear bomb.[55] The first of these appeared in June 1963, where Ironman is kidnapped by a villain called the Red Barbarian, who has the fleshy build and slicked-back black hair of Mao. The villain claimed to have stolen America's latest atomic device, which is reclaimed and returned by Ironman, after suitable heroics.[56] In a February 1964 issue of the same series, Ironman's archnemesis the Mandarin appears as an agent of "Red China," or, as the comic describes it, "seething, smoldering, secretive Red China."[57] The Mandarin claims to possess "the atomic knowledge" the Chinese Communists need, and with which Mao can "menace the world with nuclear destruction!"[58] Ironman defeats the Mandarin in his castle and dispatches a number of People's Liberation Army officers as well, taunting his nemesis as a "weak apology for Genghis Khan."[59]

Sometimes China was explicitly referenced, as in the Thor and the second Ironman issues, and other times unnamed but heavily implied, as in the first Ironman comic. In July 1965, the Avengers would tussle with "the Communist-ruled puppet state of Sin-Cong," located in Central Asia. Captain America receives a radio message for help from a Sin-Cong dissident and joins lesser heroes Quicksilver and Scarlet Witch on a mission. The soldiers of Sin-Cong wear PLA uniforms with its red-star cap, while civilians dress in nineteenth-century Chinese attire. Scarlet Witch is horrified by the contrast between the "splendor" of the leadership's palace amid a sea of "starving millions," a clear allusion to the Great Leap Forward. A villain simply known as the Commissar handily wins his initial fight with the trio of heroes, then boasts "have I not proven the superiority of communism?"[60] But the villain is defeated after Scarlet Witch realizes Commissar is a mere robot controlled by a Chinese adviser named Major Hoy, who flees the country fearing Mao will now kill him. Captain America, playing amateur anthropologist, explains to readers that "by exposing their deception, we have caused them to lose face! This is the worst fate that can befall them!" The comic ends with Captain America urging both his fellow Avengers and the comic's readers not to let their guards down, since China's "goal is nothing less than world conquest, and world enslavement!"[61]

This line serves as a belated answer to what Quicksilver asked earlier in the comic: "why need we concern ourselves with international affairs?"[62] Perhaps Marvel's mostly juvenile readers, presumably with only minimal knowledge of or interest in the course of the Cold War in Asia, felt the same way. Nonetheless, Stan Lee and those around him thought such topics as the Sino-Indian war and the Chinese nuclear program had sufficient cultural currency to be the basis for some of their superhero stories. It also allowed indulging in the yellow peril imagery they had imbibed in their youth. In appearance, the Mandarin is a carbon copy of Fu Manchu, and Radioactive Man's great power is mind control. It is also noteworthy—and symptomatic of this period—to contrast how Marvel depicted the Soviet Union. First, it appears far less frequently. In the Ironman series. It features in one issue, involving a secret mission to free Soviet political prisoners. Near the end of that comic appears a lengthy speech educating readers on how Russians are virtuous people enslaved by a cruel master, an echo of "captive nations" Cold War rhetoric. No such tribute is ever offered to Chinese civilians.

While Chinese were being vilified in American popular culture, the nation's prestige was growing among European leftists, reflected by a character in Jean-Luc Godard's 1964 film "A Band Apart" explaining that he quit his English-language class because "England's done for and the Chinese will win," and therefore he had decided to study Chinese instead.[63] Many real-life leftists identified with the Red Guards, mistakenly viewing the student militants of the Great Proletarian Cultural Revolution as kindred spirits in search of personal and political liberation. In Jean-Luc Godard's 1967 film "La Chinoise," Maoists in Paris listen to French-language broadcasts of Radio Peking, stack their apartment shelves full of Little Red Books containing Mao's quotations, and brawl in the streets with members of the Sorbonne Marxist-Leninist Group. One of the characters, in defense of Mao, claims there are two kinds of communism: "a dangerous one, and one not dangerous." Mao and China represented "a communism Johnson must fight" in Vietnam, while Brezhnev and the Soviet Union were the "one he holds out his hand to." The film memorably features the students dancing and posing to Claude Channes' 1967 French-language rock song "Mao-Mao" in a sort of proto-music video. The first verse begins with the lines "Vietnam is burning, and me I shout Mao Mao/ Johnson is laughing, and me I fly Mao Mao/ napalm leaks down and me I spin Mao Mao/ cities are dying and me I dream Mao Mao." Its chorus repeats the couplet "it's the Little Red Book/ that causes everything to finally move." Meanwhile, real-life versions of these characters inspired John Lennon to sing "and if you go carrying pictures of Chairman Mao, you ain't gonna make it with anyone anyhow" in the Beatles' 1968 single "Revolution," which criticized the excesses of some of these young activists.

In the second half of the 1960s, Hollywood continued its negative depictions of Chinese, both in contemporary life and in the past. Two very different films, "The Sand Pebbles" from 1966 and "Thoroughly Modern Millie" from 1967, were set in the 1920s. Clearly reflecting emerging doubts about the Vietnam War, the first was a lengthy epic starring Steve McQueen about an American gunboat on the Yangtze River during the early stages of the Guomindang's Northern Expedition. The movie has its now-familiar bloodthirsty Chinese hordes, in this case of the civilian variety, but they prove no less dangerous than the military variety. The clear message of the film is that Americans understood Asia then about as well in the 1920s as they did in the 1960s, which was not very well at all. The second film was a big-budget musical starring Julie Andrews and Carol Channing, with a plot centered around villainous Chinese attempting to lure white flappers into prostitution. This throwback to a mixture of both coolie and Fu Manchu stereotypes showed that they still remained acceptable to audiences.

Finally, there appeared two very different science fiction films. The first, 1967's "Battle Beneath the Earth," was a cut-rate B-movie about Chinese Communists tunneling under the Pacific Ocean with the intention of detonating atomic bombs underneath US soil to destroy the nation. The second, 1969's "The Chairman," had a far larger budget, and starred Gregory Peck as a scientist investigating attempts by the Chinese to develop an enzyme that could enable the growing of food in any climate, ending world hunger, and bestowing untold power on the nation which possessed such breakthrough technology. Both films exploited fears of increasing Chinese technological proficiency, which had been inflamed by China's 1967 detonation of a hydrogen bomb.

Chinese fictional villainy quickly vanished in the wake of Nixon's visit. In the 1980s, the bad Asians were usually Japanese, reflecting US anxieties about Japanese economic might, or, in the case of movies about the recent conflict in Indochina, Vietnamese. By the time Americans feared China again, it had become a major growth market for Hollywood, deterring filmmakers from negative depictions of Chinese for commercial reasons. Ironically, an actual threatening of China could no longer be depicted as a fictional one.

8

The Ending of Isolation 1966–76

Even when their bad boy act was seen as genuinely dangerous by the older generation—when there were deadly riots at their concerts and when British police arrested its leading duo of Mick Jagger and Keith Richards on flimsy charges of drug possession to make an example of them, the Rolling Stones were never viewed as a politically activist band, particularly in an era where protest songs were quite common in mainstream popular music. They certainly did not shy away from reflecting the events of the times in their songs. The hit singles "Gimme Shelter," "Street Fighting Man," and "You Can't Always Get What You Want" touched on the Vietnam War, race riots, countercultural violence, and protests against authority but from an outside observer's point of view. The last of these three songs seemingly poured cold water on youthful idealism, while the 1968 album track "Salt of the Earth" can be read as a sort of ode to the "Silent Majority"—the "hard working people" and the "common foot soldier."[1] Yet, at a 1970 concert at the Palais des Sports in Paris, Mick Jagger saw fit to give a speech calling for the release of jailed French Maoists.[2] Perhaps Jagger was influenced by Maoist sympathizer Jean-Luc Godard, who in 1968 spent months filming the band for his documentary "Sympathy for the Devil." More probable is that he was simply swept up in a wave of what Tom Wolfe lampooned as "Radical Chic," with Maoists as that particular moment's cause celebre.

One might assume that such enthusiasm would quickly dissipate upon first contact with what Maoism had actually wrought in China. Yet actress Shirley MacLaine led the first delegation of American women to visit China in 1973—shortly after campaigning for George McGovern's ill-fated presidential run. She drew upon her travels in the 1974 bestseller *You Can Get There from Here*, the first of several autobiographical works she would produce. In the book, a woman feeling adrift while facing the crisis of early middle age in youth-obsessed America experiences a psychic awakening after traveling to a beguiling foreign land where the people are materially poor yet spiritually fulfilled. It was a trailblazer for later bestsellers like *Eat Pray Love*, with the crucial difference being the substitution of democratic India with China in the throes of the Cultural Revolution. Because of her visit to China, MacLaine received an invitation to the White House State Dinner President Jimmy Carter held for Deng Xiaoping in January 1979, and the actress sat at the head table. During the months when MacLaine achieved enlightenment in rural China, Deng was under (relatively comfortable) house arrest in a small southern Chinese village, having been temporarily purged for alleged "Rightism" and insufficient devotion to Mao's latest revolutionary project. When MacLaine recounted a Chinese nuclear scientist telling her he was happier growing tomatoes in the countryside than he had been working in the laboratory, Deng cut her off, telling her "he lied. That was what he had to say at the time."[3]

These three moments—Mick Jagger in Paris in 1970, Shirley MacLaine in China in 1973, and Deng Xiaoping in Washington in 1979—aptly encapsulate the trajectory of the relationship between China and the West during the 1970s. Beginning in 1966, Chinese society descended into what could only seem to outsiders, and no doubt to multitudes within China, as a reign of madness, when all was chaos under Heaven. Coupled with the domestic upheaval Mao intentionally unleashed were self-imposed diplomatic isolation and global pariah status. Whatever solid allure the Chinese revolution seemed to once possess had melted into air. Or so it seemed to those in power from Washington to Moscow and points in between. Yet, among the youth, the view was quite different. China offered an exciting alternative path to the stultifying staleness of a consumerist America and a bureaucratic Soviet Union. To millions of radical foreigners, China was the shining city on a hill, even if the shining was created by the flames of destroyed temples and burned books. But when this destruction threatened to boomerang upon Mao himself, he abruptly changed course, suppressing the Chinese youth he had whipped into often homicidal frenzies and reaching out to foreign powers he had long vilified. China could not permanently survive in opposition to both superpowers. Having purposefully burned all his bridges with the Soviets, Mao turned to the Americans. His paramount concern was that his unique brand of revolution survived him, and there seemed to be no faction within his Party openly advocating China copy the American system, as was the case with the Soviets. By the end of the decade, Deng Xiaoping had replaced the now-deceased Great Helmsman, and he would begin steering the revolution down a very different path. Pragmatism would replace dogmatism, and stability supersede upheaval. Deng's goal, like Mao's, would be to transform China into a globally influential great power. The difference was, unlike Mao the uncompromising theorist, Deng did not care how China got there from here.

The primary cause for Mao's launching of the Great Proletarian Cultural Revolution in 1966 was fear of a successor denouncing him and undoing his work, as had been the case in the USSR after the death of Stalin. China's leader had experienced a taste of marginalization in the four years since the end of the Great Leap Forward when he allowed his subordinates to run a Soviet-style command economy, and he could not be sure he had much time left to reverse this trend. Mao was suffering through the early stages of Lou Gehrig's Disease, which his doctors (and foreign observers) misdiagnosed as Parkinson's Syndrome, in part because of his extreme discomfort around doctors. The chairman would purge those who might betray his legacy and replace them with those who would continue it. Such was the original intent. The secondary cause was the collapse of China's foreign policy. Since 1960, China had gone it alone in the world, estranged from the Soviets and free to "walk on two legs" without assistance. Initially this bore fruit. The world's premier non-white power enjoyed an increased presence on the African continent, a significant penetration of Southeast Asia, a military victory over India, and a general sense of growing global legitimacy. But 1965 proved to be China's *annus horribilus*. Everywhere, it lost ground, sometimes disastrously so. In Africa, coups in Algeria and Ghana deprived the Chinese of influential allies. In South Asia, Pakistan became alienated when China stood idly by as India dealt them a humiliating military defeat. Full-scale US military entry into South Vietnam denied them a quick victory in a "War of Liberation" in Southeast Asia. Most damaging of all, the overthrow of President Sukarno in Indonesia and the ensuing brutal liquidation of the world's third-largest Communist party by the Americans' close ally and new Indonesian dictator Suharto brought about a definitive end to any Chinese pretensions to regional hegemony.[4] This series of crushing setbacks caused China's leaders to turn inward.

Initially, the Cultural Revolution was an elite affair. Mao targeted Chinese Communist Party leaders he considered too close to the Soviets to prevent the establishment of a Soviet-style bureaucratic leadership, which he considered anathema to his goal of permanent revolution. First to be targeted was Mao's heir apparent, Liu Shaoqi, whose power and influence had increased as he helped stabilize the Chinese economy in the aftermath of the Great Leap Forward. But Mao's targets soon multiplied and eventually included nearly all leading Party members. From there, Mao widened his horizons. To uproot what existed of China's Soviet-style bureaucratic leadership, Mao initiated massive popular mobilization campaigns beginning in June 1966, first and foremost among the younger generation that had known nothing but his rule. Mao called for students to organize Red Guards, whom he addressed en masse in Tiananmen Square on August 18. Also present at this event was PLA leader Lin Biao, who soon replaced Liu as Mao's second-in-command and presumptive heir. Adept at pleasing Mao, Lin had compiled Mao's numerous aphorisms into the famous "Little Red Book," of which China would soon print and distribute billions of copies—more than one for every person on the planet at the time. During that gathering, Lin seconded Mao's call for the Red Guards to destroy "old ideas, old culture, old customs, and old habits."[5]

The Red Guard mobs soon began a reign of vigilante terror against Party members and other adult authority figures in the autumn of 1966 and the winter of 1967. Usually, when one speaks of politically active students, the assumption is that they are attending universities. But the ringleaders of these waves of violence were high school students who were joined by legions of middle and primary school students. A sixteen-year-old girl led a nearly successful siege of the Soviet Embassy, while sixth graders beat their music teacher to death and wrote "Long Live the Red Revolution!" in his blood on the classroom walls. By the spring of 1967, the zealous mobs had slipped beyond Mao's control, most notably during a large-scale multi-sided military battle in Wuhan in July 1967 between numerous well-armed factions, each claiming to enjoy Mao's backing. It was then that the Chairman ordered Lin to use the PLA against the Red Guards to restore order. Over the next year, the political power of the military measurably increased, and Mao formally disbanded the Red Guards in September 1968.[6] Mao now feared the establishment of a military dictatorship. Thus, in 1969, he began to turn on Lin Biao and the military faction Lin led, as he had previously turned first on Liu Shaoqi and then the Red Guards. Around this same time, Mao sought to reestablish relations with foreign powers abroad. Lin would eventually perish in October 1971 when the plane he and his family fled China crashed in Mongolia, while Liu died under house arrest. This left Zhou and Deng sitting uneasily as the final remaining remnants of the senior leadership who had participated in the Long March.

The diplomatic isolation of the early period of the Cultural Revolution resulted from actions both by the government itself and by non-governmental actors such as the Red Guards. Shortly after the Red Guards seized control of the Foreign Ministry in January 1967, Mao ordered the staffs of more than fifty Chinese embassies to return home for reeducation. In addition, Chinese mobs attacked foreign diplomats in Beijing, most notoriously burning the British Charge d' Affaires building on the night of August 22, 1967.[7] China was now more isolated than at any time since perhaps the Boxer Rebellion, while the economy and social infrastructure were in tatters. Fortunately for China, Zhou had been able to talk that sixteen-year-old girl and her thousands of well-armed Red Guard forces out of storming the Soviet Embassy. As bad as things were, they could have been worse.

Early US reactions evinced a certain schadenfreude combined with allusions to contemporaneous youthful rebellions within the United States. National Security Advisor Walt Rostow joked to President Johnson in September 1966 that "the Red Guards are getting into more trouble than Stokely Carmichael and SNICK [*sic*]."[8] Rostow's chief Chinese expert Alfred Jenkins quipped that "China is putting on one hell of a happening," and expressed "a certain exhilaration at being a leading determinant" of events, implying that the US war in South Vietnam had exacerbated tensions within the Chinese leadership.[9] State Department official Robert Barnett wrote in May 1967 that around the globe, "the lustre, the model value of this image is over."[10]

That may have been the case among those who ran nations. But among rebellious youth around the globe, Mao was suddenly hip. In 1967, a French fashion magazine ran a Chinese-themed photo spread, with scantily clad white French models dressed in pieces of Mao Suits and other recognizably East Asian garb, pointing guns and posing next to Mao's sayings. Sammy Davis Jr. wore a Mao Suit, which was being sold in fashionable shops on the Champs-Elysee in Paris and Carnaby Street in London, replacing the Nehru Jackets popular during the mid 1960s as the latest in exotic menswear. China temporarily enjoyed an amount of soft power it would not again achieve until the twenty-first century. Joseph Nye coined the term "Soft Power" in 1990 to describe a process of voluntarily emulating the culture and values of another nation which "co-opts people rather than coerces them."[11] He had in mind the supposedly benevolent unipolar United States in the Clinton era, when the world watched American movies, listened to American songs, and drank Coca-Colas at American fast food restaurants. Implicitly, soft power is positive, something no moral person would object to. After all, people are supposed to be drawn to good, not evil. For instance, the Soviet Union enjoyed substantial soft power in 1945 due to its decisive role in defeating Nazi Germany and crushing fascism.[12] But soft power is actually value-neutral. People can be attracted to nasty things, whether out of naivete or malice. Italian fascism enjoyed significant soft power in leading democracies throughout much of the 1920s and 1930s.

What worked in Mao's favor was the dullness of his American and Soviet rivals, coupled with his pose as someone supportive of young people at a time of considerable youth upheaval in Western Europe and North America. The transnational connections between the youth rebellions and protest movements of the late 1960s and early 1970s, often referred to by the shorthand of "The Global 1968," has long been recognized, as has the appeal of Cultural Revolution-era China to many of these rebellious young people.[13] By forming the Red Guards and encouraging them to attack leaders from the older generation, Mao appeared to be the one old man in a position of power who "got it" and understood the moment. Ironically, though quite numerous in the Parisian universities that were the epicenter of France's near revolution, the French Maoists failed to take part in the tumultuous events of May 1968 that nearly brought down de Gaulle's government.[14] Like the students in Godard's film from the previous year, they preferred talking and publishing to actual street action, seeming to believe that while revolution was not a dinner party, perhaps it could be an undergraduate seminar. Their influence in French culture would only flower after the events of that year, when the alliance of students and workers crumbled as Soviet Communist-affiliated unions chose pay raises over revolution. Mao represented something different and exciting, "an exit strategy to escape from the straightjacket of orthodox Marxism."[15] Fittingly, French Maoists embarked upon a cultural turn in leftist thinking. They were the first French intellectuals to champion gay and lesbian rights in their publications and also helped nurture a nascent French feminist movement.[16]

Given their outsized prominence in the public conversation, Maoists became an easy target for authority figures, leading in France to the arrests Jagger spoke out against. There was also the literal ubiquity of Mao's "Little Red Book." Functionally clad in durable red plastic, this collection of 427 quotations attributed to the Chinese leader and compiled by Lin Biao in 1965 in an act of purposeful sycophancy was the world's most-printed book in the late 1960s. An estimated 100,000 copies were sold in West Germany alone. When asked in 1969 to identify the cause of student unrest in his country, Chancellor Kurt Georg Kiesinger responded "China, China, China."[17] Maoism's appeal did stop at the Berlin Wall, and the "Little Red Book" made little impact on the Soviet Union or its European satellites.[18]

Mao also influenced the Women's Liberation Movement in the United States. In 1966, William Hinton published the book *Fanshen* about Communist-led peasant uprisings against landlords. The title's translation is roughly "to turn over," and is a metaphor for the process of social revolution. Hinton described the revolutionary upheaval in a single Chinese village in 1958.[19] This book exposed US readers to what Chinese Communists called "Speak Bitterness" sessions, where individuals would express their grievances against neighbors and colleagues. In the hands of American feminists, Speak Bitterness sessions became "Consciousness Raising" sessions.[20] Perhaps some of this affinity between these two very different political projects was Mao's quote "women hold up half the sky," which is as well-known as it is misinterpreted. Mao made the declaration on the eve of the Great Leap Forward not to champion equality of opportunity, but equality of burden. In fact, it was meant to criticize, rather than praise, Chinese women. The statement was normative, in the sense that women *should* hold up half the sky, by which he meant women should labor just as hard as men in their rural communes and urban factories.

Perhaps the most direct connection between Mao and sixties militancy in the United States was with Black militancy in general and the Black Panthers in particular. These connections existed even before the 1960s. On his ninety-first birthday in 1959, W. E. B. Du Bois spoke at Peking University, where he advocated increasing contact between China and Africa because "China is colored and knows to what a colored skin in this modern world subjects its owner."[21] But the crucial vector connecting Mao to Black militants was Robert F. Williams. A staunch advocate for armed Black self-defense, Williams fled North Carolina after a 1959 shootout with local Klansmen and police officers, first seeking refuge in Cuba and then in China. At Mao's seventieth birthday party in Beijing in October 1963, China's leader appeared with Williams as his honored guest.[22] A picture of this encounter appeared in both *Newsweek* and *Time*. Williams's presence inspired fear in some corners of white America of a rising tide of Black militants taking their cue from the Chinese and even resorting to guerrilla warfare.

Black journalist William Worthy gave voice to these fears in a 1964 *Esquire* article entitled "The Red Chinese American Negro." Worthy was a curious interlocutor for such fears. He had recently lost his passport for having traveled to Cuba, making him a martyr of sorts to left-wing activists, and inspiring protest singer Phil Ochs's 1964 song "The Ballad of William Worthy." In the article, Worthy claimed "radical Negro militants are turning to Mao Tse-tung for support in overthrowing the U.S. government," citing Williams's presence in China as proof.[23] He also noted recent favorable comments made about Mao by Malcolm X. But his main concern was the Philadelphia-based Revolutionary Action Movement, or RAM, which Worthy claimed was planning "a colonial war at home" that would feature large-scale acts of urban guerrilla warfare such as the destruction of highway bridges and overpasses.[24] Max Stanford, the founder of the RAM, came to Maoism through his admiration of Williams.[25] When RAM published the book *The World Black Revolution* in 1966, it placed the decidedly non-Black Mao on the cover.[26]

Black Panther second-in-command Bobby Seale began his political activism in the west coast branch of RAM, before meeting fellow Mao admirer and Black Panther founder Huey Newton. Formed in 1966, the Panthers soon became notorious for openly (and at the time legally) brandishing rifles and shotguns on the streets of Oakland, often in close proximity to police officers. Seale would later claim the two of them bought their first firearms with the proceeds from selling Little Red Books on the University of California-Berkeley campus, having bought them cheap in San Francisco's Chinatown and then selling them to students at a steep markup.[27] Seale reported that Newton impressed him because he "knew the Red Book sideways, backwards, and forwards," and that they shared an admiration for the militant quartet of Mao, Franz Fanon, Malcolm X, and Che Guevara.[28] It was in homage to the last of these four that the Panthers adopted their signature black berets, while Mao's book was distributed to the organization's new members to properly educate them on revolution. For Panther spokesman and propagandist Eldridge Cleaver, Mao was quite simply "the baddest motherfucker on planet earth."[29]

Yet none of this adulation ensured Mao's domestic standing or China's international security. And the Chinese were now worried about military aggression from their former Soviet allies. Before 1965, the Soviets had only stationed token forces along its lengthy borders with China. Near the end of that year, they began a pronounced buildup, both in quantity and quality.[30] The August 1968 Warsaw Pact invasion of Czechoslovakia, accompanied by the Brezhnev Doctrine justifying Soviet military action to maintain friendly Communist regimes, further alarmed Mao, causing him to seriously fear a full-scale Soviet invasion. Amid massive civil defense preparations against the perceived Soviet threat, he decided to reach out to his previous primary adversary. In February 1969, he summoned four leading generals who had been sidelined during the most intense phases of the Cultural Revolution. Dubbed the "Four Marshalls," they were instructed to evaluate China's present security posture and offer suggestions for improvement.[31] While the Marshalls conducted weekly meetings, the situation with the Soviets rapidly deteriorated. On March 2, the Chinese occupied Damasky/Zhenbao Island on the Ussuri River, triggering a substantial Soviet counterattack on March 15 that resulted in hundreds of Chinese casualties. In August, along the border of Xinjiang thousands of miles to the west, an even larger Soviet attack caused thousands of Chinese casualties. The next month, the Four Marshalls reported to Mao their recommendation that he play "the card of the United States" against the Soviets.[32]

Western observers feared war between the two Communist powers. Foreign correspondent Harrison Salisbury, who had been documenting Sino-Soviet tensions since the mid-1950s, published a book in 1969 entitled *War Between Russia and China* detailing his fear "that the two superstates are headed toward a collision course and war."[33] He argued that the only way to prevent such a monumental conflict would be for the United States to "establish a viable relationship with China."[34] Unbeknownst to him, Nixon was thinking precisely the same thing.

While the Chinese leadership lived in mortal terror of a large-scale Soviet attack, in the USSR fears of China among the intelligentsia burgeoned.[35] Around the time of the Ussuri River clashes, the dissident Andrei Amalrik published the popular underground book *Will the Soviet Union Survive until 1984?* The first half of the book detailed the USSR's internal weaknesses, particularly its economic sclerosis and ethnic tensions. Its second half predicted a war in the late 1970s with a China "seeking national revenge for the centuries of humiliation and dependence forced on her by foreign powers."[36] China would conquer eastern Siberia, leading to successful rebellions in both the eastern European satellite states and the non-Russian Soviet republics.[37] Amalrik claimed that "one can hear nowadays in Russia remarks like 'The United States will help us because we are white and the Chinese are yellow,'" though the author expressed hope that instead of taking this path the United States would eschew racial solidarity and seek a better relationship with China while working to prevent such a Sino-Soviet conflict.[38]

Whether the United States was primarily interested in "our position as 'balancer' in the evolving triangular relationship among the superpowers," to quote Kissinger aide Richard Solomon, is open to dispute.[39] The final breakdown of relations between the Chinese and Soviet Communists as represented by the border clashes in March 1969 certainly influenced the timing of subsequent US actions. But the decision to take those actions at the earliest possible moment had already been made. Nixon discussed his intentions with aides in January and ordered Kissinger to get the bureaucratic wheels spinning at the start of February, over a month before the first Red Army soldier opened fire on his People's Liberation Army counterpart along the Ussuri River. Also, discussion of the Sino-Soviet split tended to be coupled with talk of the long-term Chinese threat.

The public support for Nixon's outreach to the Chinese, and the jubilation occasioned by his trip there, were the fruits of a decade of efforts to shape public opinion. This process preceded the Vietnam War, though of course the war ultimately helped accelerate it. Fear of China had been increasing during the decade while support for allowing China in the UN had been simultaneously increasing in polls from negligible levels in 1960 to a near majority in 1966. Fear of China remained high even after Nixon announced his visit to popular acclaim. Regarding the mass public, an October 1971 Gallup poll showed a drop since 1967 in those who feared the Chinese over the Russians from 71 percent to 56 percent, but Americans by a more than two-to-one margin still claimed the Chinese would in the near future pose the greater threat to world peace.[40] The two trends were connected. Once it became clear Communist China was no passing phase, and could not be destroyed, it had to be accommodated in some form.

An important turning point was Senator Fulbright's March 1966 China hearings. Over the next month, numerous professors testified before the committee, and nearly all called for ending the policy of isolating China. On the first day, which was nationally televised on the major networks, Columbia University professor Arthur Doak Barnett, who was the older brother of State Department official Robert Barnett, called for a shift from seventeen years of "containment and isolation" to a new policy of "containment without isolation."[41] In the short term, this would entail lifting the travel and trade bans and acquiescing to UN admission. John King Fairbank focused more on history than policy, yet found time to reiterate Barnett's prescriptions, arguing the goal should be "manipulating Peking into an acceptance of the international world."[42] The press optimistically predicted the professors' testimony would bring about a sea change in Johnson administration policy in order "to meet China's future power."[43] In addition to swaying the press, the professors also influence Congress. In a speech twelve days after Barnett's testimony, moderate Republican New York Senator Jacob Javits called for "containment but not isolation of the Chinese people."[44]

Fulbright's interest in shifting China's policy toward engagement was gathering force even before the start of direct US combat in the Vietnam War, though that soon added to his worries. In November 1964, Senate Foreign Relations Committee Chief of Staff Carl Marcy forwarded an article written by George Kennan from the most recent *New York Times Magazine* entitled "A Fresh Look at Our China Policy" to his boss William Fulbright (D-AR) with the note "I think you will find this article quite worth reading."[45] In this lengthy and often meandering essay, Kennan argued that China's Communist regime would not collapse, but could be moderated through diplomatic engagement.[46] This was a frank about-face from Kennan's estimation in 1949 that "China doesn't matter very much. It's not very important. It's never going to be powerful."[47] Within a month, Fulbright began giving speeches calling for significant changes in US-China policy privileging outreach over isolation. In each of those speeches, he quoted—at length and with accreditation—Kennan's article. He called for the United States "to take a chance that China will change." This "gamble" was worth the risk because "China is too big to be isolated." It was already the leading power in the region, and "its strength is growing."[48] President Johnson responded to Fulbright's hearings by giving his first televised address on the subject of China, where he advocated outreach, arguing that "we have learned that the greatest force for opening closed societies is the free flow of ideas and people and goods."[49]

The argument that the United States reached out to China because of its growing power appears to be contradicted by the fact that between 1969 and 1972, relative Chinese power was in decline due to the effects of the Cultural Revolution. As *U.S. News* opined in late 1967, China was "more a poorhouse than a world power—and is likely to stay that way."[50] To quote former Kennedy administration official Roger Hilsman, China was a curious amalgam of "an emerging nation" and "a great power."[51] In 1971, when a foreign visitor called China a great power, Zhou Enlai disagreed, terming his country a "great power designate." Nixon certainly cared about extricating the United States from South Vietnam while preserving that state's existence and improving the strategic balance with the Soviets. But he insisted upon selling his China outreach as the best way to deal with a rising China. In a handwritten note from January 1969, he scribbled "Chinese Communists: Short range—no change. Long range—we do not want 800,000,000 living in angry isolation. We want contact."[52] On the eve of his February 1972 trip to China, Nixon wrote in his private notes the following summary of his goals: "What we want: 1. Indochina 2. Communists—to restrain Chinese expansion in Asia 3. In Future—Reduce threat of a confrontation by Chinese Super Power."[53]

Nixon recognized China's present weakness provided a window of opportunity in which a president could conduct a policy of rapprochement without it appearing to be a policy of appeasement. He also knew that America's allies in both Asia and Europe would welcome such a move. On foreign trips undertaken before his second presidential campaign in 1968, Nixon heard similar desires and arguments from key US allies along China's periphery. Their input was important because for two decades they had lived in fear of Chinese expansion and subversion. Such fears had long been used to argue any softening of US hostility to China would dishearten them. But now Singapore's Lee Kwon Yew told Nixon in 1967 that it was "a mistake for U.S. to isolate them" and that the United States "now must establish contact."[54] Most intriguing of all were Nixon's conversations with Philippine diplomat and future Foreign Minister Alberto Romulo. While meeting with Nixon in Manila in 1967, Romulo suggested that if Nixon became president he should "go to China." He then reminded Nixon he had given him identical advice when they previously met in 1966, "at a lunch in Manila" Nixon noted from memory in the margins.[55]

In Europe, Nixon met with West German vice-chancellor Willy Brandt and found China to be an "obsession" of the German politician, quoting Brandt as remarking that "12,000,000 Chinese born a year—each exists on bowl of rice," after which Brandt cupped his hand in a display of *gelbe gefahr* body language which would have made Kaiser Wilhelm II proud. What Brandt feared most was China's threat in the "future—when they have atomic weapons," by which he surely meant intercontinental ballistic missiles able to deliver the hydrogen bombs China had recently tested.[56] In a similar vein, Charles de Gaulle suggested to Nixon in 1969 that "it would be better for the U.S. to recognize China before they were obliged to do it by the growth of China."[57]

In Washington, right-wing columnist Stewart Alsop, a longtime supporter of isolating Communist China, wondered at the start of 1970 if "we perhaps take Communist China too seriously?" For the time being, the answer to him was yes. Still, "the time will no doubt come when we will have to take Chinese power very seriously indeed." Both superpowers "worry about the day when the Chinese will have a respectable arsenal of nuclear weapons and of missiles to carry them." The combination of atomic weapons and limitless manpower reserves was one "not lightly dismissed by experts."[58]

Every account of Nixon's opening to China highlights the supposed importance of his 1967 essay in *Foreign Affairs* "Asia After Vietnam." In this essay, which largely focused on how to contain China's continuing threat to incite internal Communist revolutions in the region, Nixon declared that "any American policy must come urgently to grips with the reality of China," adding "we simply cannot afford to leave China forever outside the family of nations, there to nurture its fantasies, cherish its hates and threaten its neighbors."[59] Yet the press failed to note this article until four years later, after Nixon announced his upcoming visit in July 1971. Like numerous other signals of his intentions, the media, the public, and other politicians ignored them. But in China, Mao had read "Asia After Vietnam" in 1968, recommended it to Zhou Enlai, and predicted US-China policy might change under a future Nixon administration.[60]

Nixon continued to send signals, but Americans were not listening. In October 1970 interview, Nixon told *Time* magazine that "if there is anything I want to do before I die, it is to go to China."[61] In April 1971, shortly after the beginning of Chinese diplomatic reciprocations had dramatically raised US hopes of a breakthrough, he reported to the American Society of Newspaper Editors that he wished his daughter Julie and her new husband David Eisenhower could honeymoon in China and "see the great cities, and the people, and all of that, there," adding "I hope they do. As a matter of fact, I hope I do."[62] By the summer of 1971, it could not have been any clearer to anyone paying attention that Nixon really wanted to go to China.

But the message was not getting through to the American media. On July 6, 1971, Nixon addressed a convention of media executives in Kansas City. The focus of this speech was the rise of an economically powerful China. "Inevitably," a Communist-led China would become "an enormous economic power," and "that is the reason I felt it was essential that this administration take the first steps toward ending the isolation of Mainland China from the world community." In the future, an isolated and powerful China "would be a danger to the whole world." Integrated into the global economy, the Chinese colossus would still present "an immense escalation of their economic challenge" in terms of industrial competition, but that was by far the lesser of two evils.[63] The remarks failed to make news in the United States. But they were noted in China. At Zhou Enlai's first meeting with Kissinger three days after Nixon's speech, the National Security Advisor found himself being "questioned at length" by the Chinese Premier about the text of a presidential address he did not even know existed. Swiftly recognizing his interlocutor's ignorance, Zhou Enlai provided Kissinger with an English-language copy of the speech.[64]

Due to these missed signals, Nixon's primetime address on July 15, 1971, informing Americans of Kissinger's recent visit to China and the president's upcoming trip to that nation came as a complete surprise. Over the ensuing months, Nixon continued to stress the theme of managing China's future rise. In an August news conference, he noted China was "the most populous nation in the world" and "potentially in the future could become the most powerful nation in the world." In a speech that September, he told the Economic Club of Detroit that "ten, fifteen years from now, there will be between 900 million and a billion people in Mainland China. Ten or fifteen years from now, they will be a very significant nuclear power." Considering this long-term threat, it was desirable to him "that we will talk about them [our differences] and not fight about them, now or fifteen years from now." To continue to isolate such a potential colossus would only endanger the United States and the world.[65]

"Since 1950 Washington has officially sent more men to the moon than it has to China."[66] John Fairbank wrote this in April 1971 in response to the visit earlier that month of the US Table Tennis Team to China—the first such authorized visit by American citizens since 1949. Nixon's carefully stage-managed eight-day visit ten months later was a unique media event for the period, since it was the first such diplomatic visit to occur during the age of satellite communications, meaning that the public events in Beijing could be broadcast live on US television.[67] The White House reporter for the *Washington Post* referred to it as "one of the most exciting events in all TV history." He also informed readers that the White House had worked closely with the three television networks on their presentation of these events since the previous July.[68] The Chinese also paid attention to public relations. Having vilified the United States for over two decades, Mao had to justify his rapid diplomatic reversal. With this in mind, the Chinese government presented Nixon's trip as a sort of modern-day Tribute Mission by a powerful barbarian king.

In reality, both sides acted from positions of increasing weakness. Mao and Nixon engaged in an act of mutual supplication. In *Power and Protest*, Jeremi Suri saw recent unrest and dissent—not only in the United States but also in the USSR and the PRC—as a reason for the flowering of détente. Each power needed breathing space to regroup and reassert the primacy of domestic elites before rejoining the superpower struggle in earnest. Some contemporary observers came to a similar conclusion. When meeting with Zhou Enlai in 1971, former US diplomat John Service told the Chinese premier "American youth is unhappy and alienated." This domestic unrest, coupled with a loss of "US prestige," was in his opinion a major spur for Nixon's zeal for rapprochement with the Chinese.[69] In an article published shortly before Nixon's 1972 visit, Fairbank claimed the trip was destined to succeed "because both parties are in trouble." Mao's recent purges of the Party's senior leadership, combined with "Nixon's troubles at home," would bring the two former adversaries together, leading to "a Sino-American détente, perhaps an entente."[70] Domestic discord could lead to international concord.

Coming in the immediate aftermath of US failures in South Vietnam, the American public greeted Nixon's trip and the prospect of friendly Sino-American relations with brief but barely concealed euphoria. The old missionary impulse temporarily reemerged. In the months before Nixon's visit, Edgar Snow stated "the danger is that Americans may imagine that the Chinese are giving up communism—and Mao's world view—to become nice agrarian democrats."[71] He feared this would lead to a renewed bout of disenchantment. In this, Snow was about two decades ahead of his time. In the 1970s, no leading Americans talked of a future Chinese democracy. This was as yet not a US goal. Attention remained on restraining China strategically while letting it grow economically.

China's economic prospects seemed bullish to one-time profound PRC skeptic Joseph Alsop. His dispatches in late 1972 and early 1973 from China trumpeted the nation's potential. Over the course of several months, Alsop toured parts of southeastern and southwestern China he had visited more than three decades earlier. He marveled at the people's improved standards of living, the advanced infrastructure, and what he assumed was a sophisticated and flexible approach to agricultural and industrial development. As he ended his journey, Alsop argued that "a truly successful China cannot help but be a superpower, even a supergiant power." He predicted that someday that nation would economically become "a China-sized Japan," exporting massive quantities of industrial and consumer goods across the globe and competing with existing advanced economies in North America and Western Europe. This would result by the end of the century in "a sudden tilt in the overall balance of this changing world such as no one has seen since the 18th century when the Industrial Revolution began in England."[72] Alsop would eventually be proven correct in his prediction, although only after the reforms enacted after Mao's death. Deng Xiaoping, exiled at that time to the region which Alsop visited, would eventually initiate many of these reforms. But he would not have expressed Alsop's level of optimism at the time when Mao's counterproductive economic policies kept most Chinese mired in abject poverty.

Another theme among the earliest American visitors was contrasting perceived Chinese unity and sense of purpose with what at the time seemed an exhausted and decadent America. After visiting China in the summer of 1972, future president and current House Minority Leader Gerald Ford (R-MI) returned ominously impressed by what he had seen. His compliments verged on envy. Describing "China's colossal potential," he recalled feeling "this sense of a giant stirring, a dragon waking," which gave him "much to ponder." He approved of the "State-directed conformity" he had witnessed. Ford contrasted this Chinese "unity of effort and purpose" with the current situation in his own nation, writing that "where people are free to live and work and choose and read and think and disagree as they please, there has been widespread division, discord and disillusionment and a pervasive permissiveness straining the fibers of our national character." He concluded by wondering "if our self-indulgent free society will be able to compete effectively fifty years hence with this totalitarian State," given China's population, natural resources, and "total commitment to national goals."[73]

In a similar vein, the financier David Rockefeller wrote in an August 1973 *New York Times* article how impressed he was with "the sense of national harmony" he observed in China. He commended the "very real and pervasive dedication to Chairman Mao" along with an "impressive" level of economic progress. In addition, Rockefeller claimed, "there was little sense of the constant security found in some other Communist countries."[74] Alsop, Ford, and Rockefeller all fell victim to the Chinese practice of carefully choreographing visits by prominent foreigners. These men's handlers were experts at befriending guests in order to hoodwink them.[75] One can readily imagine, and in fact surely find examples of, expressions of similar sentiments among leading American visitors to China twenty or thirty years later, or even in our own time. Americans were unsure if their nation could compete with the Chinese long before that competition had begun, generally for the same reasons, and based on the same evidence, both real and imagined.

Meanwhile, the Chinese themselves continued to struggle to recover from the Cultural Revolution, while, in his waning years, Mao sought to pit competent pragmatists like Deng and Zhou against hapless zealots like the Gang of Four. The uncertainty of succession in China combined with Nixon's Watergate-induced downfall prevented the full normalization of relations during Mao's lifetime. After his death in 1976, what China's future held was anyone's guess.

PART THREE

The Dragon Soars: 1976–2022

9

Deng Xiaoping, Before and After Tiananmen

1976–93

The year 1979 was when Jimmy Carter's already shaky presidency collapsed. Double-digit inflation at home, followed by a Federal Reserve-induced recession to bring down that inflation, coupled with the taking of fifty-four US hostages in Iran, doomed his reelection chances. That summer, Carter gave what became known as his "Malaise" speech, where he committed the unforgivable sins of telling bad news to the American people and asking them to help him fix their country's problems. Capping off those twelve unfortunate months was the Soviet invasion of Afghanistan, which seemed at the time to be yet another sign of the increasing power of America's Cold War enemy. One of the few bright spots for the president occurred at the start of the year when the United States finally established full diplomatic relations with the People's Republic of China and exchanged ambassadors. From the US side, the impetus to complete what Nixon had begun was the belated recognition that détente had long been moribund, leading to the conclusion that the United States now more than ever needed China to balance Soviet power. For China's new leader Deng Xiaoping, US support was vital to his plans for economic development. Mao may have made China strategically secure, but he left it desperately poor and in relative economic decline. In 1955, mainland China accounted for nearly 5 percent of global economic output. By the time of Mao's death in 1976, that share had fallen to a mere 1 percent.[1] Meanwhile, Japan was on its way to becoming the world's second-largest economy, and the "Asian Tigers" of South Korea, Singapore, Hong Kong, and (most humiliating for the PRC) Taiwan were growing rich at a record pace. Mao stood China up. Now, Deng needed to help China catch up.

With that in mind, China's new leader set off for the United States in late January. His ascension to power in December 1978 had already earned him *Time* magazine's "Man of the Year" award. After touching down in Washington, Deng journeyed on to Atlanta, Houston, and Seattle. More than being a diplomatic mission, this was a shopping trip combined with an advertising campaign. Before Deng could change China, he sought to change how foreigners saw his nation. What followed was a decade of good feelings and great expectations. With China seemingly abandoning Marxist economics, perhaps it might eventually jettison Leninist politics. All this seemingly ceased when Deng ordered soldiers into Tiananmen Square in June 1989 to violently suppress pro-democracy protests. In reality, while the near-term prospects for Chinese democratization had disappeared, foreign hopes for this result only increased as the 1990s progressed. What makes China in the 1980s stand out was the low level of foreign fear of China. This was by Deng's design, and he was assisted in this task by intensifying US-USSR animosity in the early 1980s, a period that historians refer to as the "Second Cold War." Communist China would never appear less threatening. Still, some underlying worries persisted about a future where a successful China might finally throw its weight around.

Carter would later call Deng's White House visit "one of the delightful experiences of my Presidency."[2] With the exception of Zhou Enlai, Deng was probably the most natural politician in the democratic sense in Communist China's history. What he lacked in urbanity he made up for in subtle flair. But in 1979, he had his work cut out for him. America's renewed honeymoon with China in 1972 had faded by mid-decade, as attempts at deepening diplomatic ties became mired in the succession struggles of Mao's final years. Five percent of Americans polled in 1967 expressed a "favorable" view of Communist China. That number jumped to 50 percent in 1972 but fell back to 20 percent in 1976.[3] Things only became worse in the post-Mao years. The arrest of the anti-American "Gang of Four" actually worsened China's image abroad by revealing the ugly underbelly of Party politics. Visitors to China in the late 1970s were underwhelmed by what they observed, and the promised dividends of access to the Chinese market remained illusory.[4] In a 1982 travelogue, longtime foreign corresponded Fox Butterfield described "a mood of introspection and self-doubt" among Communist Party cadres at the local level and claimed the brightest young Chinese all dreamed of leaving for the United States.[5] It was a rare moment where the pendulum was not oscillating between romantic hope and anxious fear, but instead resting at suspicious indifference.

Upon landing in Washington, Deng alluded euphemistically to the "period of unpleasantness between us for 30 years."[6] Quickly testing the depth of this new quasi-alliance, during his White House meeting with Carter, Deng broached the possibility of a punitive Chinese military incursion into Vietnam as a response to its recent invasion and occupation of Cambodia, which had been ruled by China's allies the Khmer Rouge. Deng promised Carter that it would be "a limited action" and that "our troops will quickly withdraw."[7] While he did not officially endorse military action, Carter did not object either, which Deng correctly viewed as tacit consent. China invaded Vietnam with 200,000 soldiers on February 17 (less than two weeks after Deng departed the United States). These forces were badly mauled by massively outnumbered but significantly more experienced and slightly better-equipped Vietnamese forces, and the Chinese withdrew after a month.[8] Perceived US support prevented Vietnam's close Soviet allies from retaliating against China along its northern border, something Deng had feared. The assault reminded Vietnam to respect its northern neighbor while also revealing the weakness of the Chinese military and its need for modernization.

Complicating any Sino-American partnership was congressional backing of Taiwanese autonomy and concerns over human rights. By linking increased trade to human rights performance, the 1974 Jackson-Vanik Amendment played a crucial role in souring the Soviets on détente. Now that the United States had formally recognized the PRC, this legislation also applied to them. Jackson-Vanik had previously expressed itself through US demands for increased emigration allowances from the USSR for dissidents, particularly persecuted Russian Jews. Carter entered office promising to make human rights the cornerstone of his foreign policy. But by 1979, his idealistic zeal had dissipated considerably. Still, Carter pressed Deng on allowing the emigration of Chinese dissidents. The ever-savvy Deng quipped in response "Oh that's easy! How many do you want? Ten million. Fifteen million?"[9] For once, fears of Chinese hordes helped defuse tensions. Deng soon departed for Atlanta, where in addition to meeting Coca-Cola executives, he toured a Ford manufacturing plant. That single factory produced 20,000 vehicles in 1978, while the entire nation of China had produced only 13,000 that year, a sign of China's profound backwardness.[10] Deng also made his first business deal in Atlanta, with Coca-Cola beating Pepsi into the Chinese market, compensating for Pepsi's monopoly in the Soviet Union.

The stop in Houston proved to be Deng's greatest challenge. When Deng arrived on the morning of February 2, he received a frosty reception. Both Senators from Texas—Republican John Tower and Democrat Lloyd Bentsen—refused to be seen with the Chinese leader. Recently elected Republican governor William Clements was present at the Houston airport that morning, but pointedly declined to personally greet Deng and immediately returned to Austin, promising only that "we will turn out in a normal show of Texas hospitality. Whether we agree with him politically, philosophically, or whether we like chop suey or not, is beside the point."[11]

Old anti-communist misgivings lingered in that conservative state. Lessening Deng's humiliation was a warm welcome by the Houston Chamber of Commerce, which sponsored this leg of the trip.[12] China possessed significant oil reserves and was a net oil exporter due to its low domestic consumption. Deng spent the morning at the Hughes Tool Company, a leading manufacturer of oil drilling equipment. In his lunchtime address to the Chamber of Commerce, Deng predicted China would need "possibly scores of billions" in foreign investment in the near term to jump-start its languishing economy. That afternoon, he visited the Johnson Space Center, where he marveled at a replica of the Apollo 11 capsule and had himself photographed sitting in a replica of the Moon Rover.[13] As in Atlanta, Deng touted the future potential of the Chinese market while highlighting China's present economic weakness.

The turning point came that evening when the Chinese delegation attended a rodeo in the tiny town of Simonton. Near the beginning of the performance, a teenage barrel racer named Martha Josey galloped over to Deng and handed him a white Stetson ten-gallon cowboy hat. Deng immediately donned the hat, smiling eagerly for the cameras. It produced the trip's indelible image and established for Deng a positive view among many Americans. A local television reporter announced on that evening's 10 o'clock news that "Deng Xiaoping not only went west, but went Western."[14] Deng added to the positive press when, after Martha's sister and fellow barrel racer fell from her horse, he sent his personal physician to check on her and confirm she was not injured.[15]

Today, that white Stetson hat has pride of place in the National Museum of China in downtown Beijing, next to Tiananmen Square. It is encased in glass in the center of the large exhibit hall devoted to the life of Deng Xiaoping.[16] Meanwhile, in a sign of things to come, despite his partial shunning of Deng, Governor Clements soon sought out Chinese deals for his own drilling company, SDCO, an effort in which he was unsuccessful. But shortly after Deng returned to China, Texas's Lieutenant Governor, Democrat William Hobby, journeyed to China, where he succeeded in striking a deal by which the Chinese began selling crude oil to Houston area refineries.[17] China's leaders no doubt realized that for all their idealistic grandstanding, Americans would ultimately put capital over principle.

Having received soda in Atlanta and sought oil in Houston, Deng next shopped for airplanes in Seattle. China's access to Soviet aircraft had ceased nearly two decades earlier with the breakdown in diplomatic relations, and the Chinese were eager to upgrade to state-of-the-art American models. Deng left the Boeing factory with a contract to purchase several 747 jumbo jets. Reviewing the situation after Deng departed the United States from Seattle, *New York Times* reporter Steven G. Roberts concluded that "China's vast size evokes" an "ambiguous response" from Americans. No longer a "yellow peril," Americans viewed the Chinese as "wise, hard-working, and amiable." Yet this admiration could be double-edged. Those who saw the Chinese as "clever" could also view them simultaneously as "deceitful." Though Americans desired improved relations, "the tradition of suspicion and ambivalence remains strong."[18] The stereotype of the inhumanly efficient and crafty Chinese dating back to the late nineteenth century remained embedded in the public consciousness.

American intelligence and military cooperation with the Chinese against the Soviets also increased significantly in 1979 and 1980. In the short term, this made obvious sense. But some questioned the long-term wisdom of providing the Chinese with military assistance and highly classified intelligence. Testifying before Congress in 1980, former US ambassador to the USSR Malcolm Toon opined that "it does not seem to me that far down the road, a China armed to the teeth, as she intends to be, with a fairly strong economy, probably is not going to be very benign in her attitude toward the United States, because they are against the sort of things we stand for."[19] International relations scholar Edward Luttwak made a similar argument in a 1978 article, asking "is it our true purpose to promote the rise of the People's Republic to superpower status?" In his view, the Soviets had already diverted all the military resources to counter China that they were ever going to, and therefore any further strengthening of China would not weaken the USSR's military posture vis-à-vis the United States. Looking well beyond the present moment, he asked "should we become the artificers of a great power which our grandchildren may have to contend with? Will they be grateful if we help to make China more powerful than it would be in the natural way of things? One thinks not."[20] But during a period of heightened fear of the Soviets, the short term was all that mattered. For instance, Chinese provided vital assistance to Afghan mujahideen, particularly the capable warlord Ahmed Shah Masood, whose base area in the Panshir Valley bordered Chinese territory and who received almost nothing from the United States on account of Pakistani suspicions of him. Ultimately, the United States would face blowback from its arming of "freedom fighters" in Afghanistan long before it would face a reckoning from aiding China's rise.

Deng opened China to market forces not to loosen the Party's grip on power, but to preserve it. The Cultural Revolution dealt a massive blow to its legitimacy and caused widespread disillusionment.[21] Just about everyone had been a victim, including the initial perpetrators. Now the Party would stake its legitimacy on improving the living standards of the people. Farmers would be able to sell some of their crops, grown on land they would essentially own. Villages could set up their own factories to produce consumer goods. In its initial stages, the focus would be internal. Deng did set up several Special Economic Zones (SEZs) to attract foreign capital and assemble products for export using inexpensive Chinese labor, but a strong focus on export-oriented growth would only come later. This meant that despite such massive changes in the world's most populous nation, strong Chinese economic growth and development would not make itself felt in the global economy for some time.

Having spent his adult life faithfully serving the Party he now led, Deng had no intention of letting its power loosen. Like Mao before him and Xi after, he talked of *zhi lu*, or "renewal."[22] Deng would use global capitalism to maintain Communist Party control.[23] A wealthier China would be a stronger China. But this would take time. Unlike Mao, Deng had patience. In embracing these reforms, Deng was far from being the path-breaking innovator his admirers in China and abroad tend to portray him as. While battling Mao's chosen successor Hua Guofeng in 1978, Deng and his supporters argued that Hua was merely a lesser Mao guided by the "Two Whatevers," meaning that Hua insisted on following whatever Mao said and whatever Mao did. But this was a willful misrepresentation. In fact, Hua began the pursuit of free-market reforms, such as the establishment of Special Economic Zones, that Deng usually receives sole credit for.[24]

Eventually, Americans took notice. In 1984, on the eve of President Ronald Reagan's visit to China, longtime China scholar Donald Zagoria published an article in *Foreign Affairs* entitled "China's Quiet Revolution." He described the far-reaching effects of the significant market reforms of the previous half-decade.[25] But Zagoria also stressed there was no indication of political liberalization accompanying market liberalization, with repression of free speech and political indoctrination still widespread. Zagoria's most important caveat was that these reforms might not survive the 79-year-old Deng were he to perish soon, since some Party elites remained skeptical of market reforms.[26] But while alive, Deng pushed forward in pursuing economic growth by any means necessary, guided by his aphorism that "it does not matter if it is a yellow cat or a black cat, as long as it catches mice."[27] In October 1984, Chinese leaders announced their nation now had "a planned commodity economy based on public ownership, in which the law of value must be consciously followed and applied," a roundabout way of announcing the gradual adoption of a capitalist approach to the laws of supply and demand.[28]

Ronald Reagan was the first president since Nixon's opening to harbor deep skepticism about rapprochement. When Nixon visited China in 1972, he dispatched the then-Governor of California to Taipei to reassure Taiwan's devastated leaders of America's commitment. In the early years of his presidency, Reagan maintained this sentimental attachment and attempted to strengthen formal ties and provide additional military aid to Taiwan, which rankled Beijing. Yet Reagan soon grudgingly accepted the existing policy approach and chose to preserve continuity in relations. It was still quite a surprise how well his visit to China went in 1984. No one expected Reagan not only to extol China's "free market spirit," but utter the phrase "so-called communist China."[29] James Mann would later write that this remark "epitomized the delusions and the China euphoria that swept America in the 1980s."[30] On its face, it recalls Professor George Taylor justifying opposition to person-to-person diplomacy with China by quoting G. K. Chesterton's quip that "nothing is so narrowing as travel."[31] Yet American conservatives had long placed free enterprise at the pinnacle of freedoms, and the antithesis of communism, meaning Reagan declaring China to no longer be an actual Communist nation because it had some significant element of market-based activity made complete sense.

American conservatives continued to cheer the Chinese on due to the possible effects of their economic success on the stagnating Soviets. Former Nixon speechwriter William Safire touted the Chinese Communist Party's "rejection of Marxism and embrace of capitalism," gloating that the Soviet leadership must view this development "with horror."[32] Ironically, Soviet and Chinese relations improved significantly in the early 1980s, with Deng reaching out to thaw the deep freeze that had set in two decades earlier. Though full diplomatic nations were not restored until 1989, between 1982 and 1985 any lingering mutual hostility vanished.[33] Much of the Soviet old guard who had risen to power during the Brezhnev era had an ingrained antipathy toward China. But Deng's outreach ensured that once Gorbachev rose to the top in 1985, he would marginalize the Soviet Union's China skeptics.[34] China was embarking on a multi-front charm offensive, which in addition to the United States and the USSR prominently included Japan, a major source of investment. Japan at this time pursued a strategy of "Friendship Diplomacy" with the Chinese.[35] The 1980s, in addition to being the peak of Japanese economic power, was the peak of Sino-Japanese relations. Deng was also savvy enough to play the "Soviet Card" to encourage a favorable economic relationship with the United States.[36] In addition to wowing Reagan on his visit, he could exploit the American president's fear of Soviet influence were the United States to treat China poorly.

By the middle of the 1980s, opinions about China began to reflect the early successes of the economic reforms and of China's newly improved international position. In his surprise 1987 bestseller *The Rise and Fall of the Great Powers*, Yale University historian Paul Kennedy, after predicting the eventual decline of both the Soviet Union and the United States, noted that China was undergoing "an economic expansion which, if it can be kept up, promises to transform the country within a few decades," concluding that "it is only a matter of time" before China became a great power in its own right.[37] Britain was the past, America the present, but China the future. Harvard University Economist Dwight Perkins predicted in 1985 that China would follow the trajectory of rapid growth previously blazed by Japan and South Korea, and claimed "few if any events in the last half of the twentieth century" were as important as the imminent rise of China.[38] Thus, within a half-decade, foreigners noted Deng's reforms and their potential to transform China in a manner that had been predicted for nearly a century. Finally, it seemed, China was on the path to live up to its immense economic potential.

The Chinese people's feelings toward the United States are not as bipolar as Americans' views of China have been, but they have always been decidedly mixed. The Chinese word for America is *Meiguo*, translated as "Beautiful Country." When Mao and other Communists denounced American imperialists, they referred to the US as *Meidi*, literally "Beautiful Imperialist."[39] Chinese intellectuals and political leaders have always admired the United States for its rapid economic development and resistance to European predation. What has long rankled the Chinese is American self-righteousness and the accompanying zeal to export its supposedly universal values. According to Deng, the United States was "waging a war without gunsmoke," seeking to corrupt Chinese society and turn its people away from the Party.[40] The British sought to exploit China through trade; the Japanese, to destroy through conquest; the Russians, to bully into subservience. But the United States was the ultimate subversive power.

Deng heartily embraced Zhou Enlai's proposals for "Four Modernizations" in the fields of agriculture, industry, defense, and science and technology. But after Deng assumed power, some Chinese argued these four could not be achieved without the "Fifth Modernization" of democracy. Deng courted these liberalizers in his battle to unseat Mao's chosen successor Hua Guofeng. Not recognizing this was a purely tactical maneuver on Deng's part, or perhaps not caring, in December 1978 a young electrician named Wei Jingsheng put up a pro-democracy poster entitled "The Fifth Modernization" on what in recent months had come to be called Beijing's "Democracy Wall."[41] Before Wei's contribution, the posters on this wall had criticized Deng's rivals, and he professed to at least tolerate this exercise in free expression. But after Wei's contribution, Deng blamed US influence. Upon returning from America, he swiftly crushed the movement, jailing Wei and the other major participants.[42] He then embarked on his first "Spiritual Pollution Campaign" to limit the influence of dangerous foreign ideas. Deng repeated this campaign in 1983 and again in 1987. Yet his targets always reemerged, bolder and more emboldened.[43] After a 1986 trip to China, Orville Schell—who had visited the country multiple times since 1980—noted the increased freedom of expression in print media, with even Party-sponsored newspapers allowing for a diversity of opinions.[44]

Part of the reason for this was that many of these US-influenced would-be liberalizers were ensconced within the Party itself. They patronized sympathetic Chinese intellectuals, giving succor to their hopes and creating an embryonic civil society. Their efforts were encouraged by none other than Deng's hand-picked successor Hu Yaobang.[45] Deng supported Hu because he spearheaded many of Deng's early market reforms. But his openness to political reform led to his purging in January 1987 and replacement with Zhao Ziyang, an economic liberalizer who did not share Hu's other beliefs.[46] Instead, Zhao allied himself with a clique known as the "New Authoritarians," who believed in following the path of autocracy and export-led growth taken by South Korea and Taiwan.[47] The problem was that by the late 1980s, both of these role models were transitioning to democracy—swiftly in South Korea's case, gradually in Taiwan's. It is important to remember that in the mid-1980s, Taiwan and mainland China appeared to be following parallel journeys of incipient political liberalization.[48] The movements against one-party rule interacted across the Taiwan Straits. However, Deng was in a much stronger position than Chiang Ching-kuo, the physically ailing son of Chiang Kai-shek who succeeded him as Taiwan's dictator. At the start of his rule, Deng outlined his "Four Basic Principles" of governance: socialism, dictatorship of the proletariat, Marxism-Leninism-Mao Zedong Thought, and party leadership. It was the fourth principle which was most concrete and important. There was only so much political pluralism Deng was willing to tolerate.

In numerous ways, the Tiananmen protests were the result of Deng's economic reforms, though not in the way traditional Western theories of democratization would imply. Based on the development of democracy in nineteenth-century Great Britain, the standard conception of democratization in modernizing societies begins with industrialization leading to the formation of a middle class which demands secure property rights, equality before the law, and some measure of political participation. In other words, the winners of economic development drive reform. But in China in 1989, the losers took to the streets in what, to paraphrase the nineteenth-century French intellectual Alexis de Tocqueville, was a "Revolution of Rising Expectations." In 1988, Zhao deepened economic liberalization through an acceleration of price reform, allowing market forces greater reign. He also sought to finally jump-start export-led industrialization.[49] The relaxation of price controls led to increased inflation, with demand for consumer goods outpacing supply. This was a recurrent problem in 1980s China, necessitating alternating cycles of liberalization and retrenchment. In addition, corruption had become endemic among Chinese officials, who saw price reform as a way to line their own pockets through hoarding and arbitrage selling, a development to which Deng turned a blind eye. These grievances were most pronounced in the burgeoning cities along China's coast, where reforms had by far the greatest impact. The April 1989 death of the deposed Hu Yaobang provided the spark for student demonstrations in Beijing. His public funeral evolved into large protests, and on April 27, 150,000 demonstrators overpowered the police and occupied Tiananmen Square.[50] Confusion among Deng's lieutenants about how to respond combined with Mikhail Gorbachev's May visit to Beijing to delay the government's response. Deng knew better than to initiate a violent crackdown while the reformist Soviet leader—who expressed his sympathy for the protesters—was in town to finally re-normalize Sino-Soviet relations (Figure 7).

Gorbachev's departure cleared the way for decisive action, provided China's leaders could come to a decision. Both Deng and Zhao sought above all else to prevent a reappearance of the chaos of the Cultural Revolution. To Deng, that meant cracking down on the protesters. To Zhao, it meant avoiding violence and listening to dissent and outside criticism so as to prevent the formation of an unthinking Mao-esque Cult of Personality. Deng's second-in-command belatedly accepted the deceased Hu's views on political reform because he decided this was the only way to ensure continued economic growth.[51] Deng removed Zhao from power, embracing those such as Li Peng

FIGURE 7 *Erected in May 1989 by demonstrators in Tiananmen Square, the "Goddess of Democracy" was a stark illustration of Deng Xiaoping's fears that the foreign ideas which had entered China over the previous decade could threaten Communist Party rule. Photo by Pat Benic, May 30, 1989, Reuters.*

who advocated a violent crackdown. Deng believed students, along with the disenchanted workers who supported them, had fallen prey to foreign ideas, threatening everything the Party stood for. Deng saw violence perpetrated by his soldiers in nationalist terms. In the days after the June 4 killings in and around Tiananmen Square that ended the occupation, he confided to Li Peng "for more than a century we were forced to feel inferior, but then, under the leadership of the Communist Party, we stood up. No behemoth out there can scare us now," adding that "our people are not going to cower before foreign invasions or threats, and neither will our children or grandchildren."[52] To Deng, it was a straightforward matter of national sovereignty. China would stand up to both foreigners and the Chinese who were in thrall to foreign ideas.

The killings in Beijing shocked the American public and had an immediate effect on how they viewed China and the Chinese government. NBC news anchor Tom Brokaw observed that no story since the Space Shuttle Challenger explosion in 1986 "so penetrated the American consciousness." In March 1989 nearly three-quarters of Americans polled expressed a favorable opinion of China. After Tiananmen, more than three-quarters reported an unfavorable opinion.[53] In China, the Tiananmen crackdown dashed hopes of greater freedoms. In the United States, such pessimism swiftly abated for reasons unrelated to events in China. It is tempting to regard the Tiananmen killings as a crucial turning point in foreign hopes for Chinese democratization. This has become the scholarly consensus, with later authoritative works referring to it as "a turning point in Western perceptions of China" and an end to US hope of "gradual, step-by-step liberalization of the PRC."[54] Yet the record of journalistic, academic, and political utterances in the 1990s thoroughly contradicts such conclusions. This was because, a few months after Tiananmen, the Communist governments of Poland, Hungary, East Germany, Czechoslovakia, Romania, and Bulgaria collapsed when their Communist rulers largely declined to suppress popular protests, while Soviet military forces based in these countries refused to become involved.

Two years later, the Soviet Union itself would cease to exist. The former Soviet satellite nations in the Warsaw Pact quickly evolved into free-market democracies, as would some of the former Soviet republics. Combined with the recent demise of dictatorships in South Korea, the Philippines, and Taiwan, along with the ongoing transformation of military dictatorships in Latin America into parliamentary democracies, it soon became apparent that there was an unprecedented wave of democratization washing over large swathes of the globe in places with little or no prior experience with democratic institutions. All too aware that the European events of 1989 had caught almost all outside observers by surprise, no one could predict which nations would be swept up next. For once in international affairs, optimism did not seem foolish. American scholar Francis Fukuyama caught the zeitgeist with his 1992 book

The End of History and the Last Man, arguing in Hegelian fashion that political development had reached its logical endpoint in free-market democracy, with all other options (monarchism, fascism, communism) vanquished forever. Such deterministic models became endemic as the 1990s progressed, with endless invocations that intelligent individuals should be "on the right side of history." Progress was now a juggernaut destined to crush all foolish enough to stand in its way. Surely, China could not be exempt. In fact, in his book, Fukuyama predicted that China would become a democracy.[55]

Even before the events in Eastern Europe, many observers saw the actions of the People's Liberation Army on June 4, 1989, as a sign of the regime's fragility. In 1990, former US ambassador to China Winston Lord told Congress that within three years "there will be a more moderate, humane government in Beijing." He expanded on this argument in a *Foreign Affairs* article, declaring that "the current discredited regime is clearly a transitional one."[56] Lord served as the translator for Kissinger's and Nixon's famous initial meetings with Zhou and Mao. As the US ambassador to China during the late 1980s, he met with reformers and democracy activists, drawing the suspicions of his Chinese hosts. This combination of expertise and advocacy was not unique in this period. Columbia University professor Andrew Nathan followed a similar path and reached similar conclusions. His 1990 book *China's Crisis* concluded that "from now on, it is doubtful that an undemocratic China can be stable and strong."[57] Once having promoted economic growth, it became the expert consensus that at some imminent point the Party would begin impeding it. Rather than protecting his legacy of growth with stability, Nathan argued that "Deng participated in the coup against his own reforms."[58]

American observers did not have a monopoly on such predictions. In the early 1990s, Japan's Foreign Minister Taro Nakayama declared that "the wave of historic changes cascading over Eastern Europe will also sweep the Asia-Pacific region, especially Communist North Korea and China," while Taiwan's Vice-Minister for Foreign Affairs Chang Shallyen offered that "this kind of situation cannot last any longer than two or three years—there will be fundamental change."[59] The last quote captured the mood of China observers during the 1990s, even after China's course defied predicted timelines. The policy goal of the US and its allies therefore became encouraging China to follow economic liberalization with political reforms that would allow for greater free speech and political participation. All assumed that a democratic China would be a friendly China. Democracy was the Saint George's Lance that would slay the dragon. In one of the first major post-Cold War books seeking to incite alarm over the rising power of China, Richard Bernstein and Ross Munro claimed that "the single most important change" which could eliminate the prospect for a future rivalry with the United States "would be for China to follow the global trend toward democracy."[60] Post-Tiananmen, the question became what was the best method of nudging China along this path—punishments, or rewards? In general, the Legislative Branch advocated the former and the Executive Branch the latter.

Within China, the aftermath of Tiananmen led to the elevation to greater power first of Li Peng and then of Jiang Zemin. Li had earned Deng's trust with his effusive support of a crackdown on demonstrators, but he lacked Deng's enthusiasm for continued market reforms. Jiang attracted Deng's attention by proactively cracking down on students in Shanghai in May 1989, proving he was no Hu Yaobang or Zhao Ziyang. At the same time, he thoroughly embraced accelerated market reforms. At the fourteenth Party Congress in October 1992, Deng announced his formal retirement, with Jiang appointed as his successor.[61] This meeting confirmed the succession policy Deng had announced in 1982. Going forward, Chinese leaders would serve two five-year terms, ensuring rotation in office and a more collegial policymaking structure. Earlier that year, Deng set a path for the future with his Southern Tour to encourage the adoption of export-led growth and establish additional SEZs to fulfill that goal. Officially dubbed the *nanxun* or "Special Inspection Tour" in emulation of similar visits to distant provinces by the early Qing emperors, during the month-long excursion Deng visited existing SEZs in the cities of Shenzhen and Zhuhai, in the far southern province of Guangdong near Hong Kong, along with a stop in Shanghai.[62]

Chinese Communists would avoid the Soviet Union's fate by establishing a new Chinese social contract: increased economic prosperity in exchange for political quiescence. Deng also believed a major cause of Soviet decline was its insistence on competing with the US militarily. China would not assume an unsustainable burden of defense spending.[63] Its military would modernize, but only within China's financial means. The success of the US military's high-technology weapons in the 1991 Gulf War against Iraq drove home to the Chinese how backward the People's Liberation Army currently was. China thus had no choice but to adopt a benevolent posture for the next generation as it strove to modernize its military. Deng articulated this strategy as *tai guang yang hui*, roughly translated as "hide our capacities/capabilities/strength and bide our time."[64] The full statement was the following: "observe developments soberly, maintain our position, meet challenges calmly, hide our capacities and bide our time, remain free of ambition, never claim leadership."[65] Though intended as a temporary tactic, the policy would remain in effect long enough to lull foreign governments into believing it could become a permanent strategy.

But some wondered how long China could remain on its upward path of growth. In late 1992, shortly after Bill Clinton won the presidency while promising a harsher and more coercive approach to China, that bellwether of elite Anglo-American conventional wisdom the *Economist* ran a cover story entitled "The Titan Stirs." In a series of articles, the magazine outlined the numerous changes which had occurred since Deng assumed power in December 1978, predicting that if China's present rate of economic growth continued, its economy would be larger than that of the United States by the 2010s.[66] Its booming economy "looks less socialist all the time."[67] But clouds were on the horizon. China's reforms were intentionally incomplete, perhaps dooming them to eventual failure. Its economy was subject to recurrent economic bubbles. Its banking sector was saddled with billions in nonperforming loans, particularly those incurred by unprofitable state-owned enterprises (SOEs).[68] Ultimately, it was the "ticking time bomb called the Communist Party of China" that was the erstwhile Middle Kingdom's Achilles Heel.[69] To succeed, "the Chinese Communist Party has to stop being Communist," and follow the path of Taiwan to political liberalization, since "sooner or later China is going to have to choose between political communism and economic growth."[70] Such beliefs strongly influenced how the world approached China over the next decade and to some extent beyond.

10

China's Peaceful Rise

1993–2008

Over the past four decades, China's economic growth has been explosive, defying all pessimists and frequently shocking informed observers. But rarely, if ever, has a nation's economy quadrupled in size in a single day. But this occurred with China in May 1993—at least on paper. A joint report by the World Bank and the International Monetary Fund decided to recalculate gross domestic product (GDP) using purchasing power parity (PPP). This measurement of a nation's output took into consideration the lower cost of goods in developing countries in an attempt to more accurately reflect living standards. China's recalculated GDP increased from slightly over $400 billion to nearly $1.7 trillion. That catapulted China from ranking as the world's tenth-largest economy to becoming the third largest, behind only Japan and the United States.[1] The nations China leapfrogged included Spain, Canada, Britain, Italy, France, and Germany. The report estimated that China would overtake both Japan and the United States in the early twenty-first century. In the words of Massachusetts Institute of Technology professor of economics Paul Krugman, this was "a reminder that China is a great power already, which is something many people haven't quite grasped yet."[2]

Later measurements, mixing PPP with valuations based on exchange rates, would place China in fourth, behind Germany, until the mid-2000s. Today, competing calculations all show the size of China's economy to be comparable to that of the United States, though the consensus is China will not be declared the world's largest economy until the late 2020s. Whichever way one tweaked the numbers, China was now an undisputed economic power, in the top tier of global economies. Nowhere was this greeted with more surprise than in China, where it "generated both elation and shock."[3] It marked the beginning of a new era in Chinese economic development and in the overall global economy. To quote *Newsweek*, "in America, 1993 has become the Year of China."[4] That year witnessed a surge of corporate interest in both selling imported products to China and building factories in China to produce exports for the American market. Before 1993, the US government paid little attention to US business interests when crafting China policy because those businesses expressed little interest in the topic. Now, corporate lobbyists swung into action, competing with those who cared about human rights or security matters.

Over the next fifteen years, China became the world's largest manufacturer, the early twenty-first century's factory floor. Consumer goods in the United States became less expensive, while low-end manufacturing jobs relocated overseas at an accelerating rate. In 1993, the big political debate regarding trade was whether or not Congress should approve the North American Free Trade Agreement (NAFTA), which former third-party presidential candidate H. Ross Perot warned would create "a giant sucking sound" as US factory jobs moved to Mexico. After China joined the World Trade Organization in 2000, many of those jobs left Mexico for China. The Chinese government would use some of its immense trade surpluses to become the world's largest foreign holder of US treasury bonds, sparking worries about China weaponizing this leverage to damage US government finances. By 2008, the two economies were hopelessly intertwined, creating what economic historian Niall Ferguson dubbed "Chimerica."

The period between 1993 and 2008 witnessed China's emergence as a true global power. Many called this a "reemergence," but even at the height of the Han, Tang, or Qing Empires, China's impact was regional. Truly global powers did not exist before the rise of regular ocean-crossing voyages in 1500. But China was the first non-Western nation to lay claim to the title.[5] The capital question of the era was what kind of global power China would become. Americans in particular held onto hopes for a future democratic China far longer than those who once subscribed to this hope now choose to admit. In its own region, Chinese wealth was welcomed, while Chinese power was feared. Leaders of countries scattered across the rest of the world shared this mix of feelings to varying degrees depending on the specific manners in which an assertive China impacted them. While 1993 could be considered the moment of "take-off," 2005 was, to extend the metaphor, when the Chinese economy reached orbit. Chinese leaders attempted to allay the fear of their nation's burgeoning power by adopting the slogan of a "Peaceful Rise," promising to follow Deng's admonition to not make waves even after it had become a mature power. It was during these fifteen years that China began to change the world more than the world changed China.

It is impossible to overstate the swiftness of this shift in the global economy. In 1993, China had just surpassed the previous apex of its share of world trade—achieved in 1928, when it stood at 2.3 percent.[6] Major metropolises like Shanghai became global hubs, with a skyline to rival New York or Tokyo. The size of less glamorous inland cities like Wuhan, Xian, and Chungking exploded as well, with populations in all three soon exceeding those of any American city. After a century of waiting, China was finally realizing its true potential. It would take time for this to spark fear abroad. The United States never felt mightier than it did in the 1990s when it was the only global power that truly mattered. It may have been "the moment of rejuvenation for history's most populous nation," but it was also "the moment of triumph for history's most powerful democracy."[7] Having graduated from superpower to "hyperpower," during these fifteen years it was the United States above all other nations that the world admired, feared, and resented.

It should also be recalled that after fearing in the 1970s that it had fallen militarily behind the Soviets, the American media and political class spent the 1980s resenting the seemingly inexorable rise of the Japanese economy. *Newsweek* argued in 1993 that the new focus on China "may be the best thing that could happen to the stormy marriage between Japan and the United States."[8] Though it took several years, by then Americans had realized how set back the Japanese economy had been by the bursting of its real estate bubble in 1990. Without the stagnation of Japan, it would have taken longer for the "China Threat" narrative to emerge.[9] Once it did, it became apparent that only China could ever challenge US global primacy. Future *New York Times* columnist Nicholas Kristof wrote in a 1993 *Foreign Affairs* article entitled "The Rise of China" that this "may be the most important trend in the world for the next century." For now, it was solely a matter of economics, but soon China would lay claim to islands in the South China Sea and threaten Taiwan. Fueling this threat would be "the sense of wounded pride" turn-of-the-twenty-first-century shared with turn-of-the-twentieth-century Germany.[10] In a 1993 cover story entitled "The Coming Power Struggle," *Newsweek* predicted that "China will become a giant version of South Korea or Taiwan," and soon "convert its wealth into political muscle." The only hope for avoiding conflict would be if China democratized as it grew wealthier.[11]

During his presidency, Bill Clinton's approach to China changed more than that of any other US president since Harry Truman. Entering the White House pledging to get tough and protect human rights, he left eight years later a champion of friendly engagement. Like many US presidents before and after, Clinton ultimately embraced concrete interests over abstract values. At his confirmation hearings, Clinton's first Secretary of State Warren Christopher bluntly told the Senate that "our policy will seek to facilitate a peaceful evolution of China from communism to democracy by encouraging the forces of economic and political liberalization," essentially declaring a policy of non-violent regime change toward the world's most populous nation.[12] In May of that year, Clinton met with forty Chinese dissidents, including representatives of the Dalai Lama and leaders of the Tiananmen protests—a provocation worthy of Ronald Reagan's condemnations of the Soviet Union as an "Evil Empire" in the early 1980s.[13]

China's leaders did not take kindly to this. Clinton's first in-person discussions with Jiang Zemin on November 19, 1993, were "somber and stiff."[14] But this posture would not last long. By the end of that year, *Time* could declare that "like Presidents before him, Clinton has learned that China is just too big to bully and too important to ignore."[15] Pushing the new president to this realization were major US-based corporations, whose desires for increased access to Chinese markets were relayed to the president by Clinton's economic adviser Robert Rubin, an investment banker who would soon become Clinton's Treasury Secretary. In addition, Anthony Lake and Samuel Berger at the National Security Council soon gained ascendancy over Secretary of State Christopher and convinced Clinton that the United States needed Chinese cooperation on important issues such as the North Korean nuclear program.[16]

But there would be substantial bumps ahead. The most formidable turned out to be Taiwan. In the spring of 1995, Bill Clinton allowed its democratically elected Premier Lien Chan to travel to the United States to attend his college reunion at Cornell University in Ithaca, New York. This was the first time such high-level travel from Taiwan to the United States had occurred since the normalization of US-PRC relations in 1979. Furthermore, the premier was the leader of the Democratic Progressive Party, which drew its support from native Taiwan residents who felt little if any connection to the Mainland (unlike the exile-dominated Guomindong membership). The DPP made little effort to conceal its desire for outright independence. Henry Kissinger, who after the Tiananmen massacre became a leading advocate of conciliating Communist China, warned that "Chinese leaders fear that America, afraid of growing Chinese economic power, is embracing a two-China policy as part of a strategy designed to contain China."[17]

China would not allow such a provocation to go unanswered. In what became known as the Third Straits Crisis, in 1995 and 1996 China fired numerous missiles across the Taiwan Strait in the direction of the island, demonstrating that attempts to defy Beijing would entail a significant cost. President Clinton dispatched aircraft carriers to the Straits in an American show of counterforce. The crisis died down only after causing considerable worries in both the United States and Taiwan. In 1996, the Clinton administration sought to reassure the Chinese by agreeing to what came to be known as the "Three Noes"—no US support for Taiwan's independence, no US support for a "Two Chinas" policy, and no US support for Taiwanese membership in the United Nations.[18] From this crisis, Clinton drew the lesson that he needed to adopt a less confrontational posture toward China.[19]

For the Chinese, the lesson was they needed to continue biding their time and strengthening their military until it could deter future American saber-rattling. Many younger Chinese began to chafe at America's swagger, and its government's willingness to tolerate this. Shortly after the crisis ended, a book came out in China entitled *China Can Say No.* It was written in three weeks by five young men without elite connections and published without overt government approval. The polemic quickly sold over one million copies and earned the praise of government officials, including Jiang Zemin. The book advocated a more independent and forceful strategic posture to counter an American bent on denying China its rightful status as a great power while interfering in China's internal affairs through human rights complaints.[20] The authors followed up their success with *China Can Still Say No* and *How China Can Say No.* These works appealed to what came to be called China's "angry youth."[21] In the coming decades, such grassroots nationalism would blossom with tacit government approval, fanned first by newspapers and then by the internet, creating an incentive for belligerent posturing by China's leaders and diplomats, lest they appear weak to their people and cost the Party prestige and legitimacy.

Shortly after securing reelection in November 1996, Clinton told an audience in Australia that "the emergence of a stable, an open, a prosperous China, a strong China confident of its place and willing to assume its responsibilities as a great nation is in our deepest interest."[22] This was the peak period of belief in the "Washington Consensus" of free trade, limited economic regulations, and global interdependence, where a rising tide would surely lift all boats in the United States and beyond. In the first Sino-American summits since the Tiananmen protests, Jiang Zemin visited Washington in October 1997 and Clinton traveled to Beijing in June 1998.[23] During a joint press conference in Washington, Clinton interrupted Jiang as the Chinese leader answered a question about theTiananmen killings and ongoing political repression in China. The US president told Jiang that when it came to human rights, China was "on the wrong side of history."[24] That Jiang refused to let such a public slight affect the bilateral relationship is a testament to China's position of relative weakness at that time, just as Clinton's utterance was a representation of American arrogance.

Jiang sought to use Clinton's return visit to highlight China's emergence as a major power, while Clinton intended to reach beyond the Chinese leadership to communicate directly with the Chinese people.[25] Jiang allowed Clinton to give a televised address at Peking University, which the US media recognized as "a testament to the Chinese government's trust in President Clinton."[26] Clinton repaid Jiang's trust by not acting as impertinent as he had in Washington. Playing the respectful guest, he gently suggested that in the upcoming century, "if you are so afraid of personal freedom" that "you limit people's freedom too much, then you pay." Clinton knew the Chinese government and the Chinese people valued stability. But, in his estimation, "stability in the 21st century will require high levels of freedom."[27] It was both classic Clintonian optimism and a reflection of the conventional wisdom of the period. In Maoist parlance, American elites believed the wind blowing from the West would remain forever strong.

The policy fruit of this approach was the approval by the US Congress in May 2000 of China's admission to the World Trade Organization. Clearing the Senate by an overwhelming margin, the vote in the House of Representatives was 237-197 in favor. Despite Clinton's heavy lobbying, the partisan breakdown was 73-138 for the Democrats, and 164-57 for the Republicans.[28] As with NAFTA at the start of his administration, Clinton had to rely on Republican votes since Democrats feared the negative effects of such free trade agreements on the dwindling number of unionized industrial jobs in the United States. Admission to the WTO changed the US-China relationship more than anything had since Carter's full normalization of relations. There was now no slowing of China's rise to becoming the world's leading exporter. In a laudatory *New York Times* story, the putative paper of record declared that "Bill Clinton has finally defined his imprint on American foreign policy, the president who cemented in place the post-cold-war experiment of using economic engagement to foster political change among America's neighbors and its adversaries."[29] The article credited Clinton for selling "a long-term vision of how America could use its economic power to change, and perhaps undermine, the nature of one-party rule in China," and claimed opponents of the bill had failed to offer an alternative strategy for how to "open up" China's "political system."[30] Like many Americans at the time, Clinton believed that in addition to trade, technology would encourage freedom, telling reporters that "Liberty will spread by cell phone and cable modem," adding that "we know how much the internet has changed America, and we are already an open society. Imagine how much it could change China."[31]

Yet this vote presented a misleadingly rosy view of the state of Sino-American relations at the turn of the millennium. It reflected a consensus that was beginning to unravel due to fears of how engagement with China might be corrupting American domestic politics and endanger national security. In certain ways, this was a reemergence of suspicions that were barely concealed even in the best of times. One of China's primary grievances with the US that decade was a symbolic 1993 Congressional resolution opposing China being awarded the 2000 Summer Olympics.[32] The United States Olympic Committee lobbied hard for Australia's competing bid on the grounds that China's human rights record was disqualifying, an argument which carried weight only four years after the Tiananmen massacre. The Chinese public saw this as a national humiliation, particularly since its neighbors South Korea and Japan had already hosted the Summer Games.[33]

Shortly after Clinton's reelection, Congress mandated the Pentagon produce annual reports assessing the state of Chinese military power.[34] By the time of the November 2000 presidential election, polls showed 57 percent of Americans holding unfavorable views of China, with 77 percent labeling China an adversary or rival.[35] The first sign of this was the 1997 campaign finance scandal where Republicans accused the Clinton campaign of accepting illegal foreign donations from Chinese sources. Heavily hyped by a media prone to distrust Clinton's ethical scruples, that summer's Republican-led congressional hearings proved to be a dud due to a lack of solid evidence. But along the way, Republicans combined their usual contempt for Clinton with casual bigotry toward Chinese, as evidenced by the *National Review's* cover depiction of the Clintons as buck-toothed Chinese caricatures. This demonstrated how little provocation was needed for the old sentiments to resurface (Figure 8).

Fears of Chinese espionage surged during Clinton's second term, particularly alleged thefts of US nuclear weapons secrets. A credulous press accepted dubious allegations as fact, fueling the sense of panic. Igniting these fears was the January 1999 Cox Committee report.[36] Long on accusations and short on evidence, this congressional investigative report claimed recent Chinese advances in nuclear weaponry and ballistic missiles were largely the result of stolen US secrets. That the report's primary accusation concerned the alleged acquisition of classified information on how to build a neutron bomb, the most useless White Elephant of Cold War-era nuclear technology, should have indicated the flimsiness of the accusations. But the media was in no mood for such disinterested logic. In a front-page article in May, the *New York Times* declared "almost everyone in the Government agrees that Chinese spies stole nuclear secrets from American weapons laboratories." Accepting conventional wisdom as fact, the *Times* legitimized the hunt for the sources of "China's ill-gotten nuclear knowledge."[37] Those with a historical perspective could not help but notice the parallels with US fears of Soviet infiltration during the first decade of the Cold War.

A *Time* magazine cover story from June 1999, entitled "Birth of a Superpower," alerted its readers to the existence of "Chinese spies" who were "eagerly vacuuming the U.S. for military secrets."[38] This hunt for Chinese nuclear spies culminated in the arrest and detention of Chinese-American scientist Wen Ho Lee. The FBI held him in solitary confinement with the lights in his cell permanently turned on for over two months before the case unraveled and the government was severely admonished for its conduct by the presiding federal judge. The press had labeled Wen Ho Lee the Chinese Rosenberg, but to Chinese-Americans, he became the Chinese Dreyfus.[39] Combined with the campaign finance scandal, this pall of suspicion galvanized

FIGURE 8 *Cover,* National Review, *March 24, 1997. The conservative flagship magazine depicted the Clintons as stereotypically Chinese "coolies" to illustrate accusations of illegal foreign campaign contributions. It reflected increased fears of Chinese infiltration prevalent in Washington during the late 1990s.*

political participation in the community. In a postmortem, the *Nation* magazine worried press coverage "reflect and fuel suspicions against all Chinese in America."[40] This trend would quickly dissipate in the new century, though by no means because American elites realized the dangers of such national security panics. For its part, the *New York Times,* which help to fuel the focus on Wen Ho Lee, largely defended its coverage even after its reporters' assertions had been thoroughly debunked, only conceding that the paper wished it had given Lee "the full benefit of the doubt" rather than having declared him guilty at the outset.[41]

China's brief reemergence as a national security villain curiously coincided with the height of American expectations of Chinese democratization. While trying to diffuse tensions in the Taiwan Straits in March 1996, Clinton's National Security Advisor Anthony Lake had the temerity to tell a Chinese official "we're going to talk about human rights because that's who we are, but frankly I don't have to convince you of democracy because history will take care of that."[42]

The theory explaining how this would occur was well-established by 1998. In an essay published the day Clinton landed in Beijing, prominent pundit Robert Kaplan outlined the arguments behind such expectations. The Chinese economy was now largely capitalist in structure, and economic development had created a sizeable middle class. It seemed preordained that "calls for political freedom to match the economic openness will undoubtedly multiply." That none of this had yet come to pass was beside the point. The goal was to expand the all-important middle class. All else would naturally follow.[43]

As one reporter put it in 1993, "it is axiomatic that successful democracy requires a society dominated by an educated middle class."[44] Explaining early in his presidential candidacy why he supported admitting China into the WTO, George W. Bush said "economic freedom creates liberty. And habits of liberty create expectations of democracy," meaning that "trade freely with China, and time is on our side."[45] At a news conference during his 1998 visit to China, Clinton recounted visiting a village that elected its own officials and meeting with "small-business people and others who are agents of change in the modern China."[46] The use of electoral mechanisms to choose village party leaders had been instituted earlier in the decade and was much trumpeted as a crucial first step on the road to political liberalization. Noted China scholar Minxin Pei saw these votes as evidence of "creeping democratization."[47] He predicted these initial reforms would be followed by an increasingly substantive role for the largely symbolic National People's Congress, with possible future elections of some of its thousands of members, and devolution of power to the provinces as part of an emerging "nascent federalist structure."[48] Another scholar approvingly cited political scientist Seymour Martin Lipset's maxim "the richer the country, the freer," concluding that "a richer China will become more democratic."[49]

Even after such certainty faded in the first decade of the next century, the hopes for a democratic China took a while to disappear. In his 2005 speech calling on China to be a "responsible stakeholder," Deputy Secretary of State Robert Zoellick began a sentence about China's future with the phrase "while not yet democratic."[50] A lot of this continued hope had to do with well-meaning desires on the part of those who knew the Chinese well and wished the best for them, including the blessings of liberty. Historian Odd Arne Westad concluded his authoritative 2003 monograph on the Chinese Civil War by opining that "sooner or later the CCP dictatorship in the People's Republic of China will have to give way to a more pluralist form of government," as had happened on Taiwan.[51]

President Bush carried on the existing policy of engaging China while containing any possible Chinese expansionist urges, what University of Pennsylvania political scientist Avery Goldstein termed the policy of "congagement," a combination of containment and engagement.[52] Many of

Bush's more hawkish foreign policy advisers entered the White House focused on the rising power of China and were determined to take a confrontational approach. Yet any desire to get tough on China disappeared after the terrorist attacks of September 11, 2001, on the World Trade Center in New York City and the Pentagon in Washington, D.C. that killed nearly 3,000 Americans. Focused first on the military response to Osama bin Laden and the Taliban in Afghanistan, and then fixated on the large-scale war he began in Iraq, Bush actually enjoyed warmer relations with China's leaders than Clinton had, since he largely left them alone. Bush's "Freedom Agenda" rarely if ever mentioned China as a target for democratization, and he refrained from singling out its dictatorship for human rights criticism.

China used the decade of US embroilment in wars in the Islamic world to quietly emerge as a second superpower. This trend became apparent by the middle of the decade, but the United States was far too distracted by the Iraq War to attempt to do much about it. Fareed Zakaria wrote in 2005 that "China's rise is no longer a prediction. It is a fact."[53] Michael O'Hanlon, a military analyst at the Brookings Institution who had risen to prominence as an advocate for a long-term counterinsurgency strategy in Iraq, wrote that "during 2005, the world took notice of China like never before."[54] Reinforcing a hands-off approach were the apparent benefits of China's economic rise. Prices for consumer goods, particularly clothing and electronics, decreased in the United States, thanks in part to cheap Chinese labor.[55] The Chinese government became the largest foreign buyer of the US government debt issued by the trillions to fund America's wars. Niall Ferguson and Moritz Schularick coined the term "Chimerica" in 2007 to explain the asset price boom in the United States over the previous half-decade. The two economies had become symbiotic. Despite its apparent double meaning, they concluded that "it is still early to dismiss Chimerica as a chimera."[56] The following year's financial panic would prove that the asset price boom Chinese investment fueled was in fact a speculative bubble.

These changes were indeed swift. China only became a financial creditor nation in 2003, but by 2007 accrued a positive current account balance of $1 trillion.[57] The United States' switch from a manufacturing to a financial center in the 1980s had made it the world's leading debtor nation and destination for foreign investment. In the 1980s, it was where Japanese corporations looked for acquisitions. By the 2000s, the Japanese had been replaced by the Chinese. The non-convertibility of China's Renminbi currency both depressed Chinese consumer demand and encouraged the investment of export earnings abroad, with the United States by far the preferred destination. This provided a significant net benefit to the American economy in terms of increased asset values and decreased interest rates.[58] The 2000s continued and if fact accentuated the belief in the positive-sum nature of the Sino-

American economic relationship. In addition, American corporations not only made products in China. They were increasingly selling goods there as well. After more than a century of unrequited hope, the fabled China market was finally no longer a mirage.

Meanwhile, the Sino-American security relationship deepened, with increased military contacts and a significant lessening of tensions along China's maritime border, at least from the American perspective. China's relations with its neighbors followed a more inconsistent trajectory. Sino-Japanese relations increasingly soured, though for reasons peculiar to that bilateral relationship. In the 1990s, Chinese education pushed a "victimization" narrative highlighting Japanese atrocities in China during the Second World War, which in China is known as the Anti-Japanese War.[59] While in power, Mao Zedong had largely avoided focusing on that war because it would have meant acknowledging that the Guomindang under the leadership of arch-enemy Chiang Kai-shek did the vast majority of the fighting. Instead, Mao promulgated a "victor narrative" centered around the Communist triumph over Chiang and the Guomindang in the civil war which followed the evacuation of Japanese forces.

Deng's post-Tiananmen "Patriotic Campaign" heightened anti-Japanese sentiment just at the moment Japan's domestic politics turned decisively in a nationalist direction. As the Chinese felt more aggrieved, Japanese politicians became far less willing to apologize for their country's past actions.[60] In the 1990s, Japan was China's largest source of foreign capital as part of a relationship defined by the themes of reciprocity and mutual benefit.[61] At the same time, Japan's leaders became increasingly cognizant of the fact that China's rising power would soon permanently shift the regional economic center of gravity from Japan to China.[62] University of Miami, Florida political scientist June Teufel Dreyer aptly described this period of relations between the neighbors as "hot economics, cold politics."[63] Still, a Japanese government survey in 2006 found that nearly 80 percent of Japanese desired improved relations with China.[64] But public opinion in both nations would nosedive over the next decade.

In India, Asia's other giant, the 2000s were both a time of strong aggregate economic growth and a moment when the world's most populous democracy realized how far behind China it had fallen, perhaps permanently. The 1962 Sino-Indian War demonstrated China's military superiority. But now China was also an economic power in ways India might never become. India's security focus shifted decisively from Pakistan, now regarded as an inferior nuisance more than a true rival, onto China, seen as India's only worthy adversary. But this was a one-sided rivalry, since the Chinese barely acknowledged India, and did not deign to consider it any sort of peer competitor. In fact, Chinese leaders were at a loss as to why Indians would ever feel threatened by China.[65] This new focus encouraged the Indian military to strengthen its relationship with the US military and its intelligence agencies, a development warmly welcomed by American presidents from both parties.

Australia's relationship with China became by far the most bifurcated in the region. Attraction and repulsion coexisted to an even higher degree than in Japan. On the positive side, the Australian economy enjoyed three recession-free decades of continuous economic growth between 1990 and 2020, carried along by the Chinese economy's insatiable demand for Australian raw materials. If China was the world's factory floor, then Australia was China's mine. Australia could no longer prosper without the Chinese market. Yet, as always, Australians feared a strong China's effects on their nation's society. But it would take a decade for these fears to become politically salient. In the meantime, the center-left Labor Party came down on the side of economic engagement, while the center-right Liberal Party banged the drums about a potential security threat. After serving as prime minister from 1990 until 1996, Labor member Paul Keating entered into a business relationship with China, which both made him extremely wealthy and led him to believe China was the key to Australia's future success.[66] Any government which antagonized China would surely cause Australia to be left behind in what was soon being termed the "Asian Century" or the "Pacific Century." In 2007, Keating's Liberal Party successor John Howard, who had been prime minister for eleven years, was trounced by Kevin Rudd. His Labor Party government would follow Keating's strategy of further deepening Australia's ties to China.

The one regional power Chinese relations truly improved with during this period was Russia. This continued the trend that began in the 1980s. After the collapse of the Soviet Union, Russia supplied the Chinese with advanced military technology, particularly jet engines for its fighter planes. The ascension to the presidency of Vladimir Putin in 2000 also created an alliance of autocratic giants to counter a United States seemingly hell-bent on fostering democratic revolutions along both nations' peripheries. Fears of Chinese encroachment in the Far East did resurface, though not in official Russian circles. With over 100 million Chinese in Manchuria but only 10 million Russians in its far eastern regions, there was occasional talk in the Russian press of China "moving to the north" to seize Russia's natural resources.[67] Surveys of Siberian Russians revealed the salience of such fears in the region, and that a small number of recent Chinese migrants could "trigger powerful latent hostilities."[68] But the Chinese threat paled in comparison to that of the American hegemon, against which only the Chinese could successfully provide significant assistance. Further west, America's allies in Europe developed a substantial economic relationship with the Chinese. In 2004, the European Union passed Japan to become China's largest trading partner. China was now the EU's second-largest export market, surpassed only by the United States.[69] The *gelbe gefahr* was now a distant memory, at least for the time being. When it came to China in the twenty-first century, for Europeans opportunity replaced peril.

At the same time, this was the decade when China returned in a decisive way to Africa, becoming the continent's leading trading partner by 2007.[70] It was a relationship borne of necessity. In 2006, China imported nearly a third of its oil from Africa.[71] China's last significant involvement in Africa was in the 1960s. But as China's zeal to export revolution dissipated, its presence on the continent receded. It now returned in a quite different capacity, not just as a trading partner, but as a purveyor of loans for infrastructure development and an employer of Africans in mines and factories. This activity soon sparked a nervous reaction in American foreign policy circles who tended to ignore Africa unless a rival expressed interest in the continent.

Closer to home, China significantly de-escalated the situation with Taiwan after the 1995–6 Straits Crisis, recognizing that it lacked the military capacity to make a more aggressive approach work. China focused instead on its weaker neighbors bordering the South China Sea, where the Chinese disputed a series of island chains primarily with Vietnam, but also with the Philippines. In 1995, China intimidated Filipino fishermen off Mischief Reef and subsequently established a makeshift military base there.[72] This action sparked the reemergence of the "China Threat" discussion in American security circles. Articles predicted an eventual Sino-American war for control of the Western Pacific.[73] Yet few in China's littoral region shared these concerns. China was yet to be viewed as a rising threat to neighborhood security.[74] In fact, during the fifteen-year period covered in this chapter, the perceptions of a Chinese threat to Southeast Asia actually receded, as China's foreign policy became more predictable and the local populations benefited from China's economic growth through trade and investment.[75]

A key element of China's grand strategy under the leadership of Jiang Zemin until 2002 and then during the stewardship of Hu Jintao during the following decade was advertising China's peaceful intentions. Chinese intellectuals, once fans of Samuel Huntington's past defenses of the autocratic developmental state, were incensed by his 1996 bestseller *The Clash of Civilizations and the Remaking of the World Order*, which posited a China hostile to the United States and seeking to aggressively defend its sphere of influence in the alleged "Confucian Civilizational Zone" while making common cause with the "Islamic Civilizational Zone" against the US-led West.[76] This "Sinic" zone supposedly included China, Vietnam, the Philippines, and the Koreas. Huntington claimed that in the 1990s Vietnam and Japan were moving away from the United States and toward the Chinese diplomatically due to these civilizational ties. With his warnings about "the fading of the West," Huntington's arguments recalled the work of Lothrop Stoddard.[77] In fact, Stoddard's follow-up to *The Rising Tide of Color Against*

White World-Supremacy was *The New World of Islam*, where, like Huntington would predict three-quarters of a century later, Stoddard predicted an alliance between the Islamic world and a rising China.

At the same time as Chinese intellectuals condemned Huntington's alleged fear-mongering, some Chinese nationalists welcomed what they saw as Huntington's portrait of a declining West and a rising China destined to dominate the twenty-first century, though these voices would not be given official sanction until after 2008.[78] In the meantime, the Chinese dismissed American concerns about rising Chinese power by labeling them part of *Zhongguo Weixielun*, literally meaning "China Threat Theory." After the mid-1990s, *Zhonggui Weixielun* replaced *Huangguo Lun* ("Yellow Peril") as the preferred Chinese term for baseless and racist foreign fears.[79] Absent before 1995, China Threat Theory would be frequently mentioned in Chinese media thereafter.[80] Its use rapidly increased between 2000 and 2005 and has plateaued at a high level ever since.[81]

China's rulers decided to counter the narrative of a threatening China with the slogan "Peaceful Rise." This term was coined by Party intellectual Zhen Bijian following his 2002 trip to the United States, where he heard frequent and unsettling references to a threatening China.[82] It would be officially adopted at the sixteenth Party Conference that same year, where Zheng explained that China did not seek conquest like Germany and Japan during the World Wars, nor did it wish to follow the militarized path of the Soviet Union. Instead, China wanted "reciprocity and mutual benefit" in its foreign relations.[83] Soon, Chinese leaders decided even this might sound too threatening, so they replaced the word "rise." Beginning in 2003, Chinese leaders began officially referring to "Peaceful Development," and that phrase was enshrined as official party doctrine at the next Party Congress in 2007.[84]

The Bush administration made an attempt at reciprocation in 2005 when Bush administration official Robert Zoellick gave a speech calling for China to be a "Responsible Stakeholder" in US-led multilateral institutions.[85] The Chinese saw this less as an offer of partnership than an attempt by America to slow China's rise by burdening it with global responsibilities it was not yet prepared to handle.[86] But Zoellick was not declaring any change in policy. Rather, he was encapsulating the approach taken for the past three decades in a new phrase. It was an approach shared by other democracies. For instance, a 2000 report by the British House of Commons endorsed efforts "to encourage and support China's closer integration into the international system, in all fields, as a friendly and responsible partner in dealing with global and regional issues."[87]

Books and articles prognosticating what kind of superpower China would become turned into a cottage industry. At first, caution reigned over alarmism in this genre. Political scientists Andrew Nathan and Robert Ross anticipated this initial tone in 1997 when they described China as "a vulnerable power" which sought to project external strength to hide internal weakness. In their view, the United States and its allies should "accommodate China when they should, persuade China when they can, and resist China when they must," an endorsement of "Congagement."[88] In 2003, Harvard professor Alastair Iain Johnston denied China was a revisionist power seeking to remake the global order, using as evidence its unwillingness to construct alternative international organizations to challenge those dominated by the United States.[89] A 2005 *Atlantic* article argued that the United States should tolerate "other great powers enjoying a sphere of influence" and that China's would include Taiwan, the rare instance of a member of the American foreign policy establishment proposing that the United States not defend Taiwan militarily.[90] Two academic articles in 2007 downplayed the prospect of Chinese military aggression, with one predicting the US and the PRC were moving toward "Managed Great Power Relations" whereby they could settle their differences amicably through a sort of dual power concert.[91] A dissenting voice emerged from a noted historian of Sino-American relations, Warren Cohen, who claimed that based on past actions by rising Chinese empires, a regionally hegemonic China would be no different from past hegemons in terms of using force to bully and brutalize weaker neighbors.[92]

For the time being, it seemed China's strategy of presenting itself as engaging in a "Peaceful Rise" or "Peaceful Development" was working. Fear of China in the 2000s was actually lower than in the 1990s, particularly in the United States. This was despite China's economy having become several times larger, and its military considerably more advanced. One cause of this was the distraction of overseas wars that did not involve China. But another cause was Chinese leaders heeding Deng's advice to present China as a power with benign intentions. The question then became when China would choose to switch gears and become more assertive. Events in 2008 would spark this switch. While China continued to rise, it appeared in that year that the United States and its allies were finally beginning to decline. Now might be China's time. Or so China's leaders began to believe.

11

From the Beijing Olympics to Wolf Warrior Diplomacy

2008–23

Few figures better represent the changes in Chinese popular culture over the past three decades than the film and stage director Zhang Yimou. He attracted the attention of US and European film critics with his daring 1991 work "Raise the Red Lantern," which focused upon the lives of concubines in 1920s China and was the first Chinese film nominated for the Academy Award for Best Foreign Language Film.[1] Over the course of the 1990s, he continually pushed the boundaries of what was considered acceptable in Chinese cinema. Because of this, he was more celebrated outside of China than within it. This all changed in 2002 when his big-budget historical action film "Hero" became a box-office success, in both China and overseas. In 2004, it became the rare foreign language film to top the weekend box-office grosses in the United States. With that film's balletic fighting sequences, reminiscent of the recent smash "Crouching Tiger, Hidden Dragon," Zhang had moved from the art house to the multiplex.

At the same time, this film finally put him in the Chinese Communist Party's good graces. Derided by some former champions of his work as an apology for authoritarianism, the film found an unlikely protagonist in Qin Shi Huangdi, China's first true emperor. He has always been a controversial figure in Chinese history and is usually viewed as an excessively tyrannical cautionary tale, much like Oliver Cromwell in English history and Julius Caesar in Roman history. As emperor, he attempted to burn most existing written works in China, including all Confucian writings, and the Qin Empire collapsed amid widespread revolts shortly after his death. In the 1996 Chinese film "The Emperor's Shadow," he was depicted as a self-destructive megalomaniac.

Mao was one of the emperor's rare enthusiastic admirers, and the film was correctly viewed as a subtle swipe at the deceased chairman. Because of this, "The Emperor's Shadow" was briefly banned in China upon release. "Hero" had no such difficulties with government censors. Inspired very loosely by an assassin's attempt to kill Qin Shi Huangdi before he could finish conquering the other six Chinese kingdoms, the climax of Zhang's film features the would-be king-killer agreeing with his arguments that the divided Chinese realm had known nothing but war, suffering, and chaos, while his unification efforts would ultimately benefit the common people. Upon this realization, the assassin willingly allows himself to be executed for the greater good. Its potential use as propaganda by the Chinese government was obvious.

With Zhang transformed from a rebel auteur into a respectable crafter of spectacles, the Chinese government tasked him with producing the opening ceremonies for the 2008 Beijing Olympics. On the night of August 8, viewers in China and around the world were treated to a lavish performance combining breathtaking visual effects and a cast of 15,000 performers seamlessly executing a series of seamless communal performances, including 2,008 drummers thumping with military precision.[2] It was simultaneously beautiful and intimidating, showcasing China's past cultural achievements and present vibrancy. US journalists quipped that the multitudes of performers served as a warning to any would-be invaders. In a subsequent episode of the animated television show "South Park," the town's resident boy bigot Eric Cartman is traumatized by viewing the ceremony, runs around town while repeatedly shrieking "The Chinese are taking us over!," and lays siege to a local restaurant owned by the one Chinese family in town.

Less than a month after the conclusion of those Olympics, the American investment bank Lehman Brothers went bankrupt, a victim of reckless speculation in an overheated housing market. Since all other major investment banks in the United States and Europe had been behaving in a similar fashion, the entire global financial system was soon on the brink of collapse in a panic the likes of which had not been seen since October 1929. The fruit of the deregulation of financial services begun in the United States and Britain three decades earlier, this near-collapse seemed at the time to herald the end of the post-Cold War "neoliberal" consensus supporting unfettered financial capitalism, just at the oil crisis of 1973 proved the death knell for the Keynesian post-Second World War system of what political economist John Ruggie termed "embedded liberalism." The United States and other wealthy nations endured a short and sharp recession, followed by a painfully slow recovery. Meanwhile, China seemed to sidestep much of the collateral damage. It was now catching up to the United States at an increasing rate. Shortly after the beginning of the financial panic, Hu Jintao announced "a major change in the balance of power."[3] The world was transitioning from unipolarity to multipolarity, with China as one of the poles. This was a declaration of a more assertive Chinese foreign policy. Brimming with confidence, China would begin to throw its weight around. It would no longer defer so readily to American demands (Figure 9).

This new assertiveness became increasingly aggressive after Xi Jinping became Hu's successor in late 2012. Gone was the suave diplomacy of Zhou Enlai and the humble pose of Deng Xiaoping. Between 2008 and 2023, the decades of comity between the United States and the PRC definitively broke down. Engagement would be labeled a failure. The election of President Donald Trump in 2016 accelerated the shift to open antagonism. In an increasingly politically polarized nation, anti-China sentiment was perhaps the only thing uniting Democrats and Republicans. Talk of a "New Cold War" was everywhere, with US-Asian policy soon revolving around often clumsy efforts to force nations to pick sides. At the same time, China sought to make friends through its "One Belt, One Road" program of massive loans for economic development across the globe. By March 2020, when Covid-19 metastasized from an outbreak in the Chinese metropolis of Wuhan into a global pandemic, the Sino-American rivalry penetrated every continent. As with the far bloodier rivalry between the Americans and the Soviets, both powers engaged in competition which often backfired on all involved. Yet there was one crucial

FIGURE 9 *Illustrating both China's glorious past and its auspicious future, the Opening Ceremonies for the 2008 Summer Olympics in Beijing featured over 10,000 performers, including 2,008 drummers. Image used with permission from Alamy.*

difference: the two rivals' economies were deeply intertwined with each other and with the economies of most other nations as well. Engagement had not succeeded in building friendship or in fostering democratic liberalization, but it had created a global economy which could not easily function without China and a Chinese economy which was dependent on the world.

Today, China's status as the world's second leading power is secure. It accounts for the majority of Asia's economic output, and about half of that continent's military spending.[4] In his 2008 speech, Hu Jintao declared "Peaceful Development" would now be replaced by the slogan "Actively Accomplishing Something," which Xi Jinping changed in 2013 to "Striving for Achievement." As explained by Chinese international relations scholar Yan Xuetong, "in the past we had to keep a low profile because we were weak," but now "we are strong and you are weak."[5] Part of this striving would be the extolling of the "China Model" of economic liberalization coupled with political authoritarianism.[6] More notably, Xi adopted another slogan—"The Chinese Dream," or *qiang zhongguo meng*, literally "strong nation dream." Xi borrowed the concept from the hit 2010 book *The China Dream*, written by PLA Colonel Liu Mingfu.[7] The full title of this work was *The China Dream: The Great Power Thinking and Strategic Positioning of China in the Post-American Age*. As opposed to the individualist "American Dream," the "Chinese Dream" is a collective desire for China to reclaim its past role as a premier power and "Central Kingdom," possessing economic and military might second-to-none.[8] Heightening this nationalism is China's heritage of both ancient might and recent exploitation, as highlighted by another leading government slogan: "Never Forget National Humiliation, Rejuvenate China."[9]

China seemed very much to be continuing along its path to national rejuvenation. In 2010, it passed Japan to become the world's second-largest economy. This was seen as a major milestone in both nations and created something of a crisis of confidence among politically influential Japanese nationalists.[10] But increasingly negative views of China extended well beyond this cohort. In a 2005 poll, 38 percent of Japanese expressed a negative view of China. A 2013 poll recorded that number soaring to 90 percent.[11] The Japanese began to feel vulnerable. This was both occasioned by, and the cause of, a quasi-militarized dispute over a group of uninhabited islands called Senkaku in Japan and Diaoyu in China.[12]

In August 2012, 150 Japanese activists, including eight members of parliament, planted flags on Uotsuri, the largest of the islands. Concurrently, the Japanese government announced its intention to purchase three of the islands from a Japanese individual, claiming they were preempting Shintaro Ishihara, the ultra-Nationalist governor of Tokyo, from doing so himself. Almost immediately, fourteen Chinese civilians journeyed to Uotsuri but were detained by Japanese officials, after planting both Chinese and—curiously—Taiwanese flags.[13] China's state-run press outlets fanned the flames of public opinion. This led to sporadic vandalism against Japanese businesses in a number of Chinese cities. Referring to these outbursts, government media argued that "Japan must take the emotion of the Chinese people seriously."[14]

State-run media publicized a series of protests planned to occur on September 18, the eighty-first anniversary of the "Mukden Incident," when Japan began its invasion of Manchuria.[15] On that day, demonstrations occurred in at least eighty Chinese cities.[16] Many turned violent, and a Chinese man in Xian was severely beaten by a mob while trying to prevent them from destroying his Toyota Corolla. This assault occurred barely 100 yards from a police station, but the authorities chose not to intervene.[17] After these demonstrations, Chinese media advised calm, with leading newspapers condemning the attack in Xian. Over the ensuing months, armed Chinese and Japanese vessels would face each other down occasionally. One wonders how official Chinese media would handle similar showdowns involving something of strategic value, like the Spratly and Paracel island groups in the South China Sea, to say nothing of Taiwan. For its part, Japanese leaders have shown no interest in backing down for fear of adding to a narrative of national decline. With this in mind, Japanese Prime Minister Shinzo Abe said in 2013 that "Japan will never be a second-tier country."[18]

China was now an economic superpower and the dominant Asian military power on both land and sea. But questions remained about China's global influence. Longtime China observer and George Washington University professor David Shambaugh labeled China a "Partial Power" which, among other shortcomings, "possesses little soft power."[19] In a similar vein, British columnist Martin Wolf of the *Financial Times* called China a "premature superpower" due to its growing but still low per capita income levels.[20] The primary method the Chinese used in the early twenty-first century to increase their soft power in the developed world was the funding of Confucius Institutes at colleges and universities across the globe. The Chinese would pay cash-strapped universities to create Chinese language programs and provide funding for research on China.

In 2005, the first Confucius Institute opened in Australia at the University of Western Australia.[21] Eventually, over a dozen were established at colleges and universities across Australia, and hundreds more worldwide. Yet scholars soon chafed at Chinese governmental meddling in research produced with Chinese funding and presented at Chinese-funded conferences. By the end of the 2010s, the demand for these institutes faded as faculty complaints began to outweigh university administrators' bottomless quest for resources in an era of decreasing public funding. Decisively tipping the balance was China's worsening image in the industrialized world, turning such funding into a political football. In May 2021, the Australian government ordered the closure of all Confucius Institutes through legislation designed to curb undue Chinese influence in Australia. This was reflective of a broader global trend.

China also sought to exercise increasing cultural influence through its film industry, though more as a major consumer of films than as a producer. Chinese leaders first allowed American movies onto Chinese screens in 1994 to boost its own lagging film industry, since at that time few Chinese were willing to pay to watch stale propagandistic domestic products. By 1998, eight Hollywood films accounted for nearly half of all Chinese box-office grosses.[22] China became by far Hollywood's leading growth market in the twenty-first century, helping shape an increasing focus on special effects-heavy blockbusters that transcended language barriers. In 2005, Chinese film receipts equaled those of Switzerland. By 2020, it was the world's largest movie market.[23]

China placed annual quotas on the number of foreign films it allowed on its screens, creating competition for these coveted spots. And since the government selected the films, US studios learned to engage in self-censorship to ensure their big-budget extravaganzas made the cut. What was more, they also learned to censor smaller film projects that were never intended for the Chinese market. If, for instance, if Disney made a film about Tibet or the Dalai Lama which drew attention to Chinese human rights violations, then its Marvel superhero films could be banned from the country, seriously impacting the studio's bottom line. This soon gave China effective veto power over the content of US cinema. Richard Nixon popularized the concept of "Linkage," arguing that friendlier relations with China would convince the PRC to discontinue support for North Vietnam, forcing the Vietnamese Communists to the negotiating table and ensuring the continued existence of South Vietnam. That form of linkage proved illusory. But when it came to the US film industry, the Chinese were able to make linkage work.

Despite these strenuous efforts to cater to the Chinese market, Hollywood may soon experience diminishing returns. In recent years, the Chinese government has reserved more screens for Chinese-made films, which it heavily subsidizes, and has encouraged the making of native blockbusters, an act of mercantilist cultural import substitution. Such efforts have borne fruit, and Chinese creators have proven equal to the task of both entertaining Chinese audiences and pleasing the government. The foremost example of this was the 2019 film "Wolf Warrior II," which quickly became the highest-grossing film in Chinese history, easily besting every American-made blockbuster. It was a new kind of Chinese film, featuring a gritty hero who bore more resemblance to Sylvester Stallone's John Rambo than any Chinese socialist realist archetype. The titular hero comes out of retirement to save Chinese citizens caught in an East African warzone. Along the way, he rescues civilians from a variety of nations and defeats an American warlord who goes by the name Big Daddy. The message hammered home to its receptive domestic audience was that China was a rising global power, beloved especially in the developing world. But while captivating domestic audiences, the film failed to attract a large audience outside China. Only 0.3 percent of the $900 million in ticket sales for "Wolf Warrior II" came from abroad.[24]

This unexpected blockbuster had an unlikely origin. It was not the product of China's subsidized cultural national champions, but rather the work of a single auteur. Hong Kong kung fu star Leng Feng wrote, directed, and starred in what was technically a sequel to his first Wolf Warrior film, which showcased the heroics of People's Liberation Army soldiers saving lives after the 2008 Sichuan earthquake.[25] It was thus the Chinese version of the earliest Hollywood action blockbusters in the 1970s, such as Steven Spielberg's "Jaws" and George Lucas's "Star Wars," rather than production-line products such as the films comprising Disney's "Marvel Cinematic Universe." China clearly has a long way to go in replicating the systemic success of cultural exports such as Indian "Bollywood" films, Japanese cartoons, or South Korean soap operas and popular music. Attempts like Zhang Yimou's 2016 historical action film "The Great Wall," featuring Matt Damon and funded by the then-largest budget in Chinese history, failed to turn a profit, doing underwhelming business in both China and the United States.

"Wolf Warrior II" also reflected China's increasing presence in Africa and other parts of the developing world, proving the old saying that trade follows the flag, and then the flag follows trade. As a massive market for the foodstuffs and natural resources of Latin America, China emerged as a major player in America's backyard, potentially threatening the monopoly of influence it had enjoyed in the region since the First World War removed British and German trade and investment. In 2009, Secretary of State Hillary Clinton noted China's "quite disturbing gains" in the region, though in 2013 her successor John Kerry downplayed the Chinese threat in the western hemisphere and dismissed calls for a resurrection of the Monroe Doctrine.[26] American diplomats took to regularly lecturing Latin American and African political leaders on the dangers of taking on excessive Chinese loans, often in a patronizing manner.

Given both their distance from China and their favorable trade terms with the Asian powerhouse, the political leaders and populations of the major European economic powers usually fail to share US fears of Chinese power and influence. In general, polls have shown a positive balance of opinion concerning China for most of this century, though this positive sentiment has eroded as China grows more assertive. British favorability ratings of China fell from 65 percent in 2006 to 48 percent in 2013, while those in France dipped from 60 percent to 48 percent over that same period. Curiously, the lowest approval ratings have been recorded in Germany, which is by far China's leading trading partner in the EU. No nation in the European Union has benefited more from China's economic growth than Germany. Yet only 56 percent of Germans expressed a favorable opinion of China in 2006, and that number plunged to 29 percent by 2013.[27] Predictably, among Europeans, Russians expressed the most consistently positive views of China, remaining stable over this period at around 60 percent.[28]

China's largest current initiative in its quest for soft power and benign influence is its Belt and Road Initiative, often confusingly referred to by Chinese leaders as "One Belt, One Road," with the "Belt" referring to roads and railroads across Eurasia and the "Road" meaning sea lanes connecting China to Africa, South Asia, and the Americas. Begun early in Xi's tenure, the program is intended to foster economic development across the globe through trillions in loans and other investments in infrastructure projects around the globe from the Chinese government, Chinese state-owned companies, and technically private Chinese business entities. The bulk of funding has gone to the developing regions of Africa and South Asia, though there are large-scale projects in Europe, particularly in Mediterranean nations such as Greece that suffered under German-enforced fiscal austerity in the aftermath of the 2008 financial crisis. In 2012, Chinese international relations scholar Wang Jisi noted that when looking East, China's strategic influence was constrained by US allies and military bases, but that these hindrances were absent to China's west. Thus, he proposed a policy of "Marching Westward," expanding Chinese influence over the Eurasian heartland.[29] He compared this Mackinder-style overland "march westward to avoid a hostile east" to pre-First World War Germany's attempt to construct a "Berlin-to-Baghdad" railway that would both increase German trade and provide a strategic outlet to the Indian Ocean, at that time effectively a British lake.[30] US leaders and media pundits have been understandably concerned by China's Marshall Plan-like efforts.

Such predictions ignore the low rate of geopolitical return on other US developmental programs during the Cold War, such as the Alliance for Progress in Latin America and the Colombo Plan in South Asia. As with Wilhelmine Germany's plans in the early 1900s, much of China's projects exist only on paper, and the desired increases in Chinese influence for completed projects have been lower than expected. In response, China has significantly scaled back future funding. In targeted nations, politics has intervened to China's detriment. In Sri Lanka, massive government indebtedness to China occasioned the overthrow of the island's pro-Chinese leaders in 2022 who fled abroad after large demonstrations and the physical occupation of the presidential palace. Something similar occurred in Malaysia in 2018 when Prime Minister Najib Razak lost power due to accusations of being too close to the Chinese.[31] In Kenyan elections in August 2022, both major candidates competed in castigating the government for its backing of a Chinese-built railroad from the port of Mombasa through the capital of Nairobi to the country's interior.[32] As with many Belt and Road projects, this was an unaffordable boondoggle that defied basic economics and can never achieve profitability, much like many such "White Elephant" projects financed by the United States and the World Bank during the Cold War.

Just as Germany's attempts in the early 1900s to throw its weight around spurred the creation of a balancing coalition in Europe of nations not previously allied with one another, China's actions in the Indian Ocean and the Western Pacific have driven the region's powers to begin to act in concert with one another. With the exception of Russia, China is not on especially good terms with any of its powerful neighbors. In India, over 60 percent of the public identified China as a "major threat" in 2015, compared to 78 percent saying the same about India's traditional nemesis Pakistan, while no other nations were identified by a significant number of respondents as a threat to India.[33] The world's two most populous nations have two long-standing border disputes. Japan spars with the Chinese over the Senkaku Islands. Australians, while more distant, have a long-standing tradition of suspicion regarding China.

This trio, along with the United States, has in recent years formed the Quadrilateral Security Dialogue, usually misidentified as the "Quad Alliance." While the United States has bilateral treaties of alliance with Japan and Australia, this quartet has yet to forge a collective security pact, and probably never will, particularly because India—like the United States in the nineteenth century—fears entanglement in others' fights, and therefore has no treaty allies. A major stumbling block on the path to strengthening this four-way partnership is the fact that each nation's conflicts with China take a different form. Indian sailors will not die for the Senkakus, just as Japanese soldiers will not risk their lives to defend Arunachal Pradesh. The United States, Japan, and Australia all wish to see the continuation of an autonomous Taiwan, though it is an open question as to how large a role the Australians and Japanese would be willing to play should a war begin in the Taiwan Strait.

The "Quad" has thus strained to find a coherent mission and geostrategic common ground. Idealistic Americans trumpet this Indo-Pacific "Diamond of Democracies," implying some sort of defense of freedom. The clear precedent for the Quad was the Cold War-era military alliance Southeast Asian Treaty Organization (SEATO), which in 1954 tied the United States and Australia to many of the nations along China's littoral. This precedent bodes poorly for the Quad's success, since SEATO folded shortly after South Vietnam, one of its charter members, ceased to exist in 1975. So long as Russia remains friendly toward the Chinese, the PRC does not face the prospect of encirclement, as Germany faced in 1914. Nor can the United States and its allies concentrate military resources on a short, contiguous frontier, as was the case with NATO against the Soviet Union. In the long run, geography, demography, and economics all weigh decisively in favor of China's ability to divide and neutralize its regional rivals.

Australia provides an important test case. With its long-standing racial, cultural, and geographic insecurities, along with deep and abiding ties to the United States, it should be the easiest partner for the United States to manage and keep in line. It was therefore no surprise that this was President Barack Obama's first stop when showcasing his "Pivot to Asia." In a November 7, 2011, speech to the Australian Parliament in Canberra, he declared that "in the Asia Pacific, in the 21st century, the United States of America is all in."[34] After receiving praise from both Labor Party Prime Minister Julia Gillard and opposition Liberal Party leader Tony Abbott, Obama headed to Australia's isolated northern coast to visit American and Australian forces at Royal Australian Air Force Base Darwin. "You are the backbone of our countries, some of the toughest people in the world," Obama told the military personnel, who gave him a "rock star welcome."[35]

That base in Darwin was the centerpiece of the "Pivot to Asia," a strategy of militarily containing China whereby the United States would withdraw forces and attention from its recent protracted wars in western and central Asia and build them up in East Asia and the Western Pacific. By 2013, three-fifths of US naval assets were stationed in the Pacific region.[36] Yet Darwin itself revealed the limits of containment since the very port where US Marines were based was soon to be run by the Chinese company Landbridge. In 2016, Abbott's right-of-center Liberal Party government, despite being prone to bashing Labor leaders like Kevin Rudd for selling Australia out to China, awarded Landbridge a 99-year lease for the Port of Darwin.[37]

For every putative partner of the United States in the Indo-Pacific, economic and security interests are at fatal cross-purposes. Japan and Australia are dependent on access to the Chinese market, providing the Chinese with enormous leverage over them. Meanwhile, India is nominally a partner of its Chinese adversary since both are members of the so-called BRICS nations of Brazil, Russia, India, China, and South Africa. The United States was able to convince Australia, New Zealand, and Japan to ban the Chinese company Huawei from installing 5G telecommunications networks in their countries, though the United States' European allies have largely refused to join them.[38] Britain's refusal was particularly galling, given the continued cherished myth of its "Special Relationship" with the United States.

The British position on the Chinese threat, or lack thereof, epitomizes the difficulties of the United States relying on even its closest European allies to support continued containment of Chinese power. In search of economic opportunity, in 2015 Conservative Party Prime Minister David Cameron called Britain China's "best partner in the west." Much to American chagrin, he made Britain a founding member of China's Asian Infrastructure Investment Bank, signing up for China's attempt to supplant and replace the US-dominated World Bank as a source of development aid. His successor Theresa May switched course and made Britain the first European nation to ban Huawei's 5 G network. Her successor, Boris Johnson, returned to David Cameron's dovish pro-business approach to China in the search for post-Brexit markets beyond Europe. In February 2021 he declared himself "fervently Sinophile" and pledged to move closer to China "whatever the occasional political difficulties."[39] But Johnson shifted course in July 2020, seeking to exploit Covid-19-based anti-Chinese sentiment.[40] It is notable that all these twists, turns, and reversals occurred among politicians belonging to the same political party. In the long term, it is highly unlikely the United States can rely on Britain, particularly when the financial stakes are so high.

As president, Barack Obama continued the rhetorical engagement of Clinton and Bush while sharpening the military edge of containment. In 2009, Deputy Secretary of State James Steinberg announced a policy of "strategic reassurance," declaring that "we are ready to accept a growing role for China on the international stage."[41] In 2011, Secretary of State Hillary Clinton claimed she was partnering "with China to build mutual trust, and to encourage China's active efforts in global problem-solving."[42] Meanwhile, Chinese power was becoming a partisan cudgel. During the 2010 congressional campaign, Republican candidates aired what became known as the "Chinese Professor" advertisement. It showed a not-too-distant future where an academic in a Beijing lecture hall explained to his students how runaway US debt led to its downfall as a great power.[43] At the time, Republicans were attacking excessive government spending, and influential academics argued the United States was on the verge of reaching sovereign debt levels that would result in a fiscal death spiral. These arguments proved to be baseless, but at the time they helped drive an elite bipartisan consensus for deficit reduction and fiscal austerity as vital for preserving American strength.

The narrative of a rising China was the flip side of the fear of American decline. This notion of "American Carnage" became the theme of Donald Trump's successful 2016 presidential campaign. Reacting to this result and the equally unexpected British vote than summer to leave the European Union, Xi Jinping confidently declared that "the world is undergoing great changes unseen in a century," and that "time and momentum are on our side."[44] Trump became the first US president in over a half-century to heap invective upon China. He charged that China's mercantilist trade policies exploited US goodwill. In the 2017 National Security Strategy, the United States officially recognized China as a "strategic competitor."[45] The United States now viewed China more as a rival than a partner. The policy of "Congagement" decisively shifted away from engagement. This has continued under President Joseph Biden, who has refused to rescind Trump's punitive tariffs on Chinese imports due to fear of a political backlash in politically competitive midwestern states such as Wisconsin, Michigan, and Pennsylvania. In both 2021 and 2022, he signed into law bipartisan bills allocating hundreds of billions of dollars to invest in US high technology industries in order to better compete with China and hopefully wean American companies off Chinese-built components.[46] American politicians discussed industrial policy when worried about a rising Japan in the 1980s, but they only began enacting it in the 2020s to compete with a rising China.

These government actions followed a decade of declining US public opinion regarding China. As late as 2012, fully three-quarters of Americans expressed their desire for a collaborative relationship with China, and 55 percent of Americans viewed China favorably.[47] In 2017, China's favorability rating still stood at 49 percent, though 73 percent viewed China as a military threat, and 63 percent as an economic threat.[48] In 2021, China's rating stood at 79 percent unfavorable. This was the most negative Americans had viewed China since before Nixon's trip. It was also notable because China had enjoyed a continuously net positive favorability rating in the United States from 1990 until 2017.[49]

This opinion environment incited a surge in political "Panda Punching," where politicians exploited legitimate fears through symbolic grandstanding.[50] In 2022, Republican-led state governments in Texas, Oklahoma, and Alabama banned the use of the popular social media application TikTok on state-owned devices, including those at state-run universities.[51] Other states soon followed suit in seeking to crack down on what had become the most popular social media platform among young Americans. This was because TikTok was created and run by ByteDance, a company based in China. Though not directly affiliated with the Chinese government, there was reason to suspect ByteDance would share user data with the Chinese government. The revelation in 2022 that ByteDance employees accessed user information without the users' consent heightened these fears. Republican Senator Josh Hawley (R-MO) referred to TikTok as "a Trojan horse for the Chinese Communist Party." By the end of the year, the application was banned from federal government devices, and Senator Marco Rubio (R-FL) introduced a bill to ban ByteDance from operating in the United States.[52]

The combination in 2016 of Britain voting to leave the European Union and Trump's election fed China's own narrative of Western decline. Speaking at the nineteenth Party Congress in October 2017, Xi Jinping began his second five-year term in office by announcing the start of "a new era" which would see China complete its rejuvenation by 2049, the Communist regime's centennial. The election results in Britain and the United States had created "a period of historic opportunity for China to expand its influence."[53] In 2016, Fu Ying, the Chair of the Foreign Affairs Committee of China's National People's Congress, published an article entitled "The US World Order is a Suit that no Longer Fits."[54] China watchers began lamenting the rise of "Wolf Warrior" diplomats who lacked the tact of the previous generation of diplomats trained by Zhou Enlai. Allegedly inspired by that film, these young diplomats were assertive to the point of rudeness. After Sweden lodged a complaint in 2019 regarding China's kidnapping in Thailand of a Hong Kong publisher who possessed Swedish citizenship, China's ambassador to Sweden appeared on that nation's national radio network to explain his country's actions. He told his shocked interviewers "for our friends, we have fine wine, but for our enemies, we have shotguns."[55] China no longer felt the need to deferentially keep its head down and play nice.

This became blatantly apparent at the opening ceremonies for the 2022 Olympic Winter Games in Beijing. The contrasts with the 2008 ceremony were glaring. China's economy was four times larger than it had been only fourteen years earlier. In the words of one Western journalist, "China no longer feels it has anything to prove."[56] The only foreign dignitary in attendance was Russian President Vladimir Putin, whose military would invade Ukraine shortly after the closing ceremonies. Once Mao had journeyed to Moscow to pay obeisance to Stalin. Now, Putin came to Xi as a supplicant. No other bilateral relationship had changed so drastically, so quickly. In 1914, Russia's economy was three times the size of China's. In 1970, the Soviet Union's economy was six times the size of China's. In 2020, Russia's economy was one-ninth the size of China's.[57] In contrast to 2008, politicians from the United States and its allies boycotted against China's mistreatment of its Uighur minority population in Xinjiang. In recent years, the Chinese government had initiated mass detentions in reeducation camps of more than 1 million ethnic Uighurs, viewed with official suspicion due to their Islamic faith. Performing the ceremony's climactic lighting of the Olympic torch were two athletes from the host nation. One was ethnically Chinese. The other was a Uighur. It was as if a Jew had lit the Olympic torch in Berlin in 1936. China was now too strong to care what the United States and its allies thought.

Conclusion

When He Wakes

That China has now entered the first rank of global powers is beyond dispute. That the naysayers who doubted the ability of China's state-directed authoritarian capitalism to achieve this result were mistaken is also clear. That those who predicted increased prosperity would produce calls for democratization which would inevitably prove irresistible were wrong is now accepted, particularly by those who had believed in this prediction most deeply. This leads to two obvious conclusions: first, that betting against the CCP's continued success has been foolish; second, that predictions about the state of China one, two, or three decades down the road tend to be wrong. China has defied expectations and predictions for over four decades. Yet that has not stopped people from continuing to make them. The impact of the rise of China to great power status is too consequential a matter not to analyze, discuss, and, yes, prognosticate over. All we can be sure of is that whatever comes to pass, China will matter, a lot, to everyone, for a long time. As one leading observer of world affairs has written, "all the world will be vitally affected by the development of Chinese affairs, which may well be a decisive factor, for good or evil, during the next two centuries." As stated by one of the foremost scholars of international relations, "China is the most powerful nation of the mainland in Asia and potentially the most powerful nation in the world." The first of these quotes was written by Bertrand Russell, in 1922. The second is from Hans Morgenthau, in 1968.[1]

As the dates of these declarations prove, fascination with Chinese power—both potential and actual—has a storied history. It is timeless, at least in the sense that from the American viewpoint, 140 years is an eternity. Judged by the raft of recent takes on China's rise, whether in the continuous stream of books published over the past decade, or the daily essays in leading newspapers and magazines, it has also never been more relevant. China in the early twenty-first century is very much like the United States in the early twentieth century—the new 800-pound gorilla everyone else views with a mix of wonder, confusion, and fear. Just as no one knew what kind of great power America would become—most of all the Americans themselves—at the start of the last century, the same seems true for China in this one. This century's first two decades witnessed an unbroken upward trajectory of growth in China's economic and military power, as well as in its global influence. Then, in March 2020, the world stopped. The previous November, people in and around Wuhan began getting hospitalized with a mysterious illness. As was the case with the mild SARS virus in 2003, Chinese authorities initially responded with a mixture of suppression and denial, allowing this far more virulent virus to spread. Only on January 23, 2020, did the Chinese government order a lockdown of Wuhan. By that point, countless thousands had left that city for other provinces to celebrate the Chinese Lunar New Year with their extended families.[2] A local outbreak became a national epidemic and soon a global pandemic.

By early 2021, when vaccines for Covid-19 became available, China appeared to have weathered the pandemic quite well. Despite having quintuple the US population, its death toll was statistically insignificant compared to that in America. This was due to stringent Chinese lockdowns of the sort which would never be tolerated in the United States. The Chinese economy had suffered in 2020 but not to the extent of other major economies. As with the 2008 financial crisis, China seemed ready to emerge from the wreckage in a position of increased relative strength. By 2022, that seemed less clear. The Chinese government only offered their people domestically developed vaccines that were markedly inferior to the others available around the world, reducing the level of the Chinese population with immune protection from the lingering and mutating virus. This led to new outbreaks, and new lockdowns, which were rightly seen by the Chinese people as signs of governmental failure. The veneer of technocratic competence cultivated by China's rulers over the past three decades began to erode, both at home and abroad. In early 2023, widespread demonstrations protesting renewed lockdowns convinced the government to swiftly abandon this approach, opening China up to both renewed economic growth and increased Coronavirus infections and hospitalizations.

The virus's place of origin revived old stereotypes of China as a source of disease. US conservatives, taking their cue from President Trump, quickly dubbed Covid-19 the "China Virus" and sought to mainstream this phrase on Twitter and other social media platforms in the spring of 2020. In the summer, Trump began jokingly referring to the pandemic as the "Kung Flu." Speculation raged inside the government and on social media as to whether the disease originated in a Chinese lab and then was released either intentionally or accidentally. On January 30, 2020, when most Americans had yet to even begin paying attention to the outbreak, Senator Tom Cotton (R-AR) asked military leaders at a Senate Armed Services Committee hearing if the virus had its origin at the Wuhan Center for Disease Control and Prevention, which studied viruses similar to Covid-19. After the United States joined other countries in instituting lockdowns and social distancing restrictions, Elise Stefanik (R-NY), then the third-ranking Republican member of the House of Representatives, said, "China lies and Americans died," reflecting the widespread feeling that the Chinese had something to hide.[3] The inability of scientists to swiftly identify the precise source of the outbreak—which is normal for viral pandemics—led mainstream media outlets like *Vanity Fair* to give the "lab-leak" theory a friendly hearing.[4] By the third anniversary of the US lockdowns in March 2023, the Federal Bureau of Investigation and the Department of Energy had both endorsed the lab-leak theory as the likeliest source of Covid-19, although the majority of federal agencies advocated a natural origin, theorizing that the disease spread to humans through a "wet market" in Wuhan that sold captured animals.

The economic effects of China's lockdowns reverberated across the globe. China's approach had been, in the words of University of Central Lancashire political scientist Jenny Clegg, "using globalization to make itself indispensable to the functioning of the world economy."[5] This protected China from economic retaliation by the United States and others while also exposing those nations to potential product shortages when global supply lines that China was central to broke down. The globalized economy's reliance on far-flung sites of manufacturing and assembly, combined with just-in-time delivery practices, rendered trade highly efficient under optimal circumstances, but deeply vulnerable to dysfunction if one or more of the many moving parts broke down. The result was protracted shortages, driving inflation in wealthy countries to levels unseen in most people's lifetimes. In the 1990s, Bill Clinton called the United States the world's "indispensable nation." Over the ensuing decades, China had assumed that role, at least economically.

China's economic rise also impacted the planet itself by fueling the warming of the planet. China is now the world's largest carbon emitter and currently contributes one-third of all annual greenhouse gas emissions.[6] Though China has invested heavily in wind turbine and solar energy technologies, for both domestic use and export, the energy needs of its population still vastly exceed what can be met by increasing the use of non-carbon sources of energy. When the world's leaders began attempting to grapple with a warming climate more than three decades ago, China was far poorer, and its carbon emissions were only a fraction of what they are today. Thus, in early treaties like the 1992 Kyoto Protocol, China was classified as a developing nation and thus bore little responsibility for reducing emissions. That burden instead fell on the long-industrialized nations in Europe and North America, as well as Australia and Japan, which collectively had contributed the overwhelming majority of excess carbon dioxide to the atmosphere over the previous decades and centuries.[7] By the time of the 2016 Paris Agreement, the Chinese faced increasing pressure to assume more responsibility for their now-significant contribution to human-caused climate change. But China has resisted taking such steps. For instance, in recent years, when the wealthy nations of Europe decided to compel one another to provide aid to poorer nations suffering the greatest from the effects of global warming, China suggested it would also possibly contribute but only on a voluntary basis.

Historians love to categorize narratives in terms of either continuity or change. Events are either a natural extension of what came before or a sharp break with the past. This book makes four major arguments. The first pair exhibit continuity, while the last two represent change. First, in the modern era, China has always been a source of mirror imaging. In the words of China scholar Michael Barr, "fears of China can often say as much about those who hold the emotion as they do about China itself."[8] The initial wave of anti-Chinese fears in the late nineteenth century imagined what would happen if the Chinese behaved like the European imperialists who bullied and exploited them. To Americans in the early twenty-first century, China is seen as disciplined, efficient, and ruthless in ways the United States no longer is. Second, the Chinese, as individuals, have long been portrayed as racially superior in a uniquely threatening manner. They are seen as able to work longer, and endure greater hardships, than other nationalities. This stereotype has been a constant, across the globe, whether used to justify preventing the immigration of Chinese "coolie labor," or to welcome "Model Minority" Chinese immigrants. On an individual level, for the last fourteen decades Chinese have been viewed as not only quantitatively superior but qualitatively so as well.

Third, after a long series of failures and false starts, China has, over the past four decades, achieved institutional durability. For most of the century before this economic take-off, the fear that the superior talents of the Chinese could be harnessed by their government to achieve global domination has been allayed by repeated Chinese institutional failures. First, the Qing failed to effectively modernize. Then the Guomindang failed to effectively mobilize. Then the Communists undercut their successes in mobilization and modernization through Mao's catastrophic capriciousness. These successive failures effectively cost China an entire century in its attempt to catch up to its adversaries. But after Mao's death, a succession of Chinese leaders borrowed from the successful examples of economic development in its home region while maintaining a monopoly on both political and economic power domestically and resisted exposure to the more destructive aspects of US-led globalization. The Chinese Communist Party has defied repeated predictions of its own demise and critiques of the limits of its state-managed developmental model.

Xi Jinping may be in the process of abandoning many of the norms and precedents established by Deng Xiaoping, most notably rule by elite consensus. In October 2022, the Party granted Xi a third five-year term as China's leader and effectively made him China's first ruler-for-life since Mao. By no means is Xi seeking a return to Maoist economic and social policies. His autocratic inclinations may slow economic growth through the creation of additional domestic inefficiencies and antagonize other nations with excessive bellicosity, but there is no sign of a reversal of China's long-term trajectory as a rising power. Fourth, and finally, this powerful, durable, and assertive China is simultaneously threatening and irresistible to outsiders. The people in all four nations of the Quad Partnership may see China as a strategic threat and even as an enemy. But they cannot resist its massive market. Their economies, and China's, are not so much entangled as they are conjoined. And if the nations most afraid of China cannot see fit to seek its isolation, what hope is there for Europe, Africa, and Latin America?

Harvard professor Joseph Nye wrote not of China's "rise" but of its "re-emergence."[9] Australian professor Hugh White called this process "less a revolution than a restoration."[10] This is a very common interpretation and seems to have much to support it. For most of the past twenty-two centuries, China has usually been the most populous polity on the planet and almost always in possession of the world's largest economy. Over the centuries, it has usually been a leading technological innovator in ways large and small. The last quarter millennium, comprising the entire history of the United States, was unique in witnessing the global economic and military dominance of European civilization. That exceptional period has now passed. Yet it would be incorrect to speak of Asia reclaiming the mantle of global leadership, with China at its center. This is because, as stated in the previous chapter, there was no such thing as a transoceanic premodern Asian power. In fact, before 1500, there was no such thing as a transoceanic power from any continent.

The premodern world differed from what followed because no civilization or empire, no matter how mighty, could impose its will beyond its immediate peripheral frontier. The Han Empire in 100 BCE was, by any measure, a superpower, and its Emperor Wu was the most powerful man on the planet. But the leaders of Rome and Parthia, and the various rulers on the Indian subcontinent, could not be coerced by him. In fact, they did not even yet know of his empire's existence. In 650 ACE, the Taizong Emperor of Tang Dynasty China was even more powerful than Wu had been, with Chinese armies roaming as far afield as modern-day South Korea and Afghanistan. His empire and civilization were well-known in the Indian subcontinent, western Asia, and the more developed parts of Europe. But beyond China's long-standing spheres of cultural influence in Japan, Korea, and Southeast Asia, the Tang only posed a threat to the Arabs, and only because the Umayyad Caliphate had pushed its own borders well into Central Asia.[11] Residents on three continents longed for Chinese silk, but their economies were fundamentally separate from China's.

Economic interdependence did not exist. Nor did global strategy. Even for the most powerful empire, the outlook was purely regional. Distant far-off lands were, at best, curiosities.

Therefore, what we are witnessing is neither a reemergence nor a restoration of Chinese power. It is the entirely new phenomenon of a "Global China" for which there is no historical precedent. Long before China became an economic superpower, hostile outsiders recognized that China could neither be crushed nor dismembered. Its eventual superpower status would have to be lived with, sometimes managed, and at other times simply endured. The salient question of what Bertrand Russell referred to as "The Problem of China" then becomes what kind of superpower China's leaders choose for it to become. As University of Virginia political scientist Jeffrey Legro put it, "The 'rising China' problem is not just about power, but purpose." Legro quoted an unnamed US Deputy Secretary of State referring to Washington's "cauldron of anxiety about China's future intentions."[12] Some have sought answers to this question by looking to a past where China viewed itself as a "Middle Kingdom" demanding respect and subservience from outsiders, but not seeking conquest or universal empire. In this vein, Hans Morgenthau predicted China would merely want "to regain the position it had occupied before it was reduced to semi-colonial status in the middle of the nineteenth century."[13] More recently, his fellow international relations scholar Robert J. Art of Brandeis University predicted China will want "its 'place in the sun,' just as every other great power that has arrived."[14] Associated with Kaiser Wilhelm II and Germany on the eve of the First World War, the phrase "place in the sun" has ominous forebodings of destructive great power war. Yet Art, like Morgenthau before him, believes China can be accommodated by the United States because, while Britain was separated from Germany only by the North Sea, the United States and China have the vast Pacific Ocean between them.[15]

Among the positive Chinese stereotypes is the idea that its leaders possess unique strategic wisdom. Peruse a popular work on Chinese strategy written by a Westerner, and it won't take long for the reader to learn that the game of *wie qi*, which the Japanese call "Go," is the Chinese equivalent of chess, except that it possesses a far greater potential number of moves, strategies, and outcomes. This will soon be followed by an assertion that whereas American leaders think in four-year increments, Chinese leaders think in terms of centuries.[16] This is not of recent vintage. A century ago, Bertrand Russell wrote "the Chinese nation is the most patient in the world; it thinks of centuries as other nations think of decades. It is essentially indestructible, and can afford to wait."[17] Such positive stereotypes are an outgrowth of the notion of a timeless, unchanging China, where history is a cycle of rising and falling dynasties, as opposed to the progressive nature of Western civilization. This is, of course, utter claptrap. China under the Communists has been no more adept at diplomacy and great power politics than other nations and has often fared far worse. To describe Chairman Mao's rule as patient is ludicrous. Taking the long view, one sees that over the past thousand years, the Han Chinese political heartland of the Yellow River Valley was under non-Han rule for nearly half that period, despite the vast numerical and economic resources possessed by the Han Chinese compared to all of its neighbors. Like all powerful peoples, the Chinese have suffered their share of humiliations, and engaged in quite a few episodes of reckless imperial overreach. To believe otherwise is to fall victim to hoary old beliefs in some timeless Eastern wisdom that produces hybrids of Confucius and Sun Tzu.[18]

Though six thousand miles of ocean separate mainland China from the mainland United States, to the leaders the two superpowers they are, strategically, barely one hundred miles apart. This is the distance separating Fujian Province from the island of Taiwan, regarded by the PRC as the breakaway province of Taipei, still undertaking a rebellion made possible by its status as a de facto US client state. While the United States no longer has a treaty of alliance with Taiwan, it is clear the US government and military ardently desire it remain outside the Communists' grasp. To American leaders, Taiwan is a vibrant democracy resisting authoritarian subjugation. To Chinese leaders, tacit US support for Taiwanese autonomy is an unacceptable infringement on China's national sovereignty. As Mao put it in 1970, "you have occupied our Taiwan Island, by I have never occupied your Long Island."[19]

Chinese leaders cannot accept a future where Taiwan is forever outside their grasp. Every year, their military gains in relative strength, particularly in terms of the naval, air, and missile assets most useful in an attack on Taiwan. Meanwhile, no prominent voices in the US foreign policy establishment advocate abandoning Taiwan to its fate. Despite its official renunciation in 1979, the commitment established by Harry Truman's sending of the Seventh Fleet into the Straits in 1950 has hardened over seven decades into a belief that a Communist conquest of Taiwan will spell the end of the United States as a great power. Having anted up for generations, Washington believes it cannot afford to fold. For example, while accepting Chinese dominance of the Asian mainland, Robert Art maintained the United States must still reign supreme at sea and that this requires protecting Taiwan at all costs. Failure to do so would supposedly shatter US "credibility" in Asia and beyond.[20] The American mindset has barely budged since the First Straits Crisis in 1954. Its leaders still see a China surrounded by dominoes waiting to tumble.

Rather than be forced to show its cards for fear it might hold a losing hand, current US strategy regarding Taiwan is based on continued bluffing in the hopes of delaying the moment of reckoning for as long as possible. This is largely couched in the notion of deterrence and "peace through strength." As Joseph Nye wrote shortly after the Third Straits Crisis, "the prospects for avoiding conflict with China look brighter the more the US maintains its strength in East Asia."[21] It is a policy of remaining faithful to Vegetius's oft-quoted maxim *qui desiderat pacem, praparet bellum*: "let him who desires peace, prepare for war." Most who use this quote are unaware that Vegetius was an armchair strategist with no firsthand military or diplomatic experience. History shows that while arms buildups can deter, they can also provoke. As Morgenthau predicted in 1962, once China gains sufficient military power, the United States will be confronted with "the painful alternative of retreat or war."[22] Morgenthau was the lone prominent US public intellectual in the 1960s calling for abandoning Taiwan to the PRC. Anyone who shared his view today would be just as isolated.

Like all hegemons in relative decline, the United States is trapped by its past successes. Having declared Taiwanese autonomy a vital US strategic interest at a time when it was easily able to enforce this desire, now that the strategic balance has decisively shifted, it feels retreat is not an acceptable option. At the same time, neither is war. This leaves as the only viable option for something changing in China. A quarter century ago, this meant China democratizing and seeing Taiwan as a kindred democracy it would not wish to conquer. More recently, it means the halting of China's rise. The PRC does face certain headwinds. Its population is rapidly aging and is expected to begin shrinking by 2050. Its economy may fall victim to the "Middle Income Trap" and stagnate.[23] Its diplomacy lacks subtlety and tact, often proving unnecessarily alienating, much as was the case with Wilhelmine Germany.[24] China may stumble. Yet, it must be remembered that over the past two decades, the United States itself has stumbled. In this century, the existing hegemon, and not the hegemon-in-waiting, has been the greatest source of global instability.[25] It is now quite difficult to convincingly argue that the United States used what *Washington Post* columnist Charles Krauthammer labeled its "Unipolar Moment" wisely. But few hegemons, if any, ever have. The temptation for squandering blood and treasure in unnecessary acts of overreach always proves too great to resist.

History does not provide parallels or predictions, but it does provide lessons, although these lessons are open to often contradictory interpretations. In 2018, Harvard's Graham Allison published *Destined for War: Can America and China Escape Thucydides's Trap?* This was a clever term for Power Transition Theory's prediction that the act of a rising power surpassing the existing premier power nearly always leads to war. It referenced the ancient Greek historian Thucydides, who remarked that the major cause of the Peloponnesian War was that a rising Athens made Sparta nervous. As reviewers pointed out, Allison's knowledge of modern East Asian and ancient Greek history were wanting, one scholar calling his work "sloppy, superficial, oversimplified, overconfident, and repetitive."[26] Allison is hardly alone in misinterpreting Thucydides. First, Athenian power was the result of the resources provided to it by its Aegean Empire. Without these colonies, it was a powerful Greek polis but lacked the ability to seek dominance.[27] Both China and the United States rely on their own internal resources.

Second, like all polities, Sparta cared most of all about preserving its domestic social and political structure, which was quite unique and vulnerable. Its government was oligarchic, and its political philosophy virulently opposed both democracy and tyranny. Most importantly, nearly nine out of ten residents of Sparta were enslaved non-Spartan Helots. A Sparta without Helots was even more inconsequential than an Athens without colonies. Sparta's domestic security was predicated on using its military power and diplomatic skill to dominate its neighbors in the Peloponnesian peninsula. So long as the poleis of nearby Arcadia and Achaea were friendly or quiescent, Sparta had little to fear. But the successful Athenian democracy which blossomed in the half-century after the Persian Wars in 480 and 479 BCE proved a deeply troubling example. When Athens' leading politician Pericles spoke of Athens as the "School of Greece," he was referring not only to the magnificent art, architecture, philosophy, and drama produced by Athenians but to their city's democratic political structure which made it all possible. So long as Athens remained a shimmering example of the virtues of *demokratia*, it encouraged the *demos* in other city-states, including ones near Sparta, to emulate the example of Athens, and a democratizing Greek world would leave Spartans feeling lonely and vulnerable. This fear can be seen as vaguely reminiscent of Chinese Communist leaders' worries in the 1980s and 1990s about the wave of democratization in East Asia and elsewhere around the globe. That wave has now subsided, and the United States is no longer the vibrant political and economic role model it once was.

Which leads to the third lesson of Thucydides. His history was couched as a dramatic tragedy, with a hubristic Athens being destroyed by nemesis. The turning point of his work—and of the war itself—was the disastrous Athenian attempt to conquer the wealthy Greek city of Syracuse on the island of Sicily, halfway across the Mediterranean and far from any existing Athenian possessions, allies, or enemies. For Thucydides, this was the ultimate manifestation of the foolishness of crowds, with democratic discourse devolving into irrational mob psychology. Athens lost thousands of soldiers, hundreds of warships, and immense wealth, none of which it could easily replace. Though its citizens grimly kept up the fight for another decade, the losses in Sicily all but ensured an Athenian defeat. Here is Thucydides' ultimate lesson: the greatest threat to a hegemon comes from within.[28] Sparta defeated Athens only after Athens had defeated itself. While the United States, its allies, and China's neighbors are correct to worry about the rise of China, first and foremost they should worry about their own domestic situations. They may fear Chinese power. The Chinese have long feared US power. But China's neighbors should fear their own myriad shortcomings even more. The same is true for the United States. And for China as well.

Notes

Introduction

1 Margaret MacMillan, *Nixon and Mao: The Week that Changed the World* (New York: Random House, 2007), 283.

2 Ron Chernow, *Grant* (New York: Penguin, 2017), 879.

3 Franck Bille, "Introduction," in *Yellow Perils: China Narratives in the Contemporary World*, ed. Franck Bille and Soren Urbansky (Honolulu: University of Hawaii, 2018), 18.

4 Ibid., 15.

5 Michael Barr, *Who's Afraid of China? The Challenge of Chinese Soft Power* (London: Zed, 2011), 127.

6 Bruce Cumings, "The World Shakes China," *National Interest* 43 (Spring 1996): 28.

7 "A Long Look at China," *Saturday Evening Post*, Final Draft, December 31, 1958, 1, Folder 0604, Box 238, Series 11, Group 628, Chester Bowles Papers, Sterling Memorial Library, Yale University, New Haven, CT.

8 John Fitzgerald, *Awakening China: Politics, Culture, and Class in the Nationalist Revolution* (Stanford, CA: Stanford University Press, 1996), 352.

9 Chester Holcombe, *China's Past & Future* (London: Morgan & Scott, 1904), xiv.

10 John Fitzgerald, *Awakening China*, 29.

11 Peter Hays Gries, *China's New Nationalism: Pride, Politics, and Diplomacy* (Berkeley, CA: University of California Press, 2004), 45.

Chapter 1

1 Bille, *Yellow Perils*, 4; Gregory Blue, "Gobineau on China: Race Theory, the 'Yellow Peril,' and the Critique of Modernity," *Journal of World History* 10, no. 1 (Spring 1999): 122.

2 Michael Keevak, *Becoming Yellow: A Short History of Racial Thinking* (Princeton, NJ: Princeton University Press, 2011), 127.

3 Ibid., 128.

4 Bille, *Yellow Perils*, 4.

5 Xiao Xiaosui, "China Encounters Darwinism: A Case of Intercultural Rhetoric," *Quarterly Journal of Speech* 81, no. 1 (1995): 84–5.

6 Halford J. Mackinder, "The Pressure of Asia," in *Yellow Peril! An Archive of Anti-Asian Fear*, ed. John Kuo Wei Tchen and Dylan Years (London: Verso, 2014), 172.

7 Christopher Frayling, *The Yellow Peril: Dr Fu Manchu & the Rise of Chinophobia* (London: Thames and Hudson, 2014), 215.

8 Keevak, *Becoming Yellow*, 26–7, 124.

9 Frank Dikotter, *The Discourse of Race in Modern China* (Stanford, CA: Stanford University Press, 1992), 55.

10 Ibid., 55, 56.

11 Keevak, *Becoming Yellow*, 130; Dikotter, *Race in Modern China*, 56.

12 Keevak, *Becoming Yellow*, 126.

13 Paul French, *Through the Looking Glass: China's Foreign Journalists from Opium Wars to Mao* (Hong Kong: Hong Kong University Press, 2009), 9.

14 "The Future of China and Japan," *Review of Reviews*, March 1895, 237.

15 T. G. Otte, "'A Very Great Gulf': Late Victorian British Diplomacy and Race in East Asia," in *Race and Racism in Modern East Asia: Western and Easter Constructions*, ed. Rotem Kowner and Walter Demel (Leiden: Brill, 2013), 143.

16 Blue, "Gobineau on China," 98, 93.

17 Ibid., 114–17.

18 Ibid., 127–9. Eulenburg left the Kaiser's inner circle in 1906 due to a scandal created by revelations in the German press of his numerous homosexual affairs with other members of the Kaiser's inner circle: John Röhl, *The Kaiser and His Court* (Cambridge: Cambridge University Press, 1994).

19 David Walker, *Anxious Nation: Australia and the Rise of Asia, 1850-1939* (Queensland: University of Queensland, 1999), 100.

20 William Ward Crane, "The Year 1899," *Overland Monthly and Out West Magazine* 21, no. 126 (June 1893): 582.

21 Ibid., 584.

22 Ibid., 587, 589.

23 Matthew P. Shiel, *The Yellow Danger* (London: Grant Richards, 1898), 4.

24 Ibid., 5, 10.

25 Ibid., 16, 108, 112.

26 Ibid., 127, 189.

27 By Fleming's admission, Fu Manchu's antagonist was the inspiration for Ian Fleming's James Bond.

28 Ibid., 343.

29 Fu Manchu was also tall, thin, and bald, with long fingernails. He also possessed a thin handlebar mustache which would thereafter be popularly known as a "Fu Manchu."

30 David Walker, "Race Building and the Disciplining of White Australia," in *Legacies of White Australia: Race, Culture and Nation*, ed. Laksiri Jayasuriya,

David Walker and Jan Gothard (Crawley, Western Australia: University of Western Australia, 2003), 42.

31 Ibid., 96.

32 Ibid., 93.

33 Taw Sein Ko, "The Chines Problem and its Solution," *Living Age*, March 30, 1901, 793.

34 In this, Europe's early modern thinkers borrowed from similar arguments made by the ancient Romans which had previously been adopted by fourteenth century Islamic polymath Ibn Khaldun.

35 Charles Pearson, *National Life and Character: A Forecast* (London: MacMillan, 1893), 31.

36 Ibid., 31, 138.

37 Ibid., 32. Pearson applied this at the country level by noting fertility rates were highest in Europe among the lower classes.

38 Ibid., 17.

39 Ibid., 137–8. By contrast, the post-British Indian subcontinent would consist of multiple states, due to the region's religious and cultural diversity. Also, Pearson refrains from ever praising the traits of the peoples of India, as he repeatedly does with the Chinese.

40 Ibid., 131–2.

41 Ibid., 49.

42 Ibid., 14.

43 Jack London, *The Asian Writings of Jack London: Essays, Letters, Newspaper Dispatches, and Short Fiction by Jack London* (Lewiston, Maine: Edwin Mellen Press, 2009), 297–305.

44 Jack London, "The Unparalleled Invasion. Earle Labor," in *Short Stories of Jack London: Authorized One-Volume Edition*, ed. Robert C. Leitz II and Milo Shepard (New York: Macmillan, 1990), 273; "The Yellow Peril," in London, *Asian Writings of Jack London*, 297, 298.

45 London, "The Unparalleled Invasion," 273.

46 Ibid., 273–4. Given China's ballooning population and extensive trade, it seems odd that it would be unaffected by a cessation of its overseas commerce, though it is necessary for the logic of the story.

47 Ibid., 275–81. At the start of the story, told in the early twenty-first century, the author explicitly connects the extermination of the Chinese to the American Bicentennial. However, his "Chinese" China, with its grow population, settler-based continental expansion, militia-based defenses, and rapid industrialization was clearly an idealized nineteenth-century America.

48 H. Bruce Franklin, *War Stars: The Superweapon and the American Imagination* (Amherst: University of Massachusetts, 2008), 33, 39, 102.

49 Jeanne Campbell Reesman, *Jack London's Racial Lives: A Critical Biography* (Athens: University of Georgia Press, 2009), 101.

50 Danel A. Metraux, "Jack London and the Yellow Peril," in London, *Asian Writings of Jack London*, 75.

51 London, "The Yellow Peril," 301–2.

52 The same probably applies to that magazine's editors and publishers, who a generation later published several of Sax Rohmer's Fu Manchu stories.

53 Larissa Heinrich, "How China Became the 'Cradle of Smallpox': Transformations in Discourse, 1726–2002," *Positions: East Asian Cultures Critique* 15, no. 1 (Spring 2007): 8; Christos Lynteris, "Yellow Peril Epidemics: The Political Ontology of Degeneration and Emergence," in Bille and Urbansky, *Yellow Perils*, 28.

54 Heinrich, "How China Became the 'Cradle of Smallpox'," 39.

55 Lynteris, "Yellow Peril Epidemics," 42–3.

56 Michael J. Devine, *John W. Foster: Politics and Diplomacy in the Imperial Era, 1873-1917* (Athens, OH: Ohio University Press, 1981), 102.

57 Ibid., 103.

58 "The Competition of Japan," *Harper's*, February 15, 1896, 147.

59 "The 'Yellow Peril'," *Living Age*, January 8, 1898, 124.

60 Gries, *China's New Nationalism*, 70–1.

61 "The Revolution in China," *Congregationalist*, August 26, 1898, 83–4.

62 "Peril of Yellow Menace," *Washington Post*, August 20, 1899.

63 "The Yellow Peril," *Review of Reviews*, August 1904, 164.

64 "The Awakening of China," *Living Age*, April 21, 1906, 131, 133.

65 "Seward on Eastern Problem," *New York Times*.

66 "Claude MacDonald's Prophecy," *Washington Post*, June 25, 1901.

67 "Warns of Yellow Peril," *Washington Post*, April 23, 1908.

Chapter 2

1 Krystyn R. Moon, *Yellowface: Creating the Chinese in American Popular Music and Performances: 1850s-1920s* (New Brunswick, NJ: Rutgers University Press, 2005), 32, 39.

2 William F. Wu, *The Yellow Peril: Chinese-Americans in American Fiction, 1850-1940* (Hampden, CT: Archon, 1982), 12.

3 Mae Ngai, *The Chinese Question: The Gold Rushes and Global Politics* (New York: W.W. Norton, 2021), 3.

4 Beth Lew-Williams, *The Chinese Must Go: Violence, Exclusion, and the Making of the Alien in America* (Cambridge, MA: Harvard University Press, 2018), 169.

5 Stanford M. Lyman, *Chinese Americans* (New York: Random House, 1974), 56.

6 Stuart Creighton Miller, *The Unwelcome Immigrant: The American Image of the Chinese, 1785-1882* (Berkeley, CA: University of California, 1969), 112.

7 Lyman, *Chinese Americans*, 56–7.

8 Moses Rachin, Forward to *The Unwelcome Immigrant*, vii.

9 Lyman, *Chinese Americans*, 57.

10 Ibid., 37.

11 Ngai, *The Chinese Question*, 62.

12 Ibid., 88.

13 Ibid., 54, 114.

14 Ibid., 87.

15 Lew-Williams, *The Chinese Must Go*, 26.

16 Ibid., 6.

17 Henry George, "The Chinese in California," *New York Tribune*, May 1, 1869, 1.

18 Ibid., 2.

19 Ngai, *The Chinese Question*, 147; Lew-Williams, *The Chinese Must Go*, 42.

20 Pierton W. Dooner, *Last Days of the Republic* (San Francisco, CA: Alta California, 1879), 151, 154.

21 Ibid., 170–3.

22 Ibid., 257.

23 Wu, *The Yellow Peril*, 40.

24 H. Bruce Franklin, *War Stars: The Superweapon and the American Imagination* (Amherst: University of Massachusetts Press, 2008), 33.

25 Lew-Williams, *The Chinese Must Go*, 45–7.

26 Ibid., 51, 171, 212.

27 Wei Tchen and Years, *Yellow Peril! An Archive of Anti-Asian Fear*, 233–4.

28 Ngai, *The Chinese Question*, 297.

29 Erika Lee, "The 'Yellow Peril' and Asian Exclusion in the Americas," *Pacific Historical Review* 76, no. 4 (November 2007): 541.

30 Lisa Rose Mar, *Brokering Belonging: Chinese in Canada's Exclusion Era, 1885-1945* (Oxford: Oxford University Press, 2010), 5.

31 John Fitzgerald, *Big White Lie: Chinese Australians in White Australia* (Sydney: University of New South Wales Press, 2007), 2; Mar, *Brokering Belonging*, 25.

32 Lee, "The 'Yellow Peril' and Asian Exclusion in the Americas," 560.

33 Ibid., 548–9.

34 Mar, *Brokering Belonging*, 5.

35 Ibid., 550.

36 Ibid., 552.

37 Lee, "The 'Yellow Peril' and Asian Exclusion in the Americas," 554.

38 Fitzgerald, *Big White Lie*, 52.

39 David Walker and Agnieszka Sobocinska, eds., *Australia's Asia: From yellow peril to Asian century* (Crawley, West Australia: University of Western Australia, 2012), 6.

40 Ngai, *The Chinese Question*, 27. As with most such influxes, most of these new arrivals did not become long-term residents.

41 Ibid., 36, 114.

42 Ibid., 167.

43 "The Yellow Peril in Queensland," *Review of Review*, August 1899, 166.

44 Ibid., 5.

45 Fitzgerald, *Big White Lie*, 13,14.

46 Ibid., 2, 13.

47 Hugh H. Lusk, "Chinese Exclusion in Australia," *North American Review* 174, no. 544 (March 1902): 370, 369, 375.

48 Carol Johnson, "Australia's Ambivalent Re-imagining of Asia," *Australian Journal of Political Science* 45, no. 1 (March 2010): 59.

49 Ngai, *The Chinese Question*, 261, 15.

50 Ibid., 190.

51 Mark O'Neill, *From the Tsar's Railway to the Red Army* (Melbourne: Penguin, 2014), 6–7.

52 "Yellow Peril for Russia," *The Sun*, November 15, 1900, 1.

53 O'Neill, *From the Tsar's Railway to the Red Army*, 10.

54 Alexander Lukin, "Russian Perceptions of the China Threat," in *The China Threat: Perceptions, Myths and Reality*, ed. Herbert Yee and Ian Story (New York: Routledge, 2022), 88.

55 Lewis H. Siegelbaum, "Another 'Yellow Peril': Chinese Migrants in the Russian Far East and the Russian Reaction before 1917," *Asian Studies* 12, no. 2 (1978): 310, 319, 321.

56 Wu, *The Yellow Peril*, 3.

57 Anne Witchard, *England's Yellow Peril: Sinophobia and the Great War* (Melbourne: Penguin, 2014), 2.

58 Frayling, *The Yellow Peril*, 222, 223.

59 "Our Yellow Peril," *Outlook*, 296.

60 George, "The Chinese in America," 2.

61 Ngai, *The Chinese Question*, 247.

62 Ibid., 190.

63 Lothrop Stoddard, *The Rising Tide of Color against White World-Supremacy* (New York: Scribner's Sons, 1920), 27.

Chapter 3

1 "China's Awakening One of the Great Events of the Age," *Wall Street Journal*, December 19, 1908, 6.

2 Judson Smith, "The Awakening of China," *North American Review*, February 1899, 230.

3 Frederic Wakeman, *The Fall of Imperial China* (New York: Free Press, 1975), 205, 213.

4 Ibid., 214.

5 Immanuel C. Y. Hsu, *The Rise of Modern China* (New York: Oxford University Press, 1970), 470.

6 "The Awakening of China," *Outlook*, August 11, 1900, 856.

7 "China's Awakening," *Los Angeles Times*, June 24, 1901, 6.

8 "Is China Awakening Herself?" *Atlanta Constitution*, August 15, 1905, 6.

9 "China's Awakening," *Washington Post*, September 16, 1905, 6.

10 K. K. Kawakami, "The Awakening of China," *North American Review*, October 5, 1906, 647, 648.

11 "All Asian Races Stir," *Washington Post*, May 17, 1908.

12 "The Mighty Awakening of the Chinese Empire," *New York Times*, April 21, 1907.

13 "After Korea—China?" *Nation*, August 1, 1907, 94.

14 "Yellow Peril Not Real," *Washington Post*, September 7, 1904.

15 D. W. Stevens, "Japan's Attitude Toward China," *Forum*, 76.

16 J. O. P. Bland, "The Yellow Peril," *The Living Age*, June 22, 1912, 708.

17 Ibid., 715.

18 Frayling, *The Yellow Peril*, 249, 222.

19 Witchard, *England's Yellow Peril*.

20 Ibid., 1, 9.

21 Urmila Seshagiri, "Modernity's (Yellow) Perils: Dr. Fu Manchu and English Race Paranoia," *Cultural Critique* 62 (Winter 2006): 169.

22 Frayling, *The Yellow Peril*, 234.

23 Sax Rohmer, *The Fu Manchu Omnibus, Volume 1* (London: Allison & Busby, 1998), 15.

24 Seshagiri, "Modernity's (Yellow) Perils," 177–8.

25 Patrick B. Sharp, *Savage Perils: Racial Frontiers and Nuclear Apocalypse in American Culture* (Norman: University of Oklahoma, 2007), 112.

26 Ibid., 113–14.

27 Ruth Mayer, *Serial Fu Manchu: The Chinese Supervillain and the Spread of Yellow Peril Ideology* (Philadelphia: Temple University, 2014), 48.

28 Ibid., 137, 148.

29 Witchard, *England's Yellow Peril*, 85.

30 Archibald R. Colquhon, "China in Transformation and the War," *North American Review*, July 1904, 12.

31 Sundara Raja, "The Future of China," *Living Age*, March 8, 1913, 613.

32 Xu Guoqi, *China and the Great War: China's Pursuit of a New National Identity and Internationalization* (Cambridge: Cambridge University Press, 2005), 93, 96.

33 Xu Guoqi, *Strangers on the Western Front: Chinese Workers in the Great War* (Cambridge: MA: Harvard University Press, 2011), 15.

34 Ibid., 1, 51, 100.

35 Ibid., 73.

36 Siegelbaum, "Another 'Yellow Peril'," 327.

37 O'Neill, *From the Tsar's Railway to the Red Army*, 25–6.

38 Ibid., 2.

39 Ibid., 63, 66.

40 Ibid., 82.

41 Ibid., 75, 86–7.

42 Guoqi, *China and the Great War*, 274.

43 Robert Bickers, *Out of China: How the Chinese Ended the Era of Western Domination* (London: Penguin, 2017), 30–3.

44 John Dewey and Alice Chipman Dewey, *Letters from China and Japan* (Coppel, TX: 1920, 2021), 37.

45 Ibid., 42–3.

46 Ibid., 48, 51.

47 Ibid., 57.

48 "'Yellow Peril': Interesting Comment on Mr. McClure's Famous Article," *Shanghai Times*, March 15, 1921, 3.

49 Richard Ellis, "Through its Rambling Millionaires, *The Great Gatsby* Satirises Racist Ideology," *Guardian*, June 13, 2022; Steve Rose, "A Deadly Ideology: How the 'Great Replacement Theory' went Mainstream," *Guardian*, June 8, 2022.

50 Madison Grant, "Introduction," in Stoddard, *The Rising Tide of Color*, 8.

51 Stoddard, *Rising Tide of Color*, vi.

52 Ibid., vii.

53 Ibid., 24, 27, 49.

54 Ibid., 228–9.

55 Ibid., 274.

56 Ibid., 232–3.

57 Bertrand Russell, *The Problem of China* (Coppel, TX: 1922, 2022), 32.

58 Ibid., 130.

59 Ibid., 134–5.

60 "China and the United States," *Chicago Daily Tribune*, November 18, 1921, 8.

61 Raymond Leslie Buell, "Against the Yellow Peril," *Foreign Affairs*, February 1923, 295.

Chapter 4

1 Andre Malraux, *The Conquerors*, trans. Winifred Stephens Whale(Boston: The Beacon Press, 1927, 1956), 1.

2 Ibid., 128.

3 Ibid., 2.

4 Ibid.

5 Orville Schell and John DeLury, *Wealth and Power: China's Long March to the Twenty-First Century* (New York: Random House, 2013), 125.

6 Marie-Claire Bergère, *Sun Yat Sen*, trans. Janet Lloyd (Stanford, CA: Stanford University Press, 1998), 5.

7 Ibid., 23–6.

8 Ibid., 59, 61, 69, 103.

9 Ibid., 154.

10 Ibid., 213–14.

11 Schell and DeLury, *Wealth and Power*, 130.

12 J. O. P. Bland, *China: The Pity of It* (Garden City, NY: Doubleday, 1932), 63.

13 Ibid., 154, 156, 158.

14 Schell and DeLury, *Wealth and Power*, 132.

15 Ibid., 352, 403.

16 Ibid., 357, 361.

17 Ibid., 373.

18 Ibid., 163, 372.

19 Ibid., 376.

20 Ibid., 389, 167.

21 Ibid., 315.

22 Lloyd E. Eastman, *The Abortive Revolution: China under Nationalist Rule, 1927-1937* (Cambridge, MA: Harvard University Press, 1974), 3.

23 C. Martin Wilbur, *The Nationalist Revolution in China, 1923-1928* (Cambridge: Cambridge University Press, 1983), 15.

24 Eastman, *The Abortive Revolution*, 37.

25 Lloyd E. Eastman, *Seeds of Destruction: Nationalist China in War and Revolution, 1937–1949* (Stanford, CA: Stanford University Press, 1984), 142.

26 Theodore H. White and Annalee Jacoby, *Thunder Out of China* (New York: William Sloane, 1946), 101.

27 Bickers, *Out of China*, 54.

28 Joe Studwell, *The China Dream: The Elusive Quest for the Greatest Untapped Market on Earth* (London: Profile, 2002, 2005), 19; John W. Garver, *China's Quest: The History of the Foreign Relations of the People's Republic of China* (New York: Oxford University, 2016), 43.

29 Ou-fan Lee, *Shanghai Modern: The Flowering of a New Urban Culture in China, 1930–1945* (Cambridge, MA: Harvard University Press, 1999), xiv.

30 Hans J. Van de Ven, *From Friend to Comrade: The Founding of the Chinese Communist Party, 1920-1927* (Berkeley, CA: University of California, 1991), 147.

31 Ibid., 3.

32 Akira Iriye, *After Imperialism: The Search for a New Order in the Far East, 1921-1931* (Cambridge, MA: Harvard University Press, 1965), 90–1.

33 Ibid., 125, 10.

34 Wilbur, *The Nationalist Revolution in China*, 62–3.

35 Iriye, *After Imperialism*, 136; Eastman, *Seeds of Destruction*, 1.

36 Iriye, *After Imperialism*, 137.

37 "Far Eastern Realities," *New Republic*, July 1, 1925, 142, 143.

38 "What China Asks," *Nation*, September 16, 1925, 294, 293.

39 "Is China Antiforeign?" *Living Age*, August 1, 1925, 24.

40 Mei Kuang-Ti, "Is the West Awakening?" *Nation*, April 21, 1926, 446.

41 "What the Chinese People Want," *Living Age*, July 25, 1925, 181.

42 Lewis S. Gannett, "Is China Being Americanized?" *Nation*, July 14, 1926, 52.

43 "Communist Victories," *Time*, October 4, 1926, 18.

44 Iriye, *After Imperialism*, 104, 107; Wilbur, *Nationalist Revolution in China*, 68.

45 Grover Clark, "The Way Out of the Chinese Muddle," *New Republic*, April 20, 1927, 240.

46 Iriye, *After Imperialism*, 227.

47 Wesley M. Bagby, *The Eagle-Dragon Alliance: America's Relations with China in World War II* (Newark, DE: University of Delaware, 1992), 48.

48 T. Christopher Jesperson, *American Images of China, 1931-1949* (Stanford, CA: Stanford University Press, 1996), 84–5.

49 "Conqueror," *Time*, April 4, 1927, 17, 18.

50 "Hero Falls," *Time*, August 22, 1927, 15.

51 "Soong Sisters," *Time*, December 12, 1927, 26.

52 "Peking Falls," *Time*, June 11, 1928, 20, 18.

53 "First President," *Time*, October 22, 1928, 22.

54 "Peking Falls," 19.

55 "A President Is Baptized," *Time*, November 3, 1930, 25.

56 "Chiang Dares," *Time*, November 9, 1936, 20.

57 "British Gift," *Time*, September 14, 1936, 24.

58 "T. V. for Victory," *New Republic*, January 26, 1942, 111.

59 "T. V.," *New Republic*, December 18, 1944, 37.

60 Hebert B. Elliston, "China in the World Family," *Foreign Affairs*, July 1929, 620.

61 Grover Clark and Henry W. Kinney, "Two Views on China," *Living Age*, February 15, 1927, 319, 321.

62 Nathaniel Peffer, "What Next in China?" *New Republic*, July 17, 1929, 225, 226.

63 Nathaniel Peffer, "What Next in China?" *New Republic*, July 31, 1929, 284.

64 "Can the Powers Keep their 'Rights' in China?" *New Republic*, December 15, 1926, 100; "Antiforeign Ferment in China," *Literary Digest*, October 16, 1926.

65 Bland, *China*, 238.

66 Bickers, *Out of China*, 63.

67 Lionel Curtis, *The Capital Question of China* (London: MacMillan, 1932), 17.

68 Ibid., 299.

69 Floyd Gibbons, *The Red Napoleon* (New York: Jonathan Cape and Harrison Smith, 1929), 23, 54, 26.

70 Ibid., 8–9.

71 Ibid., 6, 75, 181.

72 Ibid., 297.

73 Ibid., 190

74 Ibid., 5, 228.

75 Eastman, *The Abortive Revolution*, 86.

76 William C. Kirby, *Germany and Republican China* (Stanford, CA: Stanford University Press, 1984), 3–4.

77 Ibid., 152.

78 Eastman, *The Abortive Revolution*. 39–40.

79 Ibid., 46–8.

80 Ibid., 55, 62.

81 Bickers, *Out of China*, 169; Eastman, *The Abortive Revolution*, 67, 70.

82 Bickers, *Out of China*, 155; Jason Steuber, "The Exhibition of Chinese Art at Burlington House, London, 1935-36," *Burlington Magazine* 148, no. 1241 (August 2006): 529.

83 Peter Conn, *Pearl S. Buck: A Cultural Biography* (Cambridge: Cambridge University Press, 1996), 123, 131; Frayling, *The Yellow Peril*, 311.

84 Jesperson, *American Images of China*, 24.

85 Conn, *Pearl S. Buck*, xvi.

86 Kenneth E. Shewmaker, *Americans and Chinese Communists, 1927-1945* (Ithaca, NY: Cornell University Press, 1971), p. 71.

87 Bickers, *Out of China*, 172; Rana Mitter, *China's War with Japan, 1937-1945: The Struggle for Survival* (New York: Penguin, 2013), 85–6.

88 Bickers, *Out of China*, 192.

Chapter 5

1 Bagby, *Eagle-Dragon Alliance*, 53.

2 White and Jacoby, *Thunder Out of China*, 51.

3 "Japan Devours China," *New Republic*, June 26, 1935.

4 "The United States and China," *Saturday Evening Post*, March 14, 1931; A. Legendre, "Can Japan Save China?" *Living Age*, June 1931, 351.

5 Eastman, *Seeds of Destruction*, 133–6.

6 Samuel Lubell, "Is China Washed Up?" *Saturday Evening Post*, March 31, 1945.

7 The Imjin War of 1592–8, when the Chinese helped the Koreans repel a Japanese invasion, bore eerie similarities in its battlefield trajectory to the Korean War of 1950–3. The crucial difference in the results was due to the fact that the Truman's US Navy, unlike Hideyoshi's Japanese flotilla, maintained unquestioned naval superiority.

8 White and Jacoby, *Thunder Out of China*, 47; R. T. Barrett, "Chaining the Dragon," *Fortnightly Review*, July 1937, 268.

9 Richard B. Frank, *Tower of Skulls: A History of the Asia-Pacific War, July 1937–May 1942* (New York: Norton, 2020), 10.

10 Bickers, *Out of China*, 217.

11 Mitter, *China's War with Japan*, 128–30.

12 "The Dragon Licks His Wounds," *Saturday Evening Post*, April 14, 1940; "Three Years of War," *Time*, July 8, 1940, 20.

13 Eastman, *Seeds of Destruction*, 133.

14 White and Jacoby, *Thunder Out of China*, 56.

15 Eastman, *Seeds of Destruction*, 135. Japan's bombing of Chungking ceased after the United States entered the war in December 1941.

16 Jonathan Spence, *To Change China: Western Advisers in China, 1620-1960* (Boston: Little, Brown, 1969), 101.

17 Ibid., 229, 237.

18 Bagby, *Eagle-Dragon Alliance*, 40.

19 Ibid., 85–6.

20 Raymond Dawson, *The Chinese Chameleon: An Analysis of European Conceptions of Chinese Civilization* (London: Oxford University, 1967), 172.

21 Samuel Zipp, *The Idealist: Wendell Willkie's Wartime Quest to Build One World* (Cambridge, MA: Harvard University Press, 2020), 173, 176.

22 Wendell L. Willkie, *One World* (New York: Simon and Schuster, 1943), 130, 133.

23 Ibid., 150.

24 Zipp, *Idealist*, 189.

25 Nathaniel Peffer, "Two Nations Transformed," *New York Times*, July 13, 1941; Sir Frederick Whyte, "Our Chinese Ally," *Fortnightly Review*, April 1942, 284.

26 Ibid., 254.

27 Ibid., 159.

28 Ibid., 16.

29 Bickers, *Out of China*, 242.

30 Shewmaker, *Americans and Chinese Communists*, 197.

31 Schell and DeLury, *Wealth and Power*, 189–90.

32 Ibid., 159.

33 Ibid., 129, 133.

34 Ibid., 129.

35 Ibid.

36 Stephen G. Craft, *V.K. Wellington Koo and the Emergence of Modern China* (Lexington, KY: University Press of Kentucky, 2004), 170. That the Japanese felt comfortable denuding their northern sector to attack Chiang indicates how little of a threat the Chinese Communist insurgents posed.

37 Xiaoyuan Lui, *A Partnership for Disorder: China, the United States, and Their Policies for the Postwar Disposition of the Japanese Empire, 1941–1945* (New York: Cambridge University Press, 1996), 21, 208.

38 Bagby, *Eagle-Dragon Alliance*, 84.

39 Edgar Snow, *Red Star Over China* (New York: Grove Weidenfeld, 1938, 1968), 136.

40 Van de Ven, *From Friend to Comrade*, 22.

41 Cecil Beaton, *Chinese Diary & Album* (Hong Kong: Oxford University Press, 1945, 1991), 76. Snow, *Red Star*, 96; White and Jacoby, *Thunder Out of China*, 232.

42 Shewmaker, *Americans and the Chinese Communists*, 195.

43 Julia Lovell, *Maoism: A Global History* (New York: Knopf, 2019), 1.

44 Shewmaker, *Americans and the Chinese Communists*, 57.

45 Snow, *Red Star*, 95.

46 Ibid., 219.

47 Ibid., 409.

48 Shewmaker, *Americans and the Chinese Communists*, 243.

49 Ibid., 215.

50 "Chiang is China," *Time*, January 22, 1945, 21.

51 "Westward Ho!" *Time*, December 26, 1938, 16.

52 White and Jacoby, *Thunder Out of China*, xiii.

53 Ibid., 30.

54 Ibid., 234.

55 Stephen R. MacKinnon and Oris Friesen, *China Reporting: An Oral History of American Journalism in the 1930s and 1940s* (Berkeley, CA: University of California, 1987), 177.

56 Ibid., 242.

57 Ibid., 288; Craft, *Wellington Koo*, 209.

58 Jesperson, *American Images of China*, 132.

59 Eastman, *Seeds of Destruction*, 158.

60 Odd Arne Westad, *Decisive Encounters: The Chinese Civil War, 1945-1950* (Stanford, CA: Stanford University Press, 2003), 185.

61 Jesperson, *American Images of China*, 130.

62 David Allen Mayers, *Cracking the Monolith: U.S. Policy Against the Sino-Soviet Alliance, 1949–1955* (Baton Rouge, LA: Louisiana State University, 1986), 30.

63 Dean Acheson, Letter of Transmittal, Department of State, Washington July 30, 1949, in *The White Paper: August 1949, Originally Issued as United States Relations with China, With Special Reference to the Period 1944-1949* (Stanford, CA: Stanford University Press, 1967), XV, XVI.

64 Richard Bernstein, *China 1945: Mao's Revolution and America's Fateful Choice* (New York: Knopf, 2014), 393.

65 Schell and DeLury, *Wealth and Power*, 229.

66 James Kynge, *China Shakes the World: A Titan's Rise and Troubled Future—And the Challenge for America* (Boston: Houghton Mifflin, 2006), 221.

67 Brian Porter, *Britain and the Rise of Communist China: A Study of British Attitudes, 1945-1954* (London: Oxford University, 1967), 21.

68 "Who Holds China's Future?" *Business Week*, January 17, 1948, 101; Edgar Snow, "Will China Become a Russian Satellite?" *Saturday Evening Post*, April 9, 1949.

69 Snow, "Will China Become a Russian Satellite?"

70 Jack Belden, *China Shakes the World* (New York: Harper, 1949), 464–6.

71 Lorraine Boissoneault, "The True Story of Brainwashing and How It Shaped America," *Smithsonian*, May 22, 2017; David Seed, *Brainwashing: The Fictions of Mind Control* (Kent, OH: Kent State University Press, 2004), 27.

72 Seed, *Brainwashing*, 31.

73 Ibid., 67.

74 Edward Hunter, *Brainwashing: Its History; Use by Totalitarian Communist Regimes; and the Stories of American and British Soldiers and Captives Who Defied It* (New York: Pantianos Classics, 1956), 5, 36.

75 Ibid., 62–4.

76 Ibid., 145.

77 Ibid., 176.

78 Westad, *Decisive Encounters*, 323.

79 Hanson W. Baldwin, "China as a Military Power," *Foreign Affairs*, October 1951, 52.

80 Ibid., 62.

81 Ibid., 56, 61.

Chapter 6

1 James Reston, "Washington: Dean Rusk and 'The Yellow Peril'," *New York Times*, October 15, 1967.

2 Ibid.

3 John H. Averill, "McCarthy Chinese Rusk on 'Containing' China," *Los Angeles Times*, October 17, 1967, 15.

4 Joseph Kraft, "Rusk's Raising of Yellow Peril Is Truly Dangerous Escalation," *Washington Post*, October 17, 1967.

5 Robert Young, "'Yellow Peril' Talk Absurd, LBJ Asserts," *Chicago Tribune*, October 26. 1967, C4.

6 "No Place in Our Purpose," *Baltimore Afro-American*, November 4, 1967.

7 Carl T. Rowan, "There's No Place Today for Yellow-Peril Jingoism," *Washington Post*.

8 Edgar Snow, *Red China Today* (New York: Random House, 1961, 1970), 675.

9 Memorandum for General Eisenhower, Re: United States Pacific Policy, 8, 9, 3, 7, Folder Formosa (China) 1052-1957 (1), Box 10, International Series, Ann Whitman Files, DDE Library.

10 Dulles, Notes on Remarks at NSC Meeting, March 31, 1953, 2, Folder General Foreign Policy Matters (2), White House Memoranda Series, Dulles, John Foster Papers, 1951–9, DDE Library; Dulles, "Our Foreign Policies in Asia," Before the Foreign Policy Association, New York, February 16, 1955, 8, Folder 2/16/55: Speech Re, "Our Foreign Policies in Asia," Foreign Policy Association, New York, Box 333, Series Speeches, Statements, Press Conferences, etc., Dulles, JF Papers, Mudd Library, Princeton University, Princeton, NJ.

11 Report of the Van Fleet Mission to the Far East, April 26 to August 7, 1954, 7, Folder President's Papers 1954 (8), Box 2, Special Assistant Series, Presidential Subseries, OSANSA, White House Office, DDE.

12 Gen. James A. Van Fleet, "Catastrophe in Asia," *U.S. News & World Report*, September 17, 1954, 28.

13 "Taking a Look at China," *U.S. News & World Report*, February 4, 1955, 24.

14 Richard L. Walker, Communist China: Power and Prospects?" *New Leader*, October 20, 1958, 3, 32, Folder Communism—China—Printed Matter—Miscellaneous, Box 25, Christopher Emmet Papers, Hoover Institute, Stanford University, Stanford, CA.

15 Minutes, 7, Folder 271st Meeting of NSC, December 22, 1955, Box 7, NSC Series, AWF, DDE.

16 Notes, January 8, 1950, 1, 2, Folder China, People's Rep. Of, Box 47 (1950), Series Selected Correspondence, Dulles, JF, Mudd.

17 Dulles to Clare Boothe Luce, September 1, 1954, 1, Folder Dulles, John Foster Sept. 1954 (2), Box 4, Dulles-Herter Series, AWF, DDE.

18 Saturday Evening Post to Alsop, September 17, 1954, 16, Folder 1, Box 42, Joseph Alsop Papers, Library of Congress, Washington, DC.

19 Draft, NSC 148: United States Policies on the Far East, April 6, 1953, 6, 14, Folder NSC 148—Far East, Box 4, White House Office, Office of the Special

Assistant for National Security Affairs, NSC Series, Policy Papers Subseries, DDE Library.

20 NSC 146/2: U.S. Objective and Courses of Action with Respect to Formosa and the Chinese National Government, November 6, 1953, Folder NSC 146/2—Formosa & Chinese Nationalist Government (2), Box 4, White House Office, Office of the Special Assistant for National Security Affairs, NSC Series, Policy Papers Subseries, DDE Library.

21 NSC 166/1: U.S. Policy Toward Communist China, November 6, 1953, 5, 12, in Ibid.

22 Ibid., 6, 34.

23 Snow, *Red China Today*, 597.

24 Dulles to Eisenhower, February 25, 1955, Folder Dulles, John Foster Feb. 1955 (1), Box 4, Dulles-Herter Series, AWF, DDE.

25 Eisenhower to Dulles, February 10, 1955, 2, Folder Dulles, John Foster Feb. 1955 (2), Box 4, Dulles-Herter Series, AWF, DDE.

26 Eisenhower to Douglas, April 12, 1955, Folder DDE Diary April 1955 (1), Box 10, DDE Diary Series, AWF, DDE.

27 Memorandum of Conference with the President, April 4, 1955, Folder ACW Diary April 1955 (6), Box 5, ACW Diary Series, AWF, DDE.

28 Speech, Dulles, "Our Foreign Policies in Asia," Foreign Policy Association, New York, February 16, 1955, 7, Folder Dulles, John Foster Feb. 1955 (2), Box 4, Dulles-Herter Series, AWF, DDE.

29 Eisenhower to Dulles, Subject: Formosa, April 5, 1955, 5, Folder DDE Diary April 1955 (2), Box 10, DDE Diary Series, AWF, DDE.

30 Dulles to Eisenhower, February 25, 1955, 2, Folder Dulles, John Foster Feb. 1955 (1), Box 4, Dulles-Herter Series, AWF, DDE.

31 Minutes, 13, 14, Folder 232nd Meeting of NSC, January 20, 1955, Box 6, NSC Series, AWF, DDE.

32 William S. White, "New U.S. China Policy Slowly Taking Shape," *New York Times*, February 13, 1955, 170.

33 William Hopkins to Ann Whitman, Re: Correspondence Regarding Formosa, January 27, 1955, Folder Formosa (2), Box 9, International Series, AWD, DDE.

34 Excerpts of U.S. Editorial Opinion on Quemoy-Matsu, September 8, 1958, 5, Folder Quemoy-Matsu—Washburn Abbot, Box 29, Administration Series, AWF, DDE.

35 Memcon Dulles and Eisenhower, September 23, 1958, 2, Folder WH Meetings with the President July 1, 1958–December 31, 1958 (6), Box 7, WHMS, Dulles, John Foster Papers, 1951–59, DDE.

36 Niu Jun, *The Cold War and the Origin of Foreign Relations of the People's Republic of China*, trans. Zhonh Yijinh (Boston: Brill, 2018), 292; Excerpt from the Unedited Translation of Mao Zedong's Speech at the Moscow Conference of Communist and Workers' Parties, November 18, 1957, Cold War International History Project, 4; NIE 13-2-60, The Chinese Atomic Energy Program, December 13, 1960, 3.

37 "Our Long-Term Policy Toward Red China, *Kansas City Star*, September 15, 1958, Folder WH—General Correspondence 1958 (2), Box 6, White House Memoranda Series, Dulles, John Foster Papers, 1951–1959, DDE.

38 E. J. Kahn, Jr., *The China Hands: America's Foreign Service Officers and What Befell Them* (New York: Viking, 1975), 309.

39 Ruth Montgomery, "Red China in Crystal Ball," *Washington Post*, December 30, 1956, D6; Hebert Gordon, "Red China Seen Entering U.N. in 1957," *Washington Post*, December 27, 1956, A11.

40 Dulles, "Our Policies Toward Communism in China," Before the International Convention of Lions International, San Francisco, California, June 26, 1957, 7, 8, Folder Speech: "Our Policies Toward Communism in China," Box 356, Series Speeches, Statements, Press Conferences, etc., Dulles, JF Papers, Mudd.

41 Yeh to Dulles, June 30, 1957, Folder Chiang Kai-shek, Box 114 (1957), Series Selected Correspondence, Dulles, JF Papers, Mudd.

42 Qiang Zhai, "Mao Zedong and Dulles's 'Peaceful Evolution' Strategy: Revelations from Bo Yibo's Memoirs," *Cold War International History Project Bulletin*, 228–9.

43 Notes, Far East Presentation, May 10, 1955, 1, Folder China People's Republic of, Box 90 (1955), Series Selected Correspondence, Dulles, JF Papers, Mudd.

44 "Chinese Communists Held Worst Peril," *Los Angeles Times*, November 20, 1955, A6.

45 Vincent Purcell, "A 'Yellow Peril'?" *Observer*, October 12, 1958, 8.

46 Dulles, "The Threat of a Red Asia," Speech before the Overseas Press Club of America, New York, March 29, 1954, 4, Folder China, People's Republic of, Box 79 (1954), Series Selected Correspondence, Dulles, JF Papers, Mudd.

47 Hans J. Morgenthau, "The Roots of America's China Policy," *China Quarterly* 10 (April–June 1962): 49.

48 Governor's Briefing, April 27, 1954, 7, Folder 9: China People's Republic of, 1950 and 1954–5, Box 100, Series 5: Subject Files, CIA, Allen W. Dulles Papers, Mudd; Rostow, Asia Policy, 3, Report of the Quantico Vulnerabilities Panel Tab 3(b), Folder Quantico Vulnerabilities Panel, Record Group 59.15, National Archives and Records Administration, College Park, MD.

49 Chi-kwan Mark, *The Everyday Cold War: Britain and China, 1950-1972* (London: Bloomsbury, 2017), 189, 186, 190.

50 Robert Boardman, *Britain and the People's Republic of China, 1949-74* (London: MacMillan, 1976), 24.

51 Ibid., 61.

52 Donald Horne, *The Lucky Country* (Melbourne: Penguin, 1964), 2.

53 Ibid., 119–20.

54 June Teufel Dreyer, *Middle Kingdom and Empire of the Rising Sun: Sino-Japanese Relations, Past and Present* (New York: Oxford University, 2016), 361.

55 Chalmers Johnson, "How China and Japan See Each Other," in *China and Japan: Search For Balance Since World War I*, ed. Alvin D. Coox and Hilary Conroy (Santa Barbara, CA: ABC-Clio, 1978), 12.

56 Conrad Brandt, "The Passionate Pilgrimage of Simone de Beauvior," *Journal of Asian Studies* 18, no. 2 (January 1959): 277.

57 Simone de Beauvior, *The Long March: An Account of Modern China*, trans. Austryn Wainhouse (London: Phoenix, 1957), 143, 494, 124; Michael Shapiro, *Changing China* (London: Lawrence & Wishart, 1958), 46.

58 Brandt, "Passionate Pilgrimage," 279.

59 John B. Tsu, "Behind the Bamboo Curtain," *America*, April 15, 1961, 158.

60 George Gallup, "Russia Still Feared More Than Red China," *Hartford Courant*, March 22, 1961, 16.

61 William G. Mayer, *The Changing American Mind: How and Why American Public Opinion Changed between 1960 and 1988* (Ann Arbor, MI: University of Michigan Press, 1992), 422.

62 Radhe Gopal Pradham, *America and China: A Study in Cooperation and Conflict, 1962-1983* (Delhi: UDH Publishers, 1983), 49.

63 "Red Chinese Battle Plan," *Department of Defense*, 1967.

64 Thomson to Harriman, January 12, 1962, 3, Folder 1, Box 15 James Thomson Papers, John F. Kennedy Library, Boston, MA.

65 Mayers, *Cracking the Monolith*, 6.

66 Partha S. Ghosh, *Sino-Soviet Relations: U.S. Perceptions and Policy Responses* (New Delhi: Uppal Publishing House, 1981), 233; Ronald C. Keith, *The Diplomacy of Zhou Enlai* (New York: St. Martin's Press, 1989), 69.

67 Bickers, *Out of China*, 283.

68 Harold Macmillan, *Tides of Fortune: 1945-1955* (London: MacMillan, 1969), 622, 630, 648.

69 Gordon H. Chang, *Friends and Enemies: The United States, China, and the Soviet Union, 1948-1972* (Stanford, CA: Stanford University Press, 1990), 155.

70 Richard Lowenthal, "The Sino-Soviet Dispute," *Commentary*, May 1961, 393.

71 "The Wave of the Future," *Nation*, July 1, 1961, 2.

72 "How Deep the Red Feud – And a 'Summit'," *Newsweek*, December 12, 1960, 34–6.

73 Nikita Khrushchev, *Khrushchev Remembers*, trans. Strobe Talbott (Boston: Little, Brown, 1970), 461.

74 Sergey Radchenko, *Two Suns in the Heavens: The Sino-Soviet Struggle for Supremacy, 1962–1967* (Stanford, CA: Stanford University Press, 2009), 166.

75 Paul Wohl, "Soviets Sight 'Yellow Peril'," *Christian Science Monitor*, July 29, 1963, 1.

76 John K. Cooley, *East Wind Over Africa: Red China's African Offensive* (New York: Walker, 1965), 6; Bruce D. Larkin, *China and Africa, 1949-1970* (Berkeley, CA: University of California, 1971), 194.

77 Charles Burton Marshall, "The Chinese Puzzle," *Commonweal*, November 11, 1960, 167.

78 James O'Gara, "Battle of the Giants," *Commonweal*, March 22, 1963, 654.

79 "Rethinking China," *Christian Century*, September 11, 1963, 1091; Alan. L. Otten, "Bitter Clash Between China, Russia Will Have a World-Wide Impact," *Wall Street Journal*, July 1, 1963, 14.

80 Cooley, *East Wind Over Africa*, 215.

81 Saville R. Davis, "Harriman on China," *Christian Science Monitor*, September 27, 1963, 20.

82 Record of Conversation between Premier Zhou Enlai, Vice Premier Chen Yi, and Pakistani ambassador Raza, August 12, 1963, 1, in CWIHP.

83 Mao Zedong, "There Are Two Intermediate Zones," September 1963, 1, in CWIHP.

84 Rice to Harriman, June 21, 1963, 1, Subject: Inhibiting Communist China's Making and Exploiting Nuclear Weapons, Folder Nuclear Capability, Box 4, Top Secret Files Relating to the Republic of China, 1954-1965, Office of the Country Director for the Republic of China, Bureau of Far Eastern Affairs, RG 59, NARA.

85 Airgram, Hong Kong to State, Subject: Communist China and Recommendations for United States Policy, November 6, 1964, Folder Cables Volume 2, Box 238, China Country Files, National Security Files, Lyndon Baines Johnson Presidential Library, Austin, TX.

86 Frank Dikotter, *Mao's Great Famine: The History of China's Most Devastating Catastrophe, 1958–1962* (New York: Walker, 2010), 13, 48, 104, 97, 335.

87 Minutes of Chairman Mao Zedong's First Meeting with Nehru, October 19, 1954, 1; Agreement between the Republic of India and the People's Republic of China on Trade and Intercourse between the Tibet Region of China and India, April 29, 1954, 1. Both in CWIHP.

88 Robert J. MacMahon, *The Cold War on the Periphery: The United States, India, and Pakistan* (New York: Columbia University Press, 1994), 252, 257.

89 Though devoid of permanent human settlement, its parched mountainous terrain was of value to the Chinese since its occupation allowed them to build the first paved road connecting Tibet to Xinjiang.

90 A Chronology of the Sino-Indian Border Dispute, 11, Folder 19, Box 1, Roger Hilsman Papers, JFK; MacMahon, *The Cold War on the Periphery*, 292.

91 "Never Again the Same," *Time*, November 30, 1962, 23; Robert P. Martin, "Behind China's Strange Moves," *U.S. News & World Report*, December 10, 1962, 51.

92 Paul Nitze, with Ann M. Smith and Steven L. Rearden, *From Hiroshima to Glasnost: At the Center of Decision, A Memoir* (New York: Grove Wiedenfeld, 1989), 240; Telegram, Galbraith to Rusk, November 30, 1962, Folder General 11.30.62, India Country, National Security Files, JFK.

93 Rostow to Rusk, Subject: Southeast Asia and China, January 10, 1964, 2, Folder Memos Vol. 1 (1 of 2), Box 237, China Country Files, NSF, LBJ.

94 "Who Is The Real Enemy in Vietnam?" *U.S. News & World Report*, June 1, 1964, 33; "Why Hold the Line in Vietnam? Adlai Stevenson's Answer," *Newsweek*, December 27, 1965, 20.

95 Tom Wicker, "The Peking Enigma," *New York Times*, March 11, 1966.

96 "Blueprint for Conquest," *Newsweek*, September 20, 1965, 37.

97 George C. Denney to Rusk, Subject: Rand Corporation Thesis that Lin Piao Article Calls on Viet Cong to Revamp Military and Political Strategy, 3, Folder General Foreign Policy, January 1966–April 1966, Box 1, Records of Relations to Communist China, 1964–1966, Office of Asian Communist Affairs, Bureau of East Asian Affairs, RG 59, NARA.

98 Komer to McGeorge Bundy, November 23, 1964, 1, 2, Folder China—UN Representation (1964–6), Box 15, Komer Files, NSF, LBJ.

99 Benjamin Read to McGeorge Bundy, Subject: French Recognition of Communist China, January 22, 1964, Folder Political Affairs and Area Relationships, Communist China and France, 1964, Box 10, Bureau of East Asian Affairs, Central Files, 1947-1969, RG 59, NARA.

100 Central Intelligence Agency, Office of National Estimates, Subject: Implications of an Assumed French Recognition of Communist China, January 15, 1964, 2, Folder 7, Box 176, Country File—France, National Security Files, LBJ.

101 Andre Malraux, *Anti-Memoirs*, trans. Terence Kilmartin (New York: Holt, Rinehart and Winston, 1967, 1968), 137.

102 Research Memorandum, George C. Denney, Jr. to Rusk, Subject: French Recognition of Communist China, January 22, 1964, 3, Folder 7, Box 176, Country File—France, NSF, LBJ; Bureau of Intelligence and Research, Intelligence Summary, French Recognition of Communist China: Some Speculation on its Motivation, *Current Foreign Relations*, Issue No. 5, January 29, 1964, 21, CPR 64 65 66, Robert Komer Papers, NSF, LBJ.

103 Grand to William Bundy, Subject: Communist China: The Problem of Polarization, February 9, 1965, 4, 5, Folder Guidelines, Directives, Basic Studies 1-5.65, Box 1, ACA Subject Files, Lot Files, RG 59, NARA.

104 Ibid., 6.

105 Travel Letter IV, June 11, 1965, 3, Folder 12: Chinese Representation, 1961–4, Box 340, Series 5: United Nations, 1945–65, Adlai Stevenson Papers, Mudd.

106 Robert Blum to Marshall Green, February 7, 1964, 1–6, Folder 1, Box 16, Thomson Papers, JFK.

107 Folder Relations with Russia, Box 181, Office Files of Frederick Panzer, Lyndon Johnson Papers, LBJ.

108 Thomson to Bundy and Komer, Subject: U.S. Opinion regarding Communist China, August 21, 1964, 1–2, Folder CPR 64 65 66, Komer Papers, NSF, LBJ.

109 "The Future of Half the World," *Time*, June 26, 1964, 34.

Chapter 7

1 Memorandum for the Record, Michael Forrestal, Conversation with Miss Pearl Buck, December 17, 1963, 1, Folder 6, Box 23, National Security Files, JFK.

2 Ibid., 1–2.

3 "No Tickee, No Worry," *Time*, November 24, 1961, 66.

4 Eugene Franklin Wong, "On Visual Media Racism: Asians in the American Motion Pictures," Dissertation, University of Denver, 1977, 179–80.

5 Darrel Y. Hamamoto, *Monitored Peril: Asian Americans and the Politics of TV Representation* (Minneapolis: University of Minnesota, 1994), 110–11.

6 Robert A. Heinlein, *Starship Troopers* (New York: G.P. Putnam's Sons, 1959), 139, 212, 214.

7 Ibid., 246.

8 Heinlein, *Starship Troopers*, 184.

9 Arnold J. Toynbee, "Is a 'Race War' Shaping Up?" *New York Times Magazine*, September 29, 1963, 23, 26, 214, 245, 246.

10 Arnold J. Toynbee, "A War of the Races? 'No'," *New York Times Magazine*, August 7, 1960, 11, 54, 56.

11 Toynbee, "Is a 'Race War' Shaping Up?" 246.

12 Ibid., 214, 246.

13 Ibid., 246.

14 Wu, *The Yellow Peril*, 164.

15 Christina Klein, *Cold War Orientalism: Asia in the Middlebrow Imagination, 1945-1961* (Berkeley, CA: University of California, 2003), 37. Matthew Frye Jacobson and Gaspar Gonzalez, *What Have They Built You to Do? The Manchurian Candidate and Cold War America* (Minneapolis: University of Minnesota, 2006).

16 *The Manchurian Candidate* (1962), [Film], Dir. John Frankenheimer, USA: MGM.

17 Richard Condon, *The Manchurian Candidate* (New York: McGraw Hill, 1959), 28. The other two are Uzbek, and are looked down upon by their Chinese colleagues.

18 Condon, *The Manchurian Candidate*, 298.

19 Ibid., 35.

20 *The Manchurian Candidate* (1962), [Film].

21 Robert G. Lee, *Orientals: Asian Americans in Popular Culture* (Philadelphia: Temple University, 1999), 8.

22 One of Silva's Asian villains was the lead in *The Return of Mr. Moto*, a 1965 revival of a Fu Manchu knock-off popular in the 1930s, and brought back—like other Asian villains—during that decade. Jacobson and Gonzalez, *What Have They Built You To Do?*, 128.

23 Ibid., 125.

24 Arthur Knight, "The Fu Manchurian Candidate," *Saturday Review*, October 27, 1962, 65.

25 "Exclusive Interview with Frank Sinatra, John Frankenheimer, and George Axelrod," included in *The Manchurian Candidate* [DVD] MGM Home Entertainment, 1998.

26 Ian Fleming, *Doctor No* (New York: Macmillan, 1958), 8.

27 Stanley Kauffmann, "The First Roses of Summer," *New Republic*, June 15, 1963, 36.

28 Fleming, *Doctor No*, 127.

29 Brendan Gill of the *New Yorker* described Wiseman's "depraved Chinese" villain as "spooky and debonair." Brendan Gill, "Yes to 'No'," *New Yorker*, June 1, 1963, 66.

30 Fleming, *Doctor No*, 131, 133, 146.

31 Ibid., 43. Quarrel, a fisherman from the Caymans, had assisted Bond on his previous mission to Jamaica five years earlier. In the film, Bond and Quarrel are strangers.

32 Ibid., 8, 1.

33 Ibid., 50.

34 In the book, No runs a far less glamorous guano mine.

35 Fleming, *Doctor No*, 143.

36 *Dr. No* (1963), [Film], Dir. Terence Young, USA: MGM.

37 *55 Days at Peking* (1963), [Film], Dir. Nicholas Ray, USA: Allied Artists.

38 John Gregory Dunne, "Movies in Brief," *National Review*, July 30, 1963, 72. In Dunne's assessment, Yordan's scripts were "not so much written, they're manufactured."

39 *Newsweek* called the battle scenes "splashy," *Time* praised the cinematography as "magnificent," and *America* termed the production "stunning." "Nobody Eats Rats," *Newsweek*, June 3, 1963, 84; "Foreign Devils Go Home," *Time*, May 21, 1963, 80; Moira Walsh, "55 Days At Peking," *America*, July 6, 1963, 26.

40 "Foreign Devils Go Home," 80; Walsh, "55 Days at Peking," 26.

41 Dunne, "Movies in Brief," 72.

42 "Nobody Eats Rats," 84.

43 *Satan Never Sleeps* (1962), [Film], Dir. Leo McCary, USA: Twentieth Century.

44 Philip T. Hartung, "Ennui Anyone?," *Commonweal*, March 16, 1962, 645.

45 Moira Walsh, "Satan Never Sleeps," *America*, March 10, 1962, 774; Hartung, "Ennui Anyone?," 645.

46 "Nothing Sacred," *Time*, March 9, 1962, 91.

47 "Taint Funny, McCarey," *Newsweek*, March 12, 1962, 102.

48 Walsh, "Satan Never Sleeps," 775.

49 Jacobson and Gonzalez, *What Have They Built You to Do?*, 124.

50 Hamamoto, *Monitored Peril*, 117–19.

51 Norman Sklarewitz, "The New Bad Guys: Orientals Take Over As TV, Film Villains," *Wall Street Journal*, October 12, 1966, 1.

52 "The Mysterious Radio-Active Man!" Journey Into Mystery #93, June 1963. In Stan Lee and Jack Kirby, *The Mighty Thor: Journey into Mystery, Nos.*

83-100 (New York: Marvel Masterworks, 2010), 139. Thank you to Ian Abbey for supplying me with these comic book sources.

53 Ibid., 140.

54 Ibid., 143.

55 Stan Lee and Robert Berns, "Trapped by the Red Barbarian," *Tales of Suspense #42*, June 1963, Stan Lee, "The Hands of the Mandarin!," *Tales of Suspense #50*, February 1964, both in *The Invincible Ironman, Volume I: Collecting Tales of Suspense, Nos. 39-50* (New York: Marvel, 2015).

56 Lee and Berns, "Trapped by the Red Barbarian," 44, 47.

57 Lee, "The Hands of the Mandarin!," 176.

58 Ibid., 177.

59 Ibid., 181.

60 Stan Lee, "When the Commissar Commands!," *The Avengers #18*, July 1965, in *Marvel Masterworks: Volume 2, College the Avengers, Nos. 11-20* (New York: Marvel, 2009), 157, 167.

61 Ibid., 168.

62 Ibid., 156.

63 "A Band Apart," (1964), [Film], Dir. Jean-Luc Godard, France: Janus.

Chapter 8

1 Fittingly, the band played this song in the Concert for New York City at Madison Square Garden to salute the firefighters and police officers who perished on September 11, 2001.

2 Richard Wolin, *The Wind from the East: French Intellectuals, the Cultural Revolution, and the Legacy of the 1960s* (Princeton, NJ: Princeton University Press, 2010, 2018), 4.

3 Fox Butterfield, *Alive in the Bitter Sea* (New York: Bantam, 1982), 29.

4 Gregg A. Brazinsky, *Winning the Third World: Sino-American Rivalry During the Cold War* (Chapel Hill, NC: University of North Carolina, 2017), 218–27.

5 Frank Dikotter, *The Cultural Revolution: A People's History, 1962-1976* (New York: Bloomsbury Press, 2016), 57, 74, 81.

6 Ibid., 150, 164, 179.

7 Ma Jisen, *The Cultural Revolution in the Foreign Ministry of China* (Hong Kong: Chinese University, 2004), 45, 75, 188.

8 Rostow to Johnson, September 16, 1966, Folder Memos Volume 7 (3 of 3), Box 240, China Country Files, NSF, LBJ.

9 Jenkins to Rostow, Subject: Attached Memo "The Outlook in Communist China," August 20, 1967, 3, Folder 6, Box 244, China Country Files, NSF.

10 Barnett to Berger, Subject: China Strategy, May 11, 1967, 1, Folder Chicom General, Box 1, Alfred Jenkins Files, NSF, LBJ.

11 Joseph S. Nye, *Soft Power: The Means to Success in World Politics* (New York: Public Affairs, 2004), 5.

12 Ibid., 73.

13 For an early example, see Carole Fink, Philipp Gassert, and Detlef Junker, eds., *1968: The World Transformed* (New York: Cambridge University Press, 1998).

14 Wolin, *Wind from the East*, 16.

15 Ibid., 20.

16 Ibid., 147.

17 Bickers, *Out of China*, 353; Lovell, *Maoism,* 296; Alexander C. Cook, ed., *Mao's Little Red Book: A Global History* (Cambridge: Cambridge University Press, 2014), xiii.

18 Slobodian Quinn, "Badge books and brand books: The Mao Bible in East and West Germany," in Cook, *Mao's Little Red Book*, 206.

19 William Hinton, *Fanshen: A Documentary of Revolution in a Chinese Village* (New York: Monthly Review, 1966, 2008), ix, xxi.

20 Bickers, *Out of China*, 353; Lovel, *Maoism*, 39.

21 W. E. B. Du Bois, "China and Africa," February 23, 1959.

22 "Birthday Party," *Newsweek*, October 14, 1963, 45.

23 William Worthy, "The Red Chinese American Negro," *Esquire*, October 1964, 132.

24 Ibid., 174–5.

25 Lovell, *Maoism*, 280.

26 Ibid., 299.

27 Bobby Seale, *Seize the Time: The Story of the Black Panther Party and Huey P. Newton* (New York: Random House, 1970), 24, 81.

28 Ibid., 83.

29 Lovell, *Maoism*, 279.

30 NIE 11/13-69: The USSR and China, August 12, 1969, 5. In *Tracking the Dragon.*

31 Chen Jian, "China, the Vietnam War, and the Sino-American Rapprochement, 1968-1973," in *The Third Indochina War Conflict between China, Vietnam and Cambodia, 1972-79*, ed. Odd Arne Westad and Sophie Quinn-Judge (London: Routledge, 2006), 35, 45.

32 Dikotter, *Cultural Revolution*, 206; Yafeng Xia, "China's Elite Politics and the Sino-American Rapprochement, January 1969–February 1972," *Journal of Cold War Studies* 8, no. 4 (Fall 2006): 7, 17.

33 Harrison E. Salisbury, *War Between Russia and China* (New York: W.W. Norton, 1969), 9.

34 Ibid., 202.

35 Lukin, "Russian Perceptions of the China Threat," 89.

36 Andrei Amalrik, *Will the Soviet Union Survive until 1984?* (New York: Harper & Row, 1970), 47.

37 Ibid., 63.

38 Ibid., 58.

39 Solomon to Kissinger, Subject: Mao Tse-tung and the Sino-Soviet Dispute, December 7, 1971, 9, Folder PRC Briefing Papers Sent to the President February 1972, Box 91, Country Files: Far East, HAK Files, National Security Files, Richard M. Nixon Library, Yorba Linda, CA.

40 George Gallup, "Impending Talks Lessen Fear of China as a Threat to Peace," *Washington Post*, October 10, 1971, F5.

41 Statement of A. Doak Barnett, United States Senate Committee on Foreign Relations, March 8, 1966, 2, 12, Folder 38, United States Senate Committee on Foreign Relations (1), Box 5, George Taylor Papers, Washington University, Seattle, WA.

42 Statement by Professor John K. Fairbank for the Committee on Foreign Relations, United States Senate, March 10, 1966, Folder 38: United States Senate Committee on Foreign Relations (1), Box 5, Taylor Papers, Washington.

43 "U.S. Starts Rethinking Policies on Red China," *U.S News & World Report*, March 12 1966, 41.

44 Remarks, Javits, "China and the Peace of Asia, Annual Masonic Dedication Service, New York, March 20, 1966, 1–3, Folder 3/20/66: China and the Peace of Asia, Box 36, Series 1, Subseries 1, Javits Papers, State University of New York-Stony Brook, Stony Brook, NY.

45 Memo, Marcy to Fulbright, November 24, 1964, Folder 8: Misc. Speeches—Research Material (Foreign Policy), Box 5, Series 73, J. William Fulbright Papers, University of Arkansas Libraries, Special Collections, Fayetteville, AR.

46 George F. Kennan, "A Fresh Look at Our China Policy," *New York Times Magazine*, November 22, 1964, 142, 144.

47 Cumings, "The World Shakes China," 29.

48 Speech, "The Commonwealth and the United States in Eastern Asia, Parliament, Wellington, New Zealand, December 8, 1965, 4–5, Folder "The Commonwealth and the U.S. in Eastern Asia" (12/8/65), Box 25, Series 72, Fulbright Papers, Arkansas.

49 Mao Lin, "To See is to Believe?—Modernization and the U.S.-China Exchanges in the 1970s," *Chinese Historical Review* 23, no. 1 (May 2016): 30.

50 "Red Chijna: No 'Yellow Peril'—Views From Asia," *U.S. News & World Report*, December 4, 1967, 66.

51 Hilsman to Fulbright, October 14, 1966, 1, Folder Asia 1966 (2), Box 35, Series 48, Subseries 11: Asia, Fulbright Papers, Arkansas.

52 Jonathan Fenby, *Modern China: The Fall and Rise of a Great Power, 1850 to the Present* (New York: HarperCollins, 2008), 497.

53 James Mann, *About Face: A History of America's Curious Relationship with China, from Nixon to Clinton* (New York: Knopf, 1999), 14.

54 Notes, 3, Folder Far East and Middle East Trips 1967—RN's Handwritten Notes (2 of 2), Box 11, Series II: Trip File, Wilderness Years Collection, RMN.

55 Ibid., 10.

56 Notes, 2, 5, Folder Europe Trip (03/05/1967-03/15/1967)—Richard Nixon's Handwritten Notes (2 of 2), Box 9, Series II: Trip File, Wilderness Years Collection, RMN.

57 Memcon, Nixon and de Gaulle, March 1, 1969, 9, Folder Memcons—Europe Feb 23, '69, Box 447, Subject Files, NSF, RMN.

58 Stewart Alsop, "Does China Matter Much?" *Newsweek*, January 26, 1970, 84; "Red China After 20 Years of Mao: Threat to World Peace?" *U..S. News & World Report*, October 12, 1969, 66.

59 Richard Nixon, "Asia After Vietnam," *Foreign Affairs*, October 1967, 120, 121.

60 Garver, *China's Quest*, 290.

61 Folder 3: Material concerning preparations for HAK first China trip, Box 1031, China/Vietnam Negotiations, For the President's Files, NSF, RMN.

62 Nixon, Remarks, American Society of Newspaper Editors, April 16, 1971, Folder US China Policy 1969–72 [1 of 4], Box 86, Country Files: Far East, Henry A. Kissinger Files, NSF, RMN.

63 Speech, Nixon, News Media Executives, July 6, 1971, in Weekly Compilation of Presidential Documents, July 12, 1971, 1036, Folder US China Policy 1969–72 [2 of 4], Box 86, Country Files: Far East, HAK Files, NSF, RMN.

64 "The Speech Zhou En-Lai Read Before Kissinger Did," *U.S. News & World Report*, August 2, 1971, 46.

65 Nixon, News Conference, August 4, 1971, Nixon, Speech, Economic Club of Detroit, Michigan, September 23, 1971, 1, both in Folder China—United Nations Sensitive (1 of 2), Box 86, Country Files: Far East, HAK Files, NSF, RMN.

66 John K. Fairbank, "The Time Is Ripe for China to Shift Outward Again," *New York Times*, April 18, 1971, E1.

67 Richard Madsen, *China and the American Dream: A Moral Inquiry* (Berkeley, CA: University of California, 1995), 73.

68 Dan Oberdorfer, "The China TV Show," *Washington Post*, February 20, 1972, B7.

69 John Service Interview with Chou En-lai, 4, 1, Folder Contacts with Communist Representatives, Official 1971 China, Box 6, Subject Files of the Office of Asian Communist Affairs, 1961–1973, RG 59, NARA.

70 John K. Fairbank, "Getting to Know You," *New York Review of Books*, February 24, 1972.

71 Edgar Snow, *The Long Revolution* (New York: Random House, 1971), 188.

72 Joseph Alsop, "Summing Up," January 10, 1973, 4, "The East Is Red," January 17, 1973, 1, 4, both in Folder 7, Box 182, Alsop Papers, LOC.

73 Joint Report to the United States House of Representatives by Majority Leader Hale Boggs and Minority Leader Gerald R. Ford on Their Mission to the People's Republic of China, June 23 to July 7, 1972, Folder Mansfield

Reports, Impressions of the New China, June 23–July 7, 1972, Box 65, Series 21: Speeches, Reports, Michael Mansfield Papers, Maureen and Mike Mansfield Library, Archives and Special Collections, University of Montana, Missoula, Montana.

74 David Rockefeller, "From a China Traveler," *New York Times*, August 10, 1973.

75 Kynge, *China Shakes the World*, 219.

Chapter 9

1 Dong Wang, *The United States and China: A History from the Eighteenth Century to the Present, Second Edition* (London: Rowan & Littlefield, 2021), xxx.

2 Madsen, *China and the American Dream*, 129.

3 Ibid., 240 (no. 1).

4 Andrew J. Nathan, *China's Crisis: Dilemma of Reform and Prospects for Democracy* (New York: Columbia University Press, 1990), 77, 75.

5 Butterfield, *Alive in the Bitter Sea*, 447, 457.

6 Jonathan Steele, "America puts the flag out for Deng," *Guardian*, January 30, 1979.

7 Memorandum of Conversation, Jimmy Carter and Deng Xiaoping, January 29, 1979, *Foreign Relations of the United States, 1977–1980, Volume XIII: China*, 769.

8 Alexander V. Pantsov and Steven I. Levine, *Deng Xiaoping: A Revolutionary Life* (New York: Oxford University Press, 2015), 356.

9 Charles C. Foster, "Forty Years of Diplomatic Relations and Deng Xiaoping's Visit to Texas," *China Watch*, March 7, 2018.

10 Orville Schell, *"Watch Out for the Foreign Guests!" China Encounters the West* (New York: Pantheon, 1980), 88.

11 Fox Butterfield, "Teng Speaks of Plans for Imports in Billions," *New York Times*, February 4, 1979, 1, 10.

12 Charles C. Foster, "Houston Plays Key Role in U.S.-China Relations," *Houston Chronicle*, March 6, 2014.

13 Michael Schuman, "On the Time China's Leader Deng Xiaoping Went to a Rodeo in Texas," *Literary Hub*, June 10, 2020.

14 Ibid.

15 Adam Taylor, "How a 10-gallon hat Helped Heal Relations Between China and America," *Washington Post*, September 24, 2015.

16 Foster, "Forty Years of Diplomatic Relations."

17 David Kurlander, "The Honeymoon Will Continue: China, Houston, and the Euphoria of 1979," *Café*.

18 Steven G. Roberts, "Americans Provide Many Reasons for Partiality to China Over Soviet," *New York Times*, February 4, 1979.

19 Mann, *About Face*, 110.

20 Edward N. Luttwak, "Against the China Card," *Commentary*, October 1978.

21 Donald S. Zagoria, "China's Quiet Revolution," *Foreign Affairs*, Spring 1984, 880.

22 Michael Pillsbury, *The Hundred-Year Marathon: China's Secret Strategy to Replace America as the Global Superpower* (New York: St. Martin's, 2015, 2016), 17.

23 Vladislav Zubok, "The Soviet Union and China in the 1980s: Reconciliation and Divorce," *Cold War History* 17, no. 2 (2017): 140.

24 Julian Gewirtz, *Unlikely Partners: Chinese Reformers, Western Economists, and the Making of Global China* (Cambridge, MA: Harvard University Press, 2017), 23; Isabella M. Weber, *How China Escaped Shock Therapy* (London: Routledge, 2021), 108.

25 Zagoria, "China's Quiet Revolution," 889.

26 Ibid., 892, 902, 894.

27 Weber, *How China Escaped Shock Therapy*, 156.

28 Ibid., 176.

29 Lou Cannon, "Reagan Praises China's 'Free Market Spirit,' *Washington Post*, May 2, 1984, A8.

30 Mann, *About Face*, 147.

31 Letter, Taylor to Schoyer, Barnett, and Eckstein, June 26, 1972, in Folder 253, Box 33, Series 11, RG 8, National Committee on United States-China Relations Collection, Rockefeller Archive Center, Sleepy Hollow, NY.

32 William Safire, "Greatest Leap Forward," *New York Times*, December 10, 1984, A23.

33 Zubok, "The Soviet Union and China in the 1980s," 122.

34 Lukin, "Russian Perceptions of the China Threat," 91.

35 Mike M. Mochizuki, "Japan's Shifting Strategy toward the Rise of China," *Journal of Strategic Studies* 30, no. 4–5 (August–October 2007): 746.

36 Zubok, "The Soviet Union and China in the 1980s," 125.

37 Paul Kennedy, *The Rise and Fall of the Great Powers: Economic Change and Military Conflict from 1500 to 2000* (New York: Random House, 1987), 447, 458.

38 Dwight H. Perkins, *China: Asia's Next Economic Giant?* (Seattle, WA: University of Washington, 1986), 85.

39 Madsen, *China and the American Dream*, 164.

40 Rush Doshi, *The Long Game: China's Grand Strategy to Displace American Order* (New York: Oxford University Press, 2021), 52.

41 Orville Schell, *Mandate of Heaven: The Legacy of Tiananmen Square and the Next Generation of China's Leaders* (New York: Simon & Schuster, 1994), 27.

42 Robert Bernstein and Ross H. Munro, *The Coming Conflict with China* (New York: Vintage, 1997, 1998), 36; Nathan, *China's Crisis*, 2.

43 Madsen, *China and the American Dream*, 195.

44 Orville Schell, *Discos and Democracy: China in the Throes of Reform* (New York: Anchor, 1989), 29.

45 Nathan, *China's Crisis*, 12–13.

46 Ibid., 14.

47 Hall Gardner, "China and the World After Tiananmen Square," *SAIS Review* 10, no. 1 (Winter-Spring 1990): 133–47.

48 Nathan, *China's Crisis*, 17.

49 Ibid., 98–9.

50 Ibid., 116.

51 Ibid., 176–7.

52 Garver, *China's Quest*, 477.

53 Madsen, *China and the American Dream*, 2.

54 Yee and Story, *China Threat*, 3; Garver, *China's Quest*, 471.

55 Schell and DeLury, *Wealth and Power*, 305.

56 Mann, *About Face*, 229.

57 Nathan, *China's Crisis*. 211.

58 Ibid., 1–2.

59 Dennis van Vranken Hickey, "The Crises of Communism and the Prospects for Change in the People's Republic of China," *Asian Affairs: An American Review* 19, no. 4 (Winter 1993): 200.

60 Bernstein and Munro, *The Coming Conflict with China*, 204.

61 Robert L. Suettinger, *Beyond Tiananmen: The Politics of U.S.-China Relations, 1989-2000* (Washington, DC: Brookings, 2003), 136.

62 Schell and DeLury, *Wealth and Power*, 319.

63 Garver, *China's Quest*, 526.

64 Jude Woodward, *The US vs China: Asia's New Cold War?* (Manchester: Manchester University Press, 2017), 47; Doshi, *The Long Game*, 48; Susan L. Shirk, *China: Fragile Superpower* (Oxford: Oxford University Press, 2008), 104.

65 Will Hutton, *The Writing on the Wall: Why We Must Embrace China as a Partner or Face It as an Enemy* (New York: Free Press, 2006), 209.

66 Jim Rohwer, "The Titan Stirs," *Economist*, November 28, 1992, S3.

67 "Capitalism with Chinese Characteristics," *Economist*, November 28, 1992, S6.

68 "The Faltering State," *Economist*, November 28, 1992, S8.

69 "Sino Xenophila," *Economist*, November 28, 1992, S13.

70 "Land of the Living Dead," *Economist*, November 28, 1992, S15.

Chapter 10

1 "New Tally of World's Economies Catapults China Into Third Place," *New York Times*, May 20, 1993, A1.

2 Ibid., A8.

3 Suettinger, *Beyond Tiananmen*, 153.

4 Marc Levinson, "China's now the Straw that Stirs the Asian Drink," *Newsweek*, December 13, 1993, 54.

5 Between 1895 and 1945, Japan was a dominant regional military power. Between 1960 and 1990, it was a global economic power. But Japan was never both simultaneously on a global scale.

6 Studwell, *The China Dream*, 159.

7 William H. Overholt, *The Rise of China: How Economic Reform is Creating a New Superpower* (New York: Norton, 1993), 416.

8 Levinson, "China's now the Straw that Stirs the Asian Drink," 54.

9 Barr, *Who's Afraid of China*, 10.

10 Nicholas D. Kristof, "The Rise of China," *Foreign Affairs*, November/December 1993, 59.

11 Bill Powell and Steven Strasser, "The Coming Power Struggle," *Newsweek*, November 22, 1993, 40–1.

12 Overholt, *The Rise of China*, 400; Mann, *About Face*, 276.

13 Pillsbury, *Hundred-Year Marathon*, 91.

14 Suettinger, *Beyond Tiananmen*, 183.

15 Bruce W. Nelan and David Aikman, "Watch Out For China," *Time*, November 29, 1993, 36.

16 "Clinton and China: How Promise Self-Destructed," *New York Times*, May 29, 1994; Pillsbury, *Hundred-Year Marathon*, 91.

17 Henry Kissinger, "Heading for a Collision in Asia," *Washington Post*, July 26, 1995, A23.

18 Mann, *About Face*, 330.

19 Barton Gellman, "U.S. and China Nearly Came to Blows in 1996," *Washington Post*, June 21, 1998, A1.

20 Patrick E. Tyler, "Rebels' New Cause: A Book for Yankee Bashing," *New York Times*, September 4, 1996; Jing Li, *China's America: The Chinese View of the United States, 1900–2000* (Albany, NY: State University of New York, 2011), 211; Herbert Yee and Zhu Feng, "Chinese Perspectives of the China Threat: Myth or Reality?" in Yee and Story, *China Threat: Perception, Myths and Reality*, 25.

21 Suisheng Zhao, "From Affirmative to Assertive Patriots: Nationalism in Xi Jinping's China," *Washington Quarterly* 44, no. 4 (Winter 2021): 143.

22 Suettinger, *Beyond Tiananmen*, 283.

23 Li, *China's America*, 4.

24 Thomas W. Lippmann, "Clinton, Jiang Announce Security, Economic Accords," *Washington Post*, October 30, 1997, A1.

25 Suettinger, *Beyond Tiananmen*, 345–7.

26 Eric Eckholm, "With a Nod to Cultural and Historic Differences," *New York Times*, June 28, 1998, 1.

27 "The Leaders' Remarks: Hopes for a Friendship, Even if Imperfect," *New York Times*, June 28, 1998, 10.

28 Suettinger, *Beyond Tiananmen*, 397.

29 David E. Sanger, "Rounding Out a Clear Clinton Legacy," *New York Times*, May 25, 2000, 1.

30 Ibid.

31 Erich Schwartzel, *Red Carpet: Hollywood, China, and the Global Battle for Cultural Supremacy* (New York: Penguin, 2022), 59.

32 Garver, *China's Quest*, 555.

33 Avery Goldstein, *Rising to the Challenge: China's Grand Strategy and International Security* (Singapore: NUS Press, 2008), 147; Suettinger, *Beyond Tiananmen*, 355; Ted Galen Carpenter, "Confusion and Stereotypes: The U.S. Policy toward the PRC at the Dawn of the 21st Century," in *China's Future: Constructive Partner or Emerging Threat?*, ed. Ted Galen Carpenter and James A. Dorn (Washington, DC: Cato Institute, 2000), 72.

34 Chengxin Pan, *Knowledge, Desire and Power in Global Politics: Western Representations of China's Rise* (Cheltenham: Edward Elgar, 2012), 25.

35 Suettinger, *Beyond Tiananmen*, 399.

36 Ibid., 377.

37 Tim Weiner, "A Matter of Perspective," *New York Times*, May 26, 1999, A1.

38 Frank Gibney, Jr., "Birth of a Superpower," *Time*, June 7, 1999, 40.

39 Suettinger, *Beyond Tiananmen*, 362.

40 Bill Mesler, "The Spy Who Wasn't," *Nation*, August 9, 1999, 17.

41 "The Times and Wen Ho Lee," *New York Times*, September 26, 1999, A2.

42 Barton Gellman, "U.S. and China Nearly Came to Blows in 1996," *Washington Post*, June 21, 1998, A20.

43 Robert D. Kaplan, "Sometimes, Autocracy Breeds Freedom," *New York Times*, June 28, 1998, WK 17.

44 Overholt, *The Rise of China*, 402.

45 Martin Jacques, *When China Rules the World: The End of the Western World and the Birth of a New Global Order* (New York: Penguin, 2009, 2012), 462.

46 "Remarks in a Roundtable Discussion on Shaping China for the 21st Century in Shanghai, China," June 30, 1996, 1091.

47 Minxin Pei, "Creeping Democratization in China," *Journal of Democracy* 6, no. 4 (1995): 65.

48 Ibid., 76–7.

49 Ibid., 68–9.

50 Robert B. Zoellick, "Wither China: From Membership to Responsibility?" Remarks to National Committee on U.S.-China Relations, September 21, 2005.

51 Westad, *Decisive Encounters*, 331.

52 Goldstein, *Rising to the Challenge*, 218.

53 Fareed Zakaria, "Does the Future Belong to China?" *Newsweek*, May 9, 2005, 26.

54 Richard C. Bush and Michael O'Hanlon, *A War Like No Other: The Truth about China's Challenge to America* (New York: Wiley, 2007), 15.

55 "How China Runs the World Economy," *Economist*, July 30, 2005, 14.

56 Niall Ferguson and Moritz Schularick, "'Chimerica' and the Global Asset Market Boom," *International Finance* 10, no. 3 (2007): 216, 236.

57 Gregory Chin and Eric Helleiner, "China as a Creditor: A Rising Financial Power?" *Journal of International Affairs* 62, no. 1 (Fall/Winter 2008): 88.

58 Ibid., 92.

59 Gries, *China's New Nationalism*, 48.

60 Mochizuki, "Japan's Shifting Strategy Toward the Rise of China," 757.

61 Sheila A. Smith, *Intimate Rivals: Japanese Domestic Politics and a Rising China* (New York: Columbia University Press, 2015), 56.

62 Ibid., 250.

63 June Teufel Dreyer, "China and Japan: 'Hot Economics, Cold Politics'," *Orbis*, Summer 2014, 337.

64 Mochizuki, "Japan's Shifting Strategy Toward the Rise of China," 768.

65 John Garver, "Asymmetrical Indian and Chinese Threat Perceptions," *Journal of Strategic Studies* 25, no. 4 (2002): 109.

66 Johnson, "Australia's Ambivalent Re-imagining of Asia," 66.

67 Lukin, "Russian Perceptions of the China Threat," 93.

68 Mikhail Alexseev, "The Chinese are Coming: Public Opinion and Threat Perception in the Russian Far East," PONARS Policy Memo 182, San Diego State University, January 2001, 6.

69 Martin Albers and Zhong Zhong Chen, "Socialism, Capitalism, and Sino-European Relations in the Deng Xiaoping Era, 1978–1992," *Cold War History* 17, no. 2 (2017): 115.

70 Chin-Hao Huang, "China's Renewed Partnership with Africa: Implications for the United States," in *China into Africa: Trade, Aid, and Influence*, ed. Robert I. Rothberg (Washington, DC: Brookings, 2008), 296.

71 Chris Alden, *China in Africa* (London: Zed Books, 2007), 12.

72 Tilman Pradt, *China's New Foreign Policy: Military Modernisation, Multilateralism and the 'China Threat'* (New York: Palgrave, 2016), 9.

73 Denny Roy, "Hegemon on the Horizon? China's Threat to East Asian Security," *International Security* 19, no. 1 (Summer 1994): 149; Arthur Waldron, "How Not to Deal with China," *Commentary*, March 1997, 44.

74 Pradt, *China's New Foreign Policy*, 12.

75 Evelyn Goh, "Southeast Asia Perspectives on the China Challenge," *Journal of Strategic Studies* 30, no. 4–5 (August–October 2007): 810, 828.

76 Li, *China's America*, 208.

77 Samuel P. Huntington, *The Clash of Civilizations and the Remaking of the World Order* (New York: Simon & Schuster, 1996, 2001), 81.

78 Gries, *China's New Nationalism*, 41.

79 Bille, *Yellow Perils*, 27.

80 Yee and Storey, *China Threat*, 3.

81 Doshi, *The Long Game*, 107.

82 David Shambaugh, *China Goes Global: The Partial Power* (Oxford: Oxford University Press, 2013), 21.

83 Woodward, *The US vs China*, 48.

84 Guoli Liu, *China Rising: Chinese Foreign Policy in a Changing World* (New York: Palgrave, 2017), 195; Christopher Herrick, Zheya Gai, and Surain Subramanian, *China's Peaceful Rise: Perceptions, Policy and Misperceptions* (Manchester: Manchester University Press, 2016), 2.

85 Pan, *Knowledge, Desire and Power in Global Politics*, 36.

86 Shirk, *China*, 254.

87 Select Committee on Foreign Affairs, Tenth Report, House of Commons, United Kingdom, November 29, 2000.

88 Andrew J. Nathan and Robert S. Ross, *The Great Wall and the Empty Fortress: China's Search for Security* (New York: W.W. Norton, 1997), xii–xiii, 25, 237.

89 Alastair Iain Johnston, "Is China a Status Quo Power?" *International Security* 27, no. 4 (Spring 2000): 6, 39.

90 Benjamin Schwarz, "Managing China's Rise," *Atlantic*, June 2005, 28.

91 Quansheng Zhao and Guoli Liu, "The Challenges of a Rising China," *Journal of Strategic Studies* 30, no. 4–5 (August–October 2007): 590; Quangsheng Zhao, "Managed Great Power Relations: Do We See 'One-Up and One-Down'?" *Journal of Strategic Studies* 30, no. 4–5 (August–October 2007): 628.

92 Warren I. Cohen, "China's Rise in Historical Perspective," *Journal of Strategic Studies* 30, no. 4–5 (August–October 2007): 703.

Chapter 11

1 Schwartzel, *Red Carpet*, 50.

2 Jacques, *When China Rules the World*, 553.

3 Doshi, *The Long Game*, 160.

4 Ibid., 4.

5 Ibid.,160, 139.

6 Steven Halper, *The Beijing Consensus: Legitimizing Authoritarianism in our Time* (New York: Basic, 2010, 2012), 8.

7 Pillsbury, *Hundred-Year Marathon*, 27–8.

8 William A. Callahan, *China Dreams: 20 Visions of the Future* (Oxford: Oxford University Press, 2013), 58.

9 William A. Callahan, *China: The Pessoptimist Nation* (Oxford: Oxford University Press, 2010), 194, 14.

10 Dreyer, *Middle Kingdom and Empire of the Rising Sun*, 377.

11 Smith, *Intimate Rivals*, 56.

12 Ibid., 2.

13 Keith Bradsher, "Activist Chinese Group Plans More Anti-Japan Protests," *New York Times*, August 20, 2012. The Guomindong under Chiang Kai-shek also claimed these islands as Chinese territory.

14 "Japan Must Take Chinese People's Feeling Seriously," *People's Daily Online*, August 31, 2012, http://english.people.com.cn/90883/7930764.html.

15 "Japan's Two Farces are of Same Nature," *People Daily Online*, April 25, 2013, http://english.people.com.cn/90777/8222957.html; "China Calls on Japan to Face History," *Xinhua*, April 25, 2013, http://english.people.com.cn/90883/8223007.html.

16 Jane Perlez, "China Alters Its Strategy in Diplomatic Crisis with Japan," *New York Times*, September 28, 2012, A12.

17 Amy Qin and Edward Wong, "Smashed Skull Serves as Grim Symbol of Seething Patriotism," *New York Times*, October 10, 2012, A6.

18 Yang Lijum, "A Clash of Nationalisms: Sino-Japanese Relations in the Twenty-First Century," in *China-Japan Relations in the 21st Century: Antagonism Despite Interdependency*, ed. Lam Peng Er (Singapore: Palgrave MacMillan, 2017), 92.

19 Shambaugh, *China Goes Global*, 7.

20 Arvind Subramanian, "The Inevitable Superpower: Why China's Dominance is a Sure Thing," *Foreign Affairs*, September/October 2011, 69.

21 Magnus Fiskesjo, "Who's Afraid of Confucius? Fear, Encompassment, and the Global Debates over the Confucius Institutes," in Bille and Urbansky, *Yellow Perils*, 221.

22 Schwartzel, *Red Carpet*, 105, 53, 57.

23 Ibid., 73, xiii.

24 Ibid., 236.

25 Ibid., 220.

26 R. Evam Ellis, *China on the Ground in Latin America: Challenges for the Chinese and Impacts on the Region* (New York: Palgrave MacMillan, 2014), 206–7.

27 Herrick et al., *China's Peaceful Rise*, 131.

28 Ibid., 165.

29 Doshi, *The Long Game*, 235.

30 Ibid., 236.

31 Emanuel Stoakes, "Chinese Police Could Crush Solomon Islands Opposition," *Foreign Policy*, August 9, 2022.

32 Abdi Latif Dahir, "'Jewel in the Crown of Corruption': The Troubles of Kenya's China-Funded Train," *New York Times*, August 7, 2022.

33 Christopher Herrick, "China-India Relations," in Herrick et al., *China's Peaceful Rise*, 195.

34 "Barack Obama's Visit to Australia," *Sydney Morning Herald*, November 16, 2011, https://www.smh.com.au/national/barack-obamas-visit-to-australia-20111116-1ni9j.html.

35 Ibid. "In Quotes: What was said during Barack Obama's Visit," *Sydney Morning Herald*, November 18, 2011, https://www.smh.com.au/national/in-quotes-what-was-said-during-barack-obamas-visit-20111117-1nl05.html.

36 Woodward, *The US vs China*, 250.

37 Geoff Raby, *China's Grand Strategy and Australia's Future in the New Global Order* (Melbourne: Melbourne University Press, 2020), 5; Chengxin Pan, "Getting Excited About China," in *Australia's Asia: From Yellow Peril to Asian Century*, ed. David Walker and Agnieszka Sobocinska (Crawley, West Australia: University of Western Australia, 2012), 248.

38 Raby, *China's Grand Strategy*, 6.

39 Patrick Wintour, "Boris Johnson Declared he is 'Fervently Sinophile' as UK woos China," *Guardian*, February 21, 2021.

40 Tom McTague, "Why Britain Changed Its China Stance," *Atlantic*, August 2, 2022.

41 James B. Steinberg, "Diplomacy in Action: Administration's Vision of the U.S.-China Relationship," Keynote Address at the Center for a New American Security, September 24, 2009.

42 Hillary Clinton, "America's Pacific Century," *Foreign Policy*, October 11, 2011.

43 Barr, *Who's Afraid of China?* 121.

44 Doshi, *The Long Game*, 261.

45 Ellis, *China Engages Latin America*, 272.

46 Catie Edmondson, "Senate Passes $280 Billion Industrial Policy Bill to Counter China," *New York Times*, July 22, 2022.

47 Damien Ma, "Friend/Foe: The Contradictions in How Americans and Chinese See Each Other," *Atlantic*, July 13, 2012.

48 Committee of 100, "U.S.-China Public Perceptions: Hopes and Fears of Americans and Chinese People for U.S.-China Relations," 2017.

49 Gallup, "China: Gallup Historical Trends," 2022, https://news.gallup.com/poll/1627/china.aspx.

50 I use the term "Panda Punching" as an antonym to the epithet "Panda Hugger," with has long been used by China hawks to tar those advocating engagement.

51 Jared Schroeder, "The Lunacy of Banning TikTok from University Networks," *Slate*, January 20, 2023.

52 Johanna Bhuiyan, "Why did the US just ban TikTok from Government Issued Cellphones?" *Guardian*, December 31, 2022.

53 Doshi, *The Long Game*, 262.

54 Ibid., 265.

55 Ibid., 27.

56 Alec Ash, "In Beijing," *London Review of Books*, LRB Blog, February 4, 2022.

57 Adam Tooze, "How China Avoided Soviet-Style Collapse," *Noema Magazine*, September 16, 2021.

Conclusion

1 Russell, *The Problem of China*, 1; Hans J. Moregenthau, "The United States and China," *International Studies* 10, no. 1–2 (July–October 1968): 23.

2 David B. H. Denoon, *China's Grand Strategy: A Roadmap to Global Power?* (New York: New York University Press, 2021), 243.

3 John Ehrenreich, "The Lab-Leak Theory Still Can't Be Disproved. Should We Care? *Slate*, January 30, 2023.

4 Katherine Eban, "Viral Inflection," *Vanity Fair*, July/August 2021.

5 Jenny Clegg, *China's Global Strategy: Towards a Multipolar World* (New York: Pluto, 2009), 223.

6 Helen Davidson, "Is China Doing Enough to Combat the Climate Crisis," *Guardian*, November 11, 2022.

7 Maxine Joselow, Michael Birnbaum, and Lily Kuo, "How China, the World's Top Polluter, Avoids Paying for Climate Change," *Washington Post*, November 23, 2022.

8 Barr, *Who's Afraid of China?* 4.

9 Joseph S. Nye, "China's Re-Emergence and the Future of the Asia-Pacific," *Survival* 39, no. 4 (1997): 66.

10 Hugh White, *The China Choice: Why We Should Share Power* (Oxford: Oxford University Press, 2012), 30.

11 An Umayyad army's defeat of a Tang Army at the Battle of the Talas River in 751 effectively expelled Han Chinese influence from Central Asia for nearly a millennium, and helped precipitate the An Lushan rebellion, which began three years later and essentially crippled the Tang Dynasty as an expansionist power. Thus, it would be more accurate to say the Arabs were a strategic threat to the Chinese, rather than the other way around.

12 Jeffrey W. Legro, "What China Will Want: The Future Intentions of a Rising Power," *Perspectives on Politics* 5, no. 3 (September 2007): 1.

13 Hans J. Morgenthau, "The United States and China," *International Studies* 10, no. 1–2 (July–October 1968): 23.

14 Robert J. Art, "The United States and the Rise of China: Implications for the Long Haul," *Political Science Quarterly* 125, no. 3 (Fall 2010): 362.

15 Ibid., 371.

16 See Henry Kissinger, *On China* (New York: Penguin, 2011), 23.

17 Russell, *The Problem of China*, 5.

18 Once again, see the introductory chapter of Kissinger, *On China*.

19 Legro, "What China Will Want," 3.

20 Art, "The United States and the Rise of China," 375.

21 Nye, "China's Re-Emergence," 72.

22 Morgenthau, "The Roots of America's China Policy," 50.

23 Salvator Babones, "The Middling Kingdom: The Hype and the Reality of China's Rise," *Foreign Affairs*, September/October 2011, 85.

24 Jonathan E. Hillman, *The Emperor's New Road: China and the Project of the Century* (New Haven, CT: Yale University Press, 2020), 211.

25 Clegg, *China's Global Strategy*, 5.

26 Jonathan Kirshner, "Handle Him with Care: The Importance of Getting Thucydides Right," *Security Studies* 28, no. 1 (2019): 12.

27 James Lee, "Did Thucydides Believe in Thucydides' Trap? The *History of the Peloponnesian War* and its relevance to U.S.-China Relations," *Journal of Chinese Political Science* 24 (2019): 75.

28 Kirshner, "Handle Him with Care," 24.

References

Archives

University of Arkansas Libraries, Special Collections, Fayetteville, Arkansas
J. William Fulbright Papers

Cold War International History Project

Dwight Eisenhower Presidential Library, Abilene, Kansas
John Foster Dulles Papers
Office of the Special Assistant for National Security Affairs
White House Central Files
White House Office Files
Ann Whitman Files

Hoover Institution Archives, Stanford University, Palo Alto, California
Christopher Emmet Papers

Lyndon B. Johnson Presidential Library, Austin, Texas
Lyndon Johnson Papers
National Security Files

John F. Kennedy Presidential Library, Boston, Massachusetts
Roger Hilsman Papers
National Security Files
James C. Thomson Papers

Library of Congress, Manuscript Reading Room, Washington, D.C.
Joseph Alson Papers

Maureen and Mike Mansfield Library, Archives and Special Collections, University of, Montana, Missoula, Montana
Mike Mansfield Papers

Mudd Library, Princeton University, Princeton, New Jersey
Allen Dulles Papers
John Foster Dulles Papers
Adlai Stevenson Papers

National Archives and Records Administration, College Park, Maryland
Record Group 59

Richard M. Nixon Presidential Library, Yorba Linda, California
National Security Files
White House Central Files
White House Special Files
Wilderness Years Collection

Rockefeller Archive Center, Sleepy Hollow, New York
Papers of the National Committee on United States-China Relations

Sterling Memorial Archives, Yale University, New Haven, Connecticut
Chester Bowles Papers

Stony Brook University Libraries, Special Collections & University Archives, Stony Brook, New York
Jacob Javits Papers

University of Washington Libraries, Special Collections, Seattle, Washington
George Edward Taylor Papers

Films

A Band Apart
Dr. No
55 Days at Peking
Le Chinoise
Manchurian Candidate
Satan Never Sleeps

Newspapers and Periodicals

America
Atlanta Constitution
Atlantic
Baltimore Afro-American
Business Week
Cafe
Chicago Tribune
China Watch
Christian Century
Christian Science Monitor
Commentary
Commonweal
Congregationalist
Economist
Esquire
Foreign Affairs

Foreign Policy
Fortnightly Review
Forum
Guardian
Harper's
Hartford Courant
Houston Chronicle
Kansas City Star
London Review of Books
Literary Digest
Literary Hub
Living Age
Los Angeles Times
Nation
National Review
Newsweek
New Republic
New York Review of Books
New York Times
New York Times Magazine
New York Tribune
New Yorker
Noema
North American Review
Observer
Outlook
Overland Monthly and Out West Magazine
People's Daily Online
Review of Reviews
Saturday Evening Post
Saturday Review
Shanghai Times
Slate
Smithsonian
Sydney Morning Herald
Time
U.S. News & World Report
Vanity Fair
Wall Street Journal
Washington Post
Xinhua

Articles

Albers, Martin and Zhong Zhong Chen. "Socialism, Capitalism, and Sino-European Relations in the Deng Xiaoping Era, 1978–1992." *Cold War History* 17, no. 2 (2017): 115–19.

Alexseev, Mikhail. "The Chinese Are Coming: Public Opinion and Threat Perception in the Russian Far East." PONARS Policy Memo 182, San Diego State University, January 2001.
Art Robert, J. "The United States and the Rise of China: Implications for the Long Haul." *Political Science Quarterly* 125, no. 3 (Fall 2010): 359–91.
Blue, Gregory. "Gobineau on China: Race Theory, the 'Yellow Peril', and the Critique of Modernity." *Journal of World History* 10, no. 1 (Spring 1999): 93–119.
Brandt, Conrad. "The Passionate Pilgrimage of Simone de Beauvior." *Journal of Asian Studies* 18, no. 2 (January 1959): 277–80.
Chin, Gregory and Eric Helleiner. "China as a Creditor: A Rising Financial Power?" *Journal of International Affairs* 62, no. 1 (Fall/Winter 2008): 87–102.
Cohen, Warren I. "China's Rise in Historical Perspective." *Journal of Strategic Studies* 30, no. 4–5 (August–October 2007): 683–704.
Cumings, Bruce. "The World Shakes China." *National Interest* 43 (Spring 1996): 28–41.
Dreyer, June Teufel. "China and Japan: 'Hot Economics, Cold Politics'." *Orbis*, Summer 2014: 326–41.
Ferguson, Niall and Moritz Schularick. "'Chimerica' and the Global Asset Market Boom." *International Finance* 10, no. 3 (2007): 215–39.
Gardner, Hall. "China and the World after Tiananmen Square." *SAIS Review* 10, no. 1 (Winter–Spring 1990): 133–47.
Garver, John. "Asymmetrical Indian and Chinese Threat Perceptions." *Journal of Strategic Studies* 25, no. 4 (2002): 109–34.
Goh, Evelyn. "Southeast Asia Perspectives on the China Challenge." *Journal of Strategic Studies* 30, no. 4–5 (August–October 2007): 809–32.
Heinrich, Larissa. "How China Became the 'Cradle of Smallpox': Transformations in Discourse, 1726–2002." *Positions: East Asian Cultures Critique* 15, no. 1 (Spring 2007): 7–34.
Johnson, Carol. "Australia's Ambivalent Re-imagining of Asia." *Australian Journal of Political Science* 45, no. 1 (March 2010): 59–74.
Johnston Alastair, Iain. "Is China a Status Quo Power?" *International Security* 27, no. 4 (Spring 2000): 5–56.
Kirshner, Jonathan. "Handle Him with Care: The Importance of Getting Thucydides Right." *Security Studies* 28, no. 1 (2019): 1–24.
Lee, James. "Did Thucydides Believe in Thucydides' Trap? The *History of the Peloponnesian War* and its Relevance to U.S.-China Relations." *Journal of Chinese Political Science* 24 (2019): 67–88.
Lin, Mao. "To See Is to Believe? – Modernization and the U.S.-China Exchanges in the 1970s." *Chinese Historical Review* 23, no. 1 (May 2016): 23–46.
Mochizuki, Mike M. "Japan's Shifting Strategy Toward the Rise of China." *Journal of Strategic Studies* 30, no. 4–5 (August–October 2007): 739–76.
Morgenthau, Hans J. "The Roots of America's China Policy." *China Quarterly*, 10 (April–June 1962): 45–50.
Morgenthau, Hans J. "The United States and China." *International Studies* 10, no. 1–2 (July–October 1968): 23–44.
Munro, Ross H. "Awakening Dragon: The Real Danger in Asia is Coming from China." *Policy Review* 62 (Fall 1992): 10–15.
Nye Joseph, S. "China's Re-Emergence and the Future of the Asia-Pacific." *Survival* 39, no. 4 (1997): 65–79.

Pei, Minxin. "Creeping Democratization in China." *Journal of Democracy* 6, no. 4 (1995): 65–79.
Rowen, Henry S. "The Short March: China's Road to Democracy." *National Interest* 45 (Fall 1996): 61–70.
Roy, Denny. "Hegemon on the Horizon? China's Threat to East Asian Security." *International Security* 19, no. 1 (Summer 1994): 149–55.
Seshagiri, Urmila. "Modernity's (Yellow) Perils: Dr. Fu Manchu and English Race Paranoia." *Cultural Critique* 62 (Winter 2006): 162–94.
Siegelbaum, Lewis. "Another 'Yellow Peril': Chinese Migrants in the Russian Far East and the Russian Reaction before 1917." *Asian Studies* 12, no. 2 (1978): 307–30.
Steuber, Jason. "The Exhibition of Chinese Art at Burlington House, London, 1935–36." *The Burlington Magazine* 148, no. 1241 (August 2006): 528–36.
Tooze, Adam. "How China Avoided Soviet-Style Collapse." *Noema Magazine*, 16 September 2021.
Vranken Hickey, Dennis van. "The Crises of Communism and the Prospects for Change in the People's Republic of China." *Asian Affairs: An American Review* 19, no. 4 (Winter 1993): 195–205.
Xia, Yafeng. "China's Elite Politics and the Sino-American Rapprochement. January 1969–February 1972." *Journal of Cold War Studies* 8, no. 4 (Fall 2006): 83–99.
Xiao, Xiaosui. "China Encounters Darwinism: A Case of Intercultural Rhetoric." *Quarterly Journal of Speech* 81, no. 1 (1995): 83–99.
Zhao, Quangsheng. "Managed Great Power Relations: Do We See 'One-Up and One-Down'?" *Journal of Strategic Studies* 30, no. 4–5 (August–October 2007): 609–37.
Zhao, Quansheng and Guoli Liu. "The Challenges of a Rising China." *Journal of Strategic Studies* 30, no. 4–5 (August–October 2007): 609–37.
Zhao, Suisheng, "From Affirmative to Assertive Patriots: Nationalism in Xi Jinping's China." *Washington Quarterly* 44, no. 4 (Winter 2021): 585–608.
Zubok, Vladislav. "The Soviet Union and China in the 1980s: Reconciliation and Divorce." *Cold War History* 17, no. 2 (2017): 121–41.

Books

Adams, Sherman. *Firsthand Report: The Story of the Eisenhower Administration.* New York: Harper, 1961.
Alden, Chris. *China in Africa.* London: Zed Books, 2007.
Amalrik, Andrei. *Will the Soviet Union Survive until 1984?* New York: Harper & Row, 1970.
Bader, Jeffrey A. *Obama and China's Rise: An Insider's Account of America's Asia Strategy.* Washington, DC: Brookings, 2012.
Bagby, Wesley M. *The Eagle-Dragon Alliance: America's Relations with China in World War II.* Newark, DE: University of Delaware, 1992.
Barr, Michael. *Who's Afraid of China? The Challenge of Chinese Soft Power.* London: Zed, 2011.

Beaton, Cecil. *Chinese Diary & Album*. Hong Kong: Oxford University Press, 1945 (1991).

Beauvior, Simone B. *The Long March: An Account of Modern China*, trans. Austryn Wainhouse. London: Phoenix, 1957.

Belden, Jack. *China Shakes the World*. New York: Harper, 1949.

Bergère, Marie-Claire. *Sun Yat Sen*, trans. Janet Lloyd. Stanford, CA: Stanford University Press, 1998.

Bernstein, Richard. *China 1945: Mao's Revolution and America's Fateful Choice*. New York: Knopf, 2014.

Bernstein, Robert and Ross H. Munro. *The Coming Conflict with China*. New York: Vintage, 1997 (1998).

Bickers, Robert. *Out of China: How the Chinese Ended the Era of Western Domination*. London: Penguin, 2017.

Bille, Franck and Soren Urbansky, eds. *Yellow Perils: China Narratives in the Contemporary World*. Honolulu: University of Hawaii, 2018.

Bland, J. O. P. *China: The Pity of It*. Garden City, NY: Doubleday, 1932.

Boardman, Robert. *Britain and the People's Republic of China, 1949–74*. London: MacMillan, 1976.

Brazinsky, Gregg A. *Winning the Third World: Sino-American Rivalry During the Cold War*. Chapel Hill, NC: University of North Carolina, 2017.

Bush, Richard C. and Michael O'Hanlon. *A War Like No Other: The Truth about China's Challenge to America*. New York: Wiley, 2007.

Butterfield, Fox. *China: Alive in the Bitter Sea*. New York: Bantam, 1982.

Callahan, William A. *China: The Pessoptimist Nation*. Oxford: Oxford University Press, 2010.

Callahan, William A. *China Dreams: 20 Visions of the Future*. Oxford: Oxford University Press, 2013.

Chang, Gordon H. *Friends and Enemies: The United States, China, and the Soviet Union, 1948–1972*. Stanford, CA: Stanford University Press, 1990.

Chernow, Ron. *Grant*. New York: Penguin, 2017.

Chi-kwan, Mark. *The Everyday Cold War: Britain and China, 1950–1972*. London: Bloomsbury, 2017.

Clegg, Jenny. *China's Global Strategy: Towards a Multipolar World*. New York: Pluto, 2009.

Committee of 100. *U.S.-China Public Perceptions: Hopes and Fears of Americans and Chinese People for U.S.-China Relations*. 2017.

Condon, Richard. *The Manchurian Candidate*. New York: McGraw Hill, 1959.

Conn, Peter. *Pearl S. Buck: A Cultural Biography*. Cambridge: Cambridge University Press, 1996.

Cook, Alexander C., ed. *Mao's Little Red Book: A Global History*. Cambridge: Cambridge University Press, 2014.

Cooley, John K. *East Wind Over Africa: Red China's African Offensive*. New York: Walker, 1965.

Craft, Stephen G. *V.K. Wellington Koo and the Emergence of Modern China*. Lexington, KY: University Press of Kentucky, 2004.

Curtis, Lionel. *The Capital Question of China*. London: MacMillan, 1932.

Dawson, Raymond. *The Chinese Chameleon: An Analysis of European Conceptions of Chinese Civilization*. London: Oxford University Press, 1967.

"Defense of Japan: The Annual White Paper." 28 August 2021.

Denoon, David B. H. *China's Grand Strategy: A Roadmap to Global Power?* New York: New York University Press, 2021.
Devine, Michael J. *John W. Foster: Politics and Diplomacy in the Imperial Era, 1873–1917*. Athens, OH: Ohio University Press, 1981.
Dewey, John and Alice Chipman Dewey. *Letters from China and Japan*. Coppel, TX, 1920 (2021).
Dikotter, Frank. *The Discourse of Race in Modern China*. Stanford, CA: Stanford University Press, 1992.
Dikotter, Frank. *Mao's Great Famine: The History of China's Most Devastating Catastrophe, 1958–1962*. New York: Walker, 2010.
Dikotter, Frank. *The Cultural Revolution: A People's History, 1962–1976*. New York: Bloomsbury, 2016.
Dooner, Pierton W. *Last Days of the Republic*. San Francisco, CA: Alta California, 1879.
Doshi, Rush. *The Long Game: China's Grand Strategy to Displace American Order*. New York: Oxford University Press, 2021.
Dreyer, June Teufel. *Middle Kingdom and Empire of the Rising Sun: Sino-Japanese Relations, Past and Present*. New York: Oxford University Press, 2016.
Eastman, Lloyd E. *The Abortive Revolution: China under Nationalist Rule, 1927–1937*. Cambridge, MA: Harvard University Press, 1974.
Eastman, Lloyd E. *Seeds of Destruction: Nationalist China in War and Revolution, 1937–1949*. Stanford, CA: Stanford University Press, 1984.
Ellis, R. Evan. *China on the Ground in Latin America: Challenges for the Chinese and Impacts on the Region*. New York: Palgrave MacMillan, 2014.
Er, Lam Peng, ed. *China-Japan Relations in the 21st Century: Antagonism Despite Interdependency*. Singapore: Palgrave MacMillan, 2017.
Fenby, Jonathan. *Modern China: The Fall and Rise of a Great Power, 1850 to the Present*. New York: HarperCollins, 2008.
Fink, Carole, Philipp Gassert, and Detlef Junker, eds. *1968: The World Transformed*. New York: Cambridge University Press, 1998.
Fitzgerald, John. *Awakening China: Politics, Culture, and Class in the Nationalist Revolution*. Stanford, CA: Stanford University Press, 1996.
Fleming, Ian. *Doctor No*. New York: Macmillan, 1958.
Frank, Richard B. *Tower of Skulls: A History of the Asia-Pacific War, July 1937–May 1942*. New York: Norton, 2020.
Franklin, H. Bruce. *War Stars: The Superweapon and the American Imagination*. Amherst: University of Massachusetts, 2008.
Frayling, Christopher. *The Yellow Peril: Dr Fu Manchu & the Rise of Chinophobia*. London: Thames and Hudson, 2014.
French, Paul. *Through the Looking Glass: China's Foreign Journalists from Opium Wars to Mao*. Hong Kong: Hong Kong University Press, 2009.
Gallup. *China: Gallup Historical Trends*. 2022, https://news.gallup.com/poll/1627/china.aspx.
Garver, John W. *China's Quest: The History of the Foreign Relations of the People's Republic of China*. New York: Oxford University Press, 2016.
Gewirtz, Julian. *Unlikely Partners: Chinese Reformers, Western Economists, and the Making of Global China*. Cambridge, MA: Harvard University Press, 2017.
Ghosh, Partha S. *Sino-Soviet Relations: U.S. Perceptions and Policy Responses*. New Delhi: Uppal Publishing House, 1981.

Gibbons, Floyd. *The Red Napoleon*. New York: Jonathan Cape and Harrison Smith, 1929.
Gifford, Sydney. *Japan Among the Powers, 1890–1990*. New Haven, CT: Yale University Press, 1994.
Goldstein, Avery. *Rising to the Challenge: China's Grand Strategy and International Security*. Singapore: NUS Press, 2008.
Gries, Peter Hays. *China's New Nationalism: Pride, Politics, and Diplomacy*. Berkeley, CA: University of California Press, 2004.
Guoqi, Xu. *China and the Great War: China's Pursuit of a New National Identity and Internationalization*. Cambridge: Cambridge University Press, 2005.
Guoqi, Xu. *Strangers on the Western Front: Chinese Workers in the Great War*. Cambridge, MA: Harvard University Press, 2011.
Halper, Steven. *The Beijing Consensus: Legitimizing Authoritarianism in our Time*. New York: Basic, 2010 (2012).
Hamamoto, Darrel Y. *Monitored Peril: Asian Americans and the Politics of TV Representation*. Minneapolis: University of Minnesota, 1994.
Harris, Theodore F., in consultation with Pearl Buck. *Pearl S. Buck: A Biography, Volume Two: Her Philosophy as Expressed in Her Letters*. New York: John Day, 1971.
Heinlein, Robert A. *Starship Troopers*. New York: G.P. Putnam's Sons, 1959.
Herrick, Christopher, Zheya Gai, and Surain Subramanian, *China's Peaceful Rise: Perceptions, Policy and Misperceptions*. Manchester: Manchester University Press, 2016.
Hillman, Jonathan E. *The Emperor's New Road: China and the Project of the Century*. New Haven, CT: Yale University Press, 2020.
Hinton, William. *Fanshen: A Documentary of Revolution in a Chinese Village*. New York: Monthly Review, 1966 (2008).
Holcombe, Chester. *China's Past & Future*. London: Morgan & Scott, 1904.
Horne, Donald. *The Lucky Country*. Melbourne: Penguin, 1964.
Hsu, Immanuel C. Y. *The Rise of Modern China*. New York: Oxford University Press, 1970.
Hunter, Edward. *Brainwashing: Its History; Use by Totalitarian Communist Regimes; and the Stories of American and British Soldiers and Captives Who Defied It*. New York: Pantianos Classics, 1956.
Huntington, Samuel P. *The Clash of Civilizations and the Remaking of the World Order*. New York: Simon & Schuster, 1996 (2001).
Hutton, Will. *The Writing on the Wall: Why We Must Embrace China as a Partner or Face It as an Enemy*. New York: Free Press, 2006.
Iriye, Akira. *After Imperialism: The Search for a New Order in the Far East, 1921–1931*. Cambridge, MA: Harvard University Press, 1965.
Jacobson, Matthew Frye and Gaspar Gonzalez. *What Have They Built You to Do? The Manchurian Candidate and Cold War America*. Minneapolis: University of Minnesota, 2006.
Jacques, Martin. *When China Rules the World: The End of the Western World and the Birth of a New Global Order*. New York: Penguin, 2009 (2012).
Jayasuriya, Laksiri, David Walker, and Jan Gothard, eds. *Legacies of White Australia: Race, Culture and Nation*. Crawley, Western Australia: University of Western Australia, 2003.
Jesperson, T. Christopher. *American Images of China, 1931–1949*. Stanford, CA: Stanford University Press, 1996.

Jisen, Ma. *The Cultural Revolution in the Foreign Ministry of China.* Hong Kong: Chinese University Press, 2004.
Jun, Niu. *The Cold War and the Origin of Foreign Relations of the People's Republic of China*, trans. Zhonh Yijinh. Boston: Brill, 2018.
Kahn, Jr., E. J. *The China Hands: America's Foreign Service Officers and What Befell Them.* New York: Viking, 1975.
Keevak, Michael. *Becoming Yellow: A Short History of Racial Thinking.* Princeton, NJ: Princeton University Press, 2011.
Keith, Ronald C. *The Diplomacy of Zhou Enlai.* New York: St. Martin's, 1989.
Kennedy, Paul. *The Rise and Fall of the Great Powers: Economic Change and Military Conflict from 1500 to 2000.* New York: Random House, 1987.
Khrushchev, Nikita. *Khrushchev Remembers*, trans. Strobe Talbott. Boston: Little, Brown, 1970.
Kirby, William C. *Germany and Republican China.* Stanford, CA: Stanford University Press, 1984.
Kissinger, Henry. *On China.* New York: Penguin, 2011.
Klein, Christina. *Cold War Orientalism: Asia in the Middlebrow Imagination, 1945–1961.* Berkeley, CA: University of California, 2003.
Kowner, Rotem and Walter Demel, eds. *Race and Racism in Modern East Asia: Western and Easter Constructions.* Leiden: Brill, 2013.
Kynge, James. *China Shakes the World: A Titan's Rise and Troubled Future – And the Challenge for America.* Boston: Houghton Mifflin, 2006.
Larkin, Bruce D. *China and Africa, 1949–1970.* Berkeley, CA: University of California, 1971.
Lee, Ou-fan. *Shanghai Modern: The Flowering of a New Urban Culture in China, 1930–1945.* Cambridge, MA: Harvard University Press, 1999.
Lee, Robert G. *Orientals: Asian Americans in Popular Culture.* Philadelphia: Temple University Press, 1999.
Lee, Stan. *Marvel Masterworks: Volume 2, College the Avengers, Nos. 11–20.* New York: Marvel, 2009.
Lee, Stan and Robert Berns. *The Invincible Ironman, Volume I: Collecting Tales of Suspense, Nos. 39–50.* New York: Marvel, 2015.
Lee, Stan and Jack Kirby. *The Mighty Thor: Journey Into Mystery, Nos. 83–100.* New York: Marvel, 2010.
Lewis, Lionel S. *The Cold War and Academic Governance: The Lattimore Case at Johns Hopkins.* Albany, NY: State University of New York, 1993.
Lew-Williams, Beth. *The Chinese Must Go: Violence, Exclusion, and the Making of the Alien in America.* Cambridge, MA: Harvard University Press, 2018.
Li, Jing. *China's America: The Chinese View of the United States, 1900–2000.* Albany, NY: State University of New York, 2011.
Liu, Guoli. *China Rising: Chinese Foreign Policy in a Changing World.* New York: Palgrave, 2017.
London, Jack. *The Asian Writings of Jack London: Essays, Letters, Newspaper Dispatches, and Short Fiction by Jack London.* Lewiston, ME: Edwin Mellen, 2009.
Lovell, Julia. *Maoism: A Global History.* New York: Knopf, 2019.
Lui, Xiaoyuan. *A Partnership for Disorder: China, the United States, and Their Policies for the Postwar Disposition of the Japanese Empire, 1941–1945.* New York: Cambridge University Press, 1996.
Lyman, Stanford M. *Chinese Americans.* New York: Random House, 1974.

MacKinnon, Stephen R. and Oris Friesen. *China Reporting: An Oral History of American Journalism in the 1930s and 1940s*. Berkeley, CA: University of California, 1987.

MacLaine, Shirley. *You Can Get There From Here*. New York: Norton, 1975.

MacMahon, Robert J. *The Cold War on the Periphery: The United States, India, and Pakistan*. New York: Columbia University Press, 1994.

Macmillan, Harold. *Tides of Fortune: 1945–1955*. London: MacMillan, 1969.

MacMillan, Margaret. *Nixon and Mao: The Week that Changed the World*. New York: Random House, 2007.

Madsen, Richard. *China and the American Dream: A Moral Inquiry*. Berkeley, CA: University of California, 1995.

Malraux, Andre. *The Conquerors*, trans. Winifred Stephens Whale. Boston: Beacon, 1927 (1956).

Malraux, Andre. *Anti-Memoirs*, trans. Terence Kilmartin. New York: Holt, Rinehart and Winston, 1967 (1968).

Mann, James. *About Face: A History of America's Curious Relationship with China, from Nixon to Clinton*. New York: Knopf, 1999.

Mayer, Ruth. *Serial Fu Manchu: The Chinese Supervillain and the Spread of Yellow Peril Ideology*. Philadelphia: Temple University Press, 2014.

Mayer, William G. *The Changing American Mind: How and Why American Public Opinion Changed Between 1960 and 1988*. Ann Arbor, MI: University of Michigan, 1992.

Mayers, David Allen. *Cracking the Monolith: U.S. Policy Against the Sino-Soviet Alliance, 1949–1955*. Baton Rouge, LA: Louisiana State University Press, 1986.

Miller, Stuart Creighton. *The Unwelcome Immigrant: The American Image of the Chinese, 1785–1882*. Berkeley, CA: University of California, 1969.

Mitter, Rana. *China's War with Japan, 1937–1945: The Struggle for Survival*. New York: Penguin, 2013.

Moon, Krystyn R. *Yellowface: Creating the Chinese in American Popular Music and Performances: 1850s-1920s*. New Brunswick, NJ: Rutgers University Press, 2005.

Nathan, Andrew J. *China's Crisis: Dilemma of Reform and Prospects for Democracy*. New York: Columbia University Press, 1990.

Nathan, Andrew J. and Robert S. Ross. *The Great Wall and the Empty Fortress: China's Search for Security*. New York: Norton, 1997.

Ngai, Mae. *The Chinese Question: The Gold Rushes and Global Politics*. New York: W.W. Norton, 2021.

Nitze, Paul with Ann M. Smith and Steven L. Rearden. *From Hiroshima to Glasnost: At the Center of Decision, A Memoir*. New York: Grove Wiedenfeld, 1989.

O'Neill, Mark. *From the Tsar's Railway to the Red Army*. Melbourne: Penguin, 2014.

Overholt, William H. *The Rise of China: How Economic Reform is Creating a New Superpower*. New York: Norton, 1993.

Pan, Chengxin. *Knowledge, Desire and Power in Global Politics: Western Representations of China's Rise*. Cheltenham: Edward Elgar, 2012.

Pantsov, Alexander V. and Steven I. Levine. *Deng Xiaoping: A Revolutionary Life*. New York: Oxford University Press, 2015.

Pearson, Charles. *National Life and Character: A Forecast*. London: MacMillan, 1893.

Perkins, Dwight H. *China: Asia's Next Economic Giant?* Seattle, WA: University of Washington, 1986.
Pillsbury, Michael. *The Hundred-Year Marathon: China's Secret Strategy to Replace America as the Global Superpower.* New York: St. Martin's, 2015 (2016).
Porter, Brian. *Britain and the Rise of Communist China: A Study of British Attitudes, 1945–1954.* London: Oxford University Press, 1967.
Pradham, Radhe Gopal. *America and China: A Study in Cooperation and Conflict, 1962–1983.* Delhi: UDH Publishers, 1983.
Pradt. *China's New Foreign Policy: Military Modernisation, Multilateralism and the 'China Threat'.* New York: Palgrave, 2016.
Raby, Geoff. *China's Grand Strategy and Australia's Future in the New Global Order.* Melbourne: Melbourne University Press, 2020.
Radchenko, Sergey. *Two Suns in the Heavens: The Sino-Soviet Struggle for Supremacy, 1962–1967.* Stanford, CA: Stanford University Press, 2009.
Reesman, Jeanne Campbell. *Jack London's Racial Lives: A Critical Biography.* Athens: University of Georgia, 2009.
Red Star Over China. New York: Grove Weidenfeld, 1938 (1968).
Röhl, John. *The Kaiser and His Court.* Cambridge: Cambridge University Press, 1994.
Rohmer, Sax. *The Fu Manchu Omnibus, Volume 1.* London: Allison & Busby, 1998.
Rothberg, Robert I., ed. *China into Africa: Trade, Aid, and Influence.* Washington, DC: Brookings, 2008.
Russell, Bertrand. *The Problem of China.* Coppel, TX, 1922 (2022).
Salisbury, Harrison E. *War Between Russia and China.* New York: W.W. Norton, 1969.
Schell, Orville. *"Watch Out for the Foreign Guests!" China Encounters the West.* New York: Pantheon, 1980.
Schell, Orville. *Discos and Democracy: China in the Throes of Reform.* New York: Anchor, 1989.
Schell, Orville. *Mandate of Heaven: The Legacy of Tiananmen Square and the Next Generation of China's Leaders.* New York: Simon & Schuster, 1994.
Schell, Orville and John DeLury. *Wealth and Power: China's Long March to the Twenty-First Century.* New York: Random House, 2013.
Schwartzel, Erich. *Red Carpet: Hollywood, China, and the Global Battle for Cultural Supremacy.* New York: Penguin, 2022.
Seale, Bobby. *Seize the Time: The Story of the Black Panther Party and Huey P. Newton.* New York: Random House, 1970.
Seed, David. *Brainwashing: The Fictions of Mind Control.* Kent, OH: Kent State University Press, 2004.
Select Committee on Foreign Affairs. Tenth Report, House of Commons, United Kingdom. 29 November 2000.
Shambaugh, David. *Beautiful Imperialist: China Perceives America, 1972–1990.* Princeton, NJ: Princeton University Press, 1991.
Shambaugh, David. *China Goes Global: The Partial Power.* Oxford: Oxford University Press, 2013.
Shapiro, Michael. *Changing China.* London: Lawrence & Wishart, 1958.
Sharp, Patrick B. *Savage Perils: Racial Frontiers and Nuclear Apocalypse in American Culture.* Norman, OK: University of Oklahoma, 2007.

Shewmaker, Kenneth E. *Americans and Chinese Communists, 1927–1945.* Ithaca, NY: Cornell University Press, 1971.
Shiel, Matthew P. *The Yellow Danger.* London: Grant Richards, 1898.
Shirk, Susan L. *China: Fragile Superpower.* Oxford: Oxford University Press, 2008.
Smith, Sheila A. *Intimate Rivals: Japanese Domestic Politics and a Rising China.* New York: Columbia University Press, 2015.
Snow, Edgar. *Red China Today.* New York: Random House, 1961 (1970).
Snow, Edgar. *The Long Revolution.* New York: Random House, 1971.
Spence, Jonathan. *To Change China: Western Advisers in China, 1620–1960.* Boston: Little, Brown, 1969.
Steinberg, James B. "Diplomacy in Action: Administration's Vision of the U.S.-China Relationship." Keynote Address at the Center for a New American Security, 24 September 2009.
Stoddard, Lothrop. *The Rising Tide of Color Against White World-Supremacy.* New York: Scribner's Sons, 1920.
Studwell, Joe. *The China Dream: The Elusive Quest for the Greatest Untapped Market on Earth.* London: Profile, 2002 (2005).
Suettinger, Robert L. *Beyond Tiananmen: The Politics of U.S.-China Relations, 1989–2000.* Washington, DC: Brookings, 2003.
Ichen, John Kuo Wei and Dylan Yeats, eds. *Yellow Peril! An Archive of Anti-Asian Fear.* London: Verso, 2014.
Tracking the Dragon: National Intelligence Estimates on China During the Era of Mao, 1948–1976. Washington, DC: National Intelligence Council, 2004.
United States, Department of State. *The White Paper: August 1949, Originally Issued as United States Relations with China, With Special Reference to the Period 1944–1949.* Stanford, CA: Stanford University Press, 1967.
United States, Department of State. *Foreign Relations of the United States, 1977–1980, Volume XIII: China.* Washington, DC: Department of State, 2005.
Van de Ven, Hans J. *From Friend to Comrade: The Founding of the Chinese Communist Party, 1920–1927.* Berkeley, CA: University of California, 1991.
Wakeman, Frederic. *The Fall of Imperial China.* New York: Free Press, 1975.
Walker, David. *Anxious Nation: Australia and the Rise of Asia, 1850–1939.* Queensland: University of Queensland, 1999.
Walker, David and Agnieszka Sobocinska, eds. *Australia's Asia: From Yellow Peril to Asian Century.* Crawley, West Australia: University of Western Australia, 2012.
Wang, Dong. *The United States and China: A History from the Eighteenth Century to the Present*, 2nd ed. London: Rowan & Littlefield, 2021.
Weber, Isabella M. *How China Escaped Shock Therapy.* London: Routledge, 2021.
Westad, Odd Arne. *Decisive Encounters: The Chinese Civil War, 1945–1950.* Stanford, CA: Stanford University Press, 2003.
Westad, Odd Arne and Sophie Quinn-Judge, eds. *The Third Indochina War Conflict between China, Vietnam and Cambodia, 1972–79.* London: Routledge, 2006.
White, Hugh. *The China Choice: Why We Should Share Power.* Oxford: Oxford University Press, 2012.
White, Theodore H. and Annalee Jacoby. *Thunder Out of China.* New York: William Sloane, 1946.

Wilbur, Martin C. *The Nationalist Revolution in China, 1923–1928*. Cambridge: Cambridge University Press, 1983.
Willkie, Wendell L. *One World*. New York: Simon and Schuster, 1943.
Witchard, Anne. *England's Yellow Peril: Sinophobia and the Great War*. Melbourne: Penguin, 2014.
Wolin, Richard. *The Wind from the East: French Intellectuals, the Cultural Revolution, and the Legacy of the 1960s*. Princeton, NJ: Princeton University Press, 2010 (2018).
Wong, Eugene Franklin. "On Visual Media Racism: Asians in the American Motion Pictures." Dissertation, University of Denver, 1977.
Woodward, Jude. *The US vs China: Asia's New Cold War?* Manchester: Manchester University Press, 2017.
Wu, William F. *The Yellow Peril: Chinese-Americans in American Fiction, 1850–1940*. Hampden, CT: Archon, 1982.
Yee, Herbert Yee and Ian Story, eds. *The China Threat: Perceptions, Myths and Reality*. New York: Routledge, 2022.
Zhang, Shu Guang. *Deterrence and Strategic Culture: Chinese-American Confrontations, 1949–1958*. Ithaca, NY: Cornell University Press, 1992.
Zipp, Samuel. *The Idealist: Wendell Willkie's Wartime Quest to Build One World*. Cambridge, MA: Harvard University Press, 2020.

Index